Boyhood and Delinquency
in 1920s Chicago

ALSO BY ROGER A. SALERNO

Sociology Noir: Studies at the University of Chicago in Loneliness, Marginality and Deviance, 1915–1935 (McFarland, 2007)

Boyhood and Delinquency in 1920s Chicago

A Sociological Study of Juvenile Jack-Rollers and Gender

ROGER A. SALERNO

McFarland & Company, Inc., Publishers
Jefferson, North Carolina

Stories in Chapter Six courtesy Institute for Juvenile Research (Illinois). Taken from: Life Histories Collection, the Chicago History Museum, Archives and Manuscript Division. Transcripts are undated.

Names contained in these oral histories have been changed to assure anonymity of the authors. The following provides a collection reference for each of these stories: the Lone Wolf: Box 42, folder 9; the Boy Scout: Box 55, folder pv; and the Beaver: Box 45, folder 21.

LIBRARY OF CONGRESS CATALOGUING-IN-PUBLICATION DATA

Names: Salerno, Roger A., author.
Title: Boyhood and delinquency in 1920s Chicago : a sociological study of juvenile jack-rollers and gender / Roger A. Salerno.
Description: Jefferson, North Carolina : McFarland & Company, Inc., Publishers, 2017 | Includes bibliographical references and index.
Identifiers: LCCN 2016051904 | ISBN 9781476663418 (softcover : acid free paper) ∞
Subjects: LCSH: Juvenile delinquents—Illinois—Chicago—Social conditions—20th century. | Juvenile delinquency—Illinois—Chicago—History—20th century. | Juvenile corrections—Illinois—Chicago—History—20th century. | Street children—Illinois—Chicago—Social conditions—20th century. | Boys—Illinois—Chicago—Social conditions—20th century.
Classification: LCC HV9106.C4 S25 2017 | DDC 364.360977311/09042—dc23
LC record available at https://lccn.loc.gov/2016051904

BRITISH LIBRARY CATALOGUING DATA ARE AVAILABLE

ISBN (print) 978-1-4766-6341-8
ISBN (ebook) 978-1-4766-2717-5

© 2017 Roger A. Salerno. All rights reserved

No part of this book may be reproduced or transmitted in any form or by any means, electronic or mechanical, including photocopying or recording, or by any information storage and retrieval system, without permission in writing from the publisher.

Front cover photograph by Lewis Hine (Library of Congress)

Printed in the United States of America

McFarland & Company, Inc., Publishers
Box 611, Jefferson, North Carolina 28640
www.mcfarlandpub.com

For Sandi, Bennie, Rosie and the Moose

Acknowledgments

I'd like to acknowledge the assistance given to me by Pace University, particularly the Office of the Provost and the Dean of Dyson College of Arts and Sciences, for providing me with needed scholarly release time. I'd also like to thank the Scholarly Research Committee of the New York Faculty Council for believing in this project and supporting me on this work over the past several years. I thank all of the faculty members of this committee for their patience and assistance. I'd also like to thank my department chair, Amy Foerster, for enabling me to have a teaching schedule to accommodate this project, and Steven Goldleaf, for his broad-ranging help and insights.

This work has been important to me. Over the past several years my training in psychoanalysis had a considerable impact on the direction this project took. The influence of fellow students and teachers at the National Institute for the Psychotherapies helped enrich my thinking. Conversations with my students in my gender and intimacy classes also contributed significantly to the way I came to envision this project.

Howard Becker deserves particular gratitude for helping me to better understand the importance of labeling in the construction of the delinquent. And I would also like to thank Jon Snodgrass not only for the groundbreaking work he has done with his research on *The Jack-Roller* and his book *The Jack-Roller at Seventy*, and for his assistance in helping me think more clearly about some of these matters, but also for his important insights into this type of sociological research. I am particularly grateful to my spouse and best friend, Sandi, for her suggestions, understanding and patience with me as I often threw myself into this work behind closed doors for hours and days at a time. This book could not have been completed without her personal encouragement and support.

Table of Contents

Acknowledgments vi
Preface 1
*Introduction: Boyhood and
the Criminological Imagination* 3

ONE. Jack-Roller Stories   19

TWO. Decoding *The Jack-Roller*   41

THREE. Shaw's Other Boys   61

FOUR. Exclusions of Convenience   82

FIVE. Inclusions of Convenience   103

SIX. Introduction to the Institute
for Juvenile Research Oral Histories   111

THE LONE WOLF   113

THE BOY SCOUT   132

THE BEAVER   163

Conclusion: Delinquency and the End of Boyhood   182
Bibliography   189
Index   195

Preface

This is a book about juvenile delinquency in the city of Chicago at the beginning of the twentieth century. It is also an examination of boyhood and masculinity at that time. It deals principally with the lives of boys, their social class, race and the courts. It examines the ways they saw their world. But it also looks at progressive advocates of juvenile justice and social reform and the role they played in helping to construct stories of immigrant children's lives.

This work is the result of an extensive study of juvenile crime during this period and the narratives of boyhood that were inimically linked to criminal character traits. This connection between masculinity and criminality is viewed as a product of early gender socialization and emerges from fanciful myths of boyhood imposed by a predatory capitalistic culture. It is a study of power and powerlessness and examines criminology, scholarship, immigration and race.

The social science scholarship at the University of Chicago and its impact on theories of crime emerged as a part of what was then called the Chicago school of sociology. This was a liberal or progressive sociology that established academic dominance among theoretical perspectives of its time, particularly when it came to examining social relations in American cities. Under the direction of renowned scholars like Robert E. Park, W.I. Thomas and Ernest W. Burgess, this group of people were to influence succeeding generations of urban social theorists and criminologists. They were among the first academics to oppose the essentialist notions of crime advanced by such people as Cesare Lombroso, who saw the criminal mind as a product of bad genes. They substituted an environmental perspective in which the social environment played a paramount role in behavioral outcomes. Criminals were made, they were not born.

While these theories were indeed superior to those that had come before, these scholars became bogged down in "depersonalizing" crime and seeing criminal behavior as a consequence of what they referred to as "ecological variables." These impersonal elements or social factors were structural in nature and included things like poor housing and a breakdown of social institutions, such as family, community and religion. Since much of the funding for their projects came from the very wealthy in society through their established foundations, they turned away from the conditions of inequality and this enabled them to study social problems without being political. While they recognized poverty as harmful, much of their emphasis was on the violations of social norms. Most took offense to programs of direct social action. Robert E. Park had a particular disdain for what he called "do-gooders" like the women of Hull House and other community based reform groups. While he marginally participated in some of the more conservative civic organizations aimed at improving lives of the poor, he saw the role of sociologist as restricted to objective research. He opposed political action organizations like the NAACP. While not a biological essentialist, he was an ardent anti-racist who believed in gradualism which was inspired through his work for Booker T. Washington (Matthews 1977, Bulmer 1984).

His students and those students of his departmental colleagues became some of America's leading criminologists. These included Edwin Sutherland (1883–1950), Clifford Shaw (1895–1957), Henry McKay (1899–1980), John Landesco (1890–1954), Walter Reckless (1899–1988) and many others. We will explore some of their ideas in the chapters ahead. The ecological and environmental models developed by these scholars raised the level of scholarship. But it was Sutherland who recognized the important connection of gender to crime, describing boys as "less controlled" than girls and recognizing male behavior as more "rough and tough" (Sutherland 1947, p. 101).

This research is an attempt to make some connections between gender and social deviance. While this orientation is not new, it is historically based and gives us some insights into how the definition of boyhood and delinquency were united during the early decades of the twentieth century. In the Introduction on boyhood and the criminological imagination, I establish why a work like this is so necessary for contemporary sociologists interested in the mass violence associated with alienated boys.

Introduction
Boyhood and the Criminological Imagination

Over 35 years ago social historian James Bennett (1981) published a brilliant analysis of juvenile delinquency research taken from archival oral histories of incarcerated boys. His book has become an invaluable resource for those of us interested in the history of American juvenile justice, especially the lives of incarcerated young males at the beginning of the twentieth century. How did such boys find their way into a system of courts and corrections intended to salvage their lives through physical discipline and punishment? How did these efforts help put them on a straight and narrow path and protect their communities from their apparent danger and viciousness?

Towards the opening of the twentieth century there was considerable scholarly debate over the causes of antisocial behavior. Enrico Ferri (1900), Cesare Lombroso (1911) and others were among those who saw the crime problem as inherent, deeply embedded in the particular biological make-up of certain individuals, primarily males. More progressive medical criminologists such as Charles Goring (1913) attempted to refute such a hypothesis by countering with their own research but it took some time before crime was viewed as rooted in dysfunctional social relations. Criminal sociologists in the first decades of the twentieth century such as Edwin Sutherland (1924) began to see crime as emanating from "bad social environments." Still, well into the 1930s there were proposals for a policy of eugenics, in part an outcome of Lombroso's earlier findings, aimed at ridding society of criminal genes through widespread programs of sterilization particularly aimed at the "feeble minded" and immigrant populations (Hansen and King 2013).

If as Sutherland and his colleagues suggested that the social environment was indeed the cause of antisocial behavior and not genes, why were boys overwhelmingly seen as more problematic, more violent than girls. Some progressive sociologists of that time advised us that juvenile crime was due to cultural conflict by immigrants flooding into cities and adjusting to a new way of life. But why weren't girls in these families in the same sort of trouble? Could the reason boys got into mischief be attributed to hormones or anatomy? Perhaps boys are just constituted as more predatory. We know they have been portrayed this way.

Even today boyhood is seen as vitally connected to most delinquency in society. In the U.S. over 80 percent of all homicides are committed by young men or boys. The arrest rates for boys for assault, property crime, sex crimes and even drug-related offenses dwarfs the rate of arrests for girls for such offenses (UCR 2013). Boys are overwhelmingly more likely than girls to physically abuse animals, siblings and friends (Hensley and Tallichet 2009). Over 70 percent of young people who are arrested and brought to court are boys. And over 80 percent of those serving time in juvenile facilities are boys as well (UCR 2013). While 15 percent of police officers in the U.S. are female, a study by the *Washington Post* done in 2015 revealed in their survey in 2005 that all but one of the of 57 officers who drew their guns that year and fatally shot a suspect were men. But so were their victims; and more than half those victims were shot in the back. Nearly all of the police officers charged with "excessive force" have been men and the victims have been overwhelmingly boys and young men. Boys account for 81 percent of teen suicides. Many more boys than girls are attracted to violent pornography and video games glorifying human sadism and brutality (CDC 2014).

The overwhelming majority of corporate criminals are men. According to Cynthia Barnett (2000) of the U.S. Department of Justice most white collar criminals are disproportionately young white men in their 20s and 30s. The economic costs attributed to male antisocial behavior, including damages to property, fraud, disability and medical expenses, judicial processing, incarceration costs, economic and financial failures runs into hundreds of billions of dollars each year. And as we see an upward spike in mass homicides committed by school age boys with guns, sociologists are asking themselves about the overall social cost associated with learning to be a man in American society (Klein 2012). Men themselves are by and large the most likely to be victims of a violent crime. Young men of color are disproportionately victims of violence perpetrated by criminals and police alike (Sered 2014; Liberman and Fontaine 2015).

Yet most young men are not criminals. They are just as capable of love, generosity and affection as are women, but these traits are not considered masculine characteristics by many; men are frequently considered exceptional if they possess such traits. Still many men who appear to be compassionate and law abiding, often seem to be empathetically stunted, unable to allow themselves to be vulnerable or sensitive to the needs of others who they see as different from themselves (Kimura 1999). Could it be that delinquency is defined in large part by notions of masculinity? Such a tautology is not rare and this one might be a natural consequence of gender labeling.

Unlike Bennett's ground-breaking work on the history of male delinquency or even the classical nineteenth and early twentieth century studies he reports on, this book attempts to connect his and other findings to the phenomenological history of boyhood and masculinity. It is proposed here that if we examine the early lives of boys who supposedly were incorrigible we can find the source of many contemporary social problems. This is not to imply that boyhood is the sole cause of violence in our society, but it must certainly be considered an important factor. How we teach our boys to be men and how boys respond to such treatment is a central component of this work. "What has been seen as 'uniting' men," notes criminologist Richard Collier, "is an overwhelming propensity, relative to women, toward criminality as testified by both criminal statistics and lived experience" (Collier 1998/1999, p. 21). And according to some criminologists, "traditionally masculine persons may be more delinquent than those who are less masculine because individuals with masculine orientations are less committed to and involved in conventional action, and less likely to believe that social rules should be obeyed than persons with expectations that are less traditionally masculine" (Thornton and James 1979, p. 225). What it takes to be a boy is what it takes to be a delinquent.

Some scholars have understood a recent uptick in female crime, particularly more violent crime, as associated with girls taking on more "masculine" or predatory characteristics (Irwin and Chesney-Lind 2008). Instead of the early and mid–twentieth century crimes associated with girls, such as petty theft, shoplifting, drugs and prostitution, the 1970s and 1980s saw a major rise in arrests of girls for more violent activities. Freda Adler (1975) a feminist criminologist looking at this trend in the early 1970s, viewed this phenomenon as a "masculinization" of female behavior brought on by fewer social constraints on women's civility.

Giordano, Cernkovich and Rudolph (2002) found a definite link between so-called gender traits and crime. In their research they conclude "the notion that there may be gendered pathways into crime leads us to assume that there are gendered pathways out of crime" (p. 996).

It is important to keep in mind that most sociologists see gender as a social construction and is something quite distinct from one's sexual anatomy. But it is interesting to note that there is little written about a decline in violent male crime as reflective of the "feminization" of men. In this case framing masculinity as "predatory-aggressiveness" and femininity as "victim-passivity" reveals more about the tautological construction of gender than it does physiology and sex. Obviously, narratives of juvenile crime have deeply embedded gender tropes.

The perception of masculinity is critical to research of this sort. We can observe that studies and reports on juvenile crime promoted images of male predator and female victim. But we understand that boyhood and girlhood are defined differently depending on class and culture. The contentious nature of defining boyhood, masculinity or manhood as cultural signifiers has its place in historical, religious and literary texts. It is culturally relative and "standpoint" related. Masculinities are culturally constructed and therefore ethnically and linguistically defined. But they are also defined by class, education, social and cultural capital. While it must me acknowledged that there are as many masculinities as femininities it must also be understood that boyhood and masculinity are proscriptive, particularly in patriarchal societies. Being a boy is for the most part performative (Butler 1999). How boyhood evolved in the turn of the twentieth century is particularly important in this study. The fear of "a loss of masculinity" permeated a great deal of literature and social science in this era. One can view twentieth century American masculinity as a reaction to the loss of nineteenth century definitions of what it was to be a man.

The American male of the nineteenth century narrative was an adventurer and frontiersman. He carried a gun and often used it against wild animals and lesser men who got in his way. He was rugged and aggressive, not the powdered-wig dandy of the previous generation of bourgeois noblemen. He was "self-reliant," "self-made" and not in the least "refined." He was for the most part native born, holding women, blacks and immigrants as his inferiors or property or both. He was above all else white and phallocentric. Andrew Jackson represented the new rugged man, uncultured, poorly educated military hero who treated those he perceived weaker than himself with disdain. Toughness was essential to masculinity as much as suppleness was essential to femininity. Men were crusty, insensitive and hard. Anti-intellectualism and crude physicality separated real men from lesser ones. Intimidation and bullying were much more important than intellect.

The Progressive Era feminist movement was a direct challenge to male hegemony. Women were already making substantial political and social gains by 1910. They were beginning to become more sexually liberated, could speak more freely about sex and were now entering into what had been strictly male professions and challenging men's monopolistic power. They were entering higher education in increasing numbers and recruits to their cause were rapidly increasing (Kitch 1999). At the same time there was considerable unease in large sectors of the male community with these advances of women. What historian John Higham was to call the "muscular spirit" was a reaction not only to the ascendancy of female rights, but the influx of immigrants from Europe into American society who brought with them matriarchal ways.

The fear of feminization of young men was a challenge to patriarchy (Kimmel 1996; Bederman 1995). Instead of gender becoming more fluid, the fear of the loss of male sexual and political dominance created a backlash and an even more restrictive definition of what it was to be a man. The result was an over-emphasis on male aggression as the central component of masculinity. To a large extent the only emotions men could readily display toward others were pity, hatred and anger; and even these had serious restrictions. Here is a real disdain for all forms of weakness and dependency. The bottling up of emotions could lead to a type of masculinist pathology with periodic outbursts of rage. Masculine traits such as these still find acceptability in American politics and remote corners of corporate culture.

Writing about "toxic masculinity" behind bars, psychologist Terry A. Kupers has taken to task the lack of psychological treatment for conditions responsible for young men even prior to getting incarcerated. He proposes prisons encourage if not require a type of macho callousness of inmates as a key to survival. To avoid a fight, one must convey a type of toughness in appearance, manner and interaction with others. Likewise, Kupers suggests that men seeking mental health treatment (whether in prison or not) are stigmatized in masculinist culture. This is well documented especially in police culture where police officers are required to interact with tough males (Fox, Desai, Britten, Lucas, Luneau and Rosenthal 2012). There is a general disdain for psychological treatment and a general distrust for psychotherapists among police officers. For Kupers, "unfortunate male proclivities associated with toxic masculinity include insensitivity to or lack of consideration of experiences and feelings of others, a strong need to dominate and control others, an incapacity to nurture, a dread of dependency, a readiness to resort to violence, and the stigmatization and subjugation of women, gays and men who exhibit feminine characteristics" (Kupers 2005, p. 217). In fleshing out the production of toxic masculinity, Kurpers focuses on the inability of people in jail to gain respect, and therefore the extreme importance they attach to it. In fact the need to dominate others comes from an attempt to gain self-respect through bullying and physical intimidation.

In the introduction to *Oral History and Delinquency*, James Bennett (1981) makes clear how difficult it was for him to collect more contemporaneous autobiographical accounts of juvenile offenders. He himself worked closely with boys and young men who served time for dangerous and violent crimes. But since 1967 children brought before juvenile courts have been given "due process" and represented by court appointed attorneys who understand that any information they reveal related to a crime could be used in the courts in the future against their defendants. The public narrative confession of one boy could have a devastating impact on his incarcerated friends, placing them and the boy who tells his story in real physical or legal danger. And for Bennett there was a reticence to inflict any more damage on the interviewee. However, he cites some wonderful studies that have been done despite such legal and ethical constraints. By unearthing the accounts of boys lives collected by Clifford Shaw and others in the 1920s, he was able to give his readers a deep appreciation for the personal story as well as the manner in which these stories were collected over time. Missing from Bennett's findings on boys' inaccessibility is the general notion of male mistrust.

There is ample evidence that early socialization of baby boys in American working class families, particularly, engenders deep feelings of disconnectedness and insecurity. Boys are taught to dissociate from their feelings (Chodorow 1978; Shamir and Travis 2002). And if race was to enter into this picture, the mistrust especially among poor young black men, of white academics and social researchers in positions of authority is particularly high (Wilson 2011).

Like Bennett's book this work constitutes an examination of the studies that were done with young boys by Clifford Shaw, a world renowned criminologist of his time affiliated with the University of Chicago. He was a progressive and an advocate for boys in trouble and asked them to confide in him by sharing their life stories. However, what separated Clifford Shaw's studies of male delinquents from most other studies of his time is that he took these stories primarily from boys who were incarcerated. He did not mingle with gang members on the street to get these first person narratives as did Frederic Thrasher for his ethnographic study of Chicago street gangs. Nor did he like Phillipe Bourgeois live for five years with crack dealers, drug addicts and petty thieves in one of the most dangerous urban neighborhoods in America. His interviewees for the most part were boys behind bars. Many were enticed to tell their stories with the hope of early release or parole, perhaps even some degree of celebrity. Some of them were on parole while they were being interviewed. As will be noted in later chapters, much was being made during this time of first person crime narratives.

While one need not read Shaw's sampling of young men as coercive, a social scientist might speculate on the impact such power disparity would have on such elicitation. Shaw had served time as part of the system that incarcerated boys, as a part-time parole officer at the St. Charles School for Boys (where he met his first interviewee), and later as a juvenile probations officer. He then served as a director at the Institute for Juvenile Research with government and foundation funding. He had a research staff and was politically connected. Rarely was his work radical. His orientation was in keeping with what was at that time referred to as "child savers" looking to address juvenile delinquency by saving boys from their toxic environments. This orientation was influenced by his own Christian upbringing and focus on redemption narratives. He understood the "neighborhood" to be an ecological variable that contaminated the lives of those who lived in it. Coming from a small farming community in rural Indiana, he viewed cities like Chicago as toxic centers of anomie.

In his books, Bennett spends much of his time examining the way case material was collected and analyzed in the 1920s and 1930s by Clifford Shaw and Henry McKay. The cases Bennett draws upon were oral histories of poor boys from deteriorating sections of Chicago and its environs who wound up on the other side of the law. There is no mention of the Leopold and Loeb murder case; two wealthy and highly intelligent teenage college graduates (Leopold from the University of Chicago where both Shaw and McKay studied), who kidnapped and murdered a 14-year-old acquaintance for the sake of proving themselves intellectually superior and capable of committing a "perfect crime." Richard Loeb was murdered in prison and Nathan Leopold, paroled after 36 years, worked briefly with and for Shaw from prison.

While Bennett makes some attempt to critique the early nineteenth century liberal narrative of poverty and dysfunctional families as mechanisms for "decommissioning the soul" there was little in the way of psychodynamic focus in Shaw's work or any deep analysis in his commentaries on the lives of the boys he interviewed. Despite the personal nature of some of the stories, his treatment of each "case" was considerably detached. Still he was deeply sensitive to the struggles of immigrant families living in poverty.

His motif of delinquency was in line with what sociologist Robert Nisbet (1976) saw as a literary theme of that era. For Nisbet, sociological motifs often parallel artistic and literary ones. The Dickensian vision of poor orphan boys being forced into lives of crime by greedy adult overseers doesn't always tell the complete story. Many liberal sociologists have rested far too easily on indicting poverty as the singular cause of personal and social dysfunction rather than examining the psychosocial complexity of this phenomena and its relationship to the economic system. Such limited understandings of young male criminal behavior often misses countervailing accounts of the viciousness of the rich, and the thugs who pass as professional businessmen, or young middle class boys involved in hate crimes and senseless acts of vandalism. All of this surrounded Shaw at the time. More importantly, brutal crime as a consequence of poverty ignores the fact that poor young women are much less likely to engage violent behavior, including acts of homicide, armed robbery, mugging, torture of animals, acts against property and the like, although this is beginning to change. Still, when women are accused of such offenses, it is viewed as exceptional. We readily expect troubled girls to be prostitutes and boys to be thugs. This book challenges the popular notion of the innate ferocity of boys that was nearly universally accepted at the time in American popular culture.

Modern Discourse and the Gender Narrative

In examining first person narratives of boys whose early lives were affected by violence and domestic exile, this study additionally focuses on the importance of gender construction and discourse in the most formative years of these interviewees. How these boys relate their stories, who enables or encourages them to do so, what elements of story-telling they employ and how they depict their unique life experiences through a masculine lens informs us about the cultural significance of boyhood. The ways in which a boy develops his sense of gender identity, intimacy and sexuality are essential components of his socialization, and for every boy each experience is unique.

Narrative analysis has become an important instrument of qualitative social research. As Jane Elliot (2005) asserts, its origins in more contemporary social science can be traced back to Daniel Bertaux (1981) and his work in biography. It gained a solid position in sociological research with the work of Elliot Mishler (1986) and his discussions of narrative in interviews. Examining narrative gives to the researcher something that remains unattainable through social surveys. My work is an attempt to better understand boyhood at a particular time and place in American social history through such personal accounts. While a number of studies of gender have attempted to systemize the binary, it is important to understand that each person's autobiography is rooted in her or his identity (imposed or otherwise) as a gendered person. It is the process of gender socialization that lies at the heart of most boy trouble. Here boys are assumed to understand what is expected of them as boys and therefore comply accordingly in their autobiographical recollections. I make no hermeneutic claim, or even suggest statistical probability. Quantification is not even attempted, nor is this seen as desirable here. This work calls upon the reader or listener to take from the autobiographical narrative what one might see as gender informative, descriptive or significant.

In her study of boys, masculinities and juvenile justice in the United States, law professor Nancy E. Dowd (2008, p. 117) has noted that "the juvenile justice system is one that we have constructed as a gender-specific system to manage, control and respond to boys. It reflects and operates upon assumptions of masculinities and reflects masculinities norms."

Gender socialization is a life-long process that takes place through those social institutions that comprise each particular society. Sociologists and psychologists contend that most behavior, particularly gendered behavior, is learned through processes of interaction. The same may be said for the gendered use of language. One learns and unlearns expected gender roles and expected gendered language that are critical to one's self-identity at particular points in time. Bravado, grandiosity, swearing and other characteristics that are more particular to male autobiographies than to female autobiographies are presumed to be unconscious for the most part and often highly developed defense mechanisms to cover deep insecurities, just as female concern with feelings of others remains a common but typically unconscious trope in the autobiographies of women. Nevertheless, these are important to one's gender identification. We can observe in such studies a confirmation of the well regarded understanding in oral history and its reporting that girls tend to remember more detail and personal experiences than boys. As Valerie Raleigh Yow (2015, p. 56) has noted: "Researchers observed that men's accounts of personal histories tend to be more purposeful and linear than women's accounts." And she suggests that this is a function of gender socialization and culture.

Kenneth B. Kidd's excellent study of American boyhood has provided a deep analysis of the cultural construction of youthful masculinity in late nineteenth and early twentieth century fiction. Kidd explores the important power that certain literary motifs, such as savagery, have in helping to present an image of American boyhood. In examining how the white discourse of savagery distinguishes between those savages who can and cannot be tamed because of their race, he draws parallels between Anglo-American colonialism and the domestic repression of children. One weakness that might be found in Kidd's thesis, however, is his assertion that the psychoanalytic paradigm as well as psychological and sociological ones predominantly present boys as innately untamed, immature, wild animals (Kidd 2004). However, it is important to recognize that the social sciences and psychoanalysis looked upon *all children* as innately untamed and in need of strict control; girl babies were not exempt from this particular view. But the dangers they presented to societies were seen very differently. Bram Dijkstra's brilliant exploration of the cultural motifs of the dangers inherent in women's sexuality in the early twentieth century is a case in point (Dijkstra 1996). So is Freud's emphasis on the dangers inherent female sexuality and their pathologies such as hysteria (Freud 1925). Likewise, Lombroso (1893) located social pathology in female anatomy.

While girls were seen as more malleable and easier to control because of some perceived innate differences, particularly intellectual inferiority, they were definitely was in need of discipline and very tight control thought to be needed to be exercised over their sexuality. Gustav LeBon (1879), the French psychologist who wrote about the dangers of human instincts, especially crowds and rabble, wrote: "All psychologists who have studied the intelligence of women recognize today that they represent the most inferior forms of human evolution and that they are closer to children and savages than to an adult, civilized man" (pp. 60–61). Accordingly, just as the savage might be civilized, so might most children and women. But all needed to be civilized according to a rigid formula imposed by white American patriarchy. Anthony Platt's book *The Child Savers* (2009) looks at progressives who were instrumental in the juvenile justice movement as imposing strict social control over boys and particularly girls so as to serve the needs of the upper classes and maintain a particular type of social order.

Platt saw the progressive movement at the beginning of the twentieth century as a concept over the barbarity of the lower classes and the dread of witnessing the unleashing of its innate savagery. There was social outrage and indignation expressed by progressive reformers who viewed themselves keepers of the moral code when the jazz age began promoting the sexual liberation of women. When so-called "animal dances" and "ragtime" music became popular in the early 1900s, men and women, boys and girls were seen as morally endangered, gyrating to "jungle music." Progressives viewed the appropriation of black music as a "white descent" into a sexualized, primitive, uncivilized depths of African culture (George-Graves 2009 and Wall 2013). Progressive efforts to impose civility and order on what appeared to them as a disorderly "dangerous class" could not be imposed by immigrant families who knew no better. They themselves were the problem. Settlement houses were developed to help Americanize and pacify the European rabble flooding cities at the turn of the century. Classes in English, parenting, values and manners were among those provided, as were courses in music appreciation.

Girls play a minor role in this study for two main reasons. First, it is my intention to focus this study on boyhood and the sociological construction of masculinity as evidenced in a particular set of interviews of young men who were studied by Clifford Shaw and his staff at the Institute for Juvenile Research in Chicago in the 1920s and 1930s. Second, although there exist some remarkable studies of girl delinquents, boys were considered far more dangerous than girls and still are. It was young white men studying younger white men that makes this set of studies particularly interesting. Yet I have no pretense at objectivity, since I am an old white man studying younger white men studying still younger white men. The tradition goes on!

Gendered Dungeons for Children

The first juvenile detention center in Chicago was established for boys in the mid–nineteenth century. A center for girls which opened later was more of an afterthought. Girls were seen as far less dangerous than boys and were primarily portrayed as victims of unmonitored city life. White girls particularly were viewed as inherently virginal, non-sexual. The "white slave trade," as it became known, was the idea that white young girls were being kidnapped off the streets and taken to work as prostitutes against their will. There was little sense at this time that girls might use their bodies, as had boys, to make money. Still the overwhelming majority of girls brought before juvenile court at the beginning of the twentieth century were brought there for moral offenses.

Mary Odem's study of delinquent girls in the late nineteenth and early twentieth centuries reveals how most social reform movements of that period were targeted particularly at young white girls. Girls of color were never granted the same consideration. Much of this reform was directed toward preventing female promiscuity by both denying their sexual desire and agency and attempting to relegate girls to lives of domesticity (Odem 1995). There was a push on the part of many social reformers to raise the age of consent for girls to protect their virginity. But at the same time, there was enormous fear on the part of men who worked in the criminal justice system of the power of young women's sexuality. This concern was also expressed in a growing body of noir fiction in the 1920s that portrayed women either as predators or as saints. The *femme fatal* was basically a white male trope expressing paranoia related to the growing power of women.

Gender socialization establishes the groundwork for American boyhood. The values embedded in our social institutions, in family, religion, governance, commerce, the arts, etc., attempt to impose strict regimens that distinguish male from female, boy from girl in thinking, sociability, looks and behavior.

Total institutions, particularly the military and prisons are powerful instruments when it comes to imposing an ordered system of physical and psychological characteristics, especially when children enter into them at a very early stage of their developing years. While we can observe institutionalized examples of this, many of our assumptions about gender are deeply imbedded in our unconscious minds. As Kidd himself points out, we constructed a gender binary that encourages the "savagery" of boys while repressing it or denying it in girls very early in our history. Few would argue today that girls are innately incapable of savage, and diabolical acts no more than they would argue that boys are incapable of gentle loving and nurturing ones. Neuroscientists are well aware today that infant brain plasticity and how a child is raised establishes a "gendered brain" and can pattern aggressive or nurturing behavior along socially established protocols (Eliot 2009).

Still, women are viewed by many political, corporate and military leaders as incapable of performing as aggressively as men. That girls and their bodies remain the targets of religious, political, commercial, and institutional control is part of America's sexual legacy. But as Kidd notes, boys are called upon to both reject and devalue qualities this culture associates with femininity. The inability of the child to incorporate certain gender specific qualities (this foreclosure) has long been discussed in the psychoanalytic literature. While it has been primarily examined in terms of object-choice and sexual desire, I believe that the foreclosure of choice runs much deeper and is embedded in the culture of gender identification which mostly precedes erotic object-choice and is perhaps even shaped by it in most cases. Unlike Judith Butler (1999) who privileges sexual desire in her use of the notion of melancholy, I feel that the foreclosure of certain gender-identified attributes brings us closer to an understanding of the enormous power gender socialization has in shaping sexual desire.

Ken Corbett (2009), a psychotherapist who deals with children attempting to navigate the gender terrain established for them by society, articulately describes the ways in which boys particularly struggle. But there are as many boyhoods as there are masculinities and Corbett recognizes this. He finds much of the theoretical basis for the male-female binary in the early work of Freud, which eventually led to notions advanced later by Robert Stoller (1965), Nancy Chodorow (1978) and Jessica Benjamin (1988). The closeness of a boy to his mother, the rejection of the mother as an icon of powerlessness, the struggle to identify with the father all emerge in psychoanalytic theory as ways of understanding rigid separations that constitute gender in American culture. His psychotherapeutic work reveals just how significant this process of indoctrination is for the perceived health and wellbeing of the child on the part of parents, and how a male child who is directed by his own cognitive and emotional sensibilities is frequently encouraged to deny what appears to be a vital sets of attributes and preferences in order to be "properly gendered" for his "own well-being." It is no accident that the harshest punishments are meted out to boys by their peers and adult males, who have difficulty denying their own uniqueness.

A variety of gender theorists see this denial in terms of gender melancholy and loss; that is, the social control and denial of human attributes and potentialities that can result in feelings of loss, resentment, and anger. The stage of human development we refer to as boyhood holds potential as a place of self-discovery, and Corbett provides such opportunities to his young male patients in consultation with their families. But there is always the recognition on the part of children and adults, conscious or not, that to allow oneself to be different often means to be stigmatized and devalued by the society in which one lives.

This book sets out to contextualize the lives of male juvenile delinquents in a rapidly changing urban society that was Chicago in the 1920s and 1930s. In doing so, it explores the tales of a small number of boys who shared their life stories with sociologists. It also examines proper male behavior prescribed for them in the social code. Boyhood is tough enough for some, but with the rapid currents of social change come many challenges affecting the meaning of boyhood and masculinity. And while gender fluidity might be considered more reasonable today, in the 1920s is was considered quite pathological.

Each of the first three chapters in this book deals with the treatment of young men and boys who often found their way into the juvenile justice system because of their socially unacceptable behaviors. These chapters examine how the research was done, and how these studies sometimes overlooked important elements of each boy's unique biographical narrative. I also support Jonathan Snodgrass (2012) in his contention that the lives of these children were subordinated to the needs of social scientists who hoped to make discoveries without considering the sometimes exploitive nature of their methodologies.

Chapter four deals with important factors that were significantly overlooked in these studies and speculates as to why there was an invisibility of girls, drug addicts, black youth, and gay boys among those interviewed by Shaw. My conclusion here is that these categories were viewed as anomalies. Not that they were unworthy of Shaw's studies, but rather that they would not fit into his theory of juvenile delinquency, which was vitally connected to the ideas of cultural conflict and social disorganization that characterized the sociological tradition up until this point. But by not focusing on these excluded groups, Shaw and his readers come away with an unrealistic picture of juvenile delinquency.

In a similar fashion, chapter five deals with those inclusions that had a distorting influence on the outcome of Shaw's research. This is not to assume that he was unaware of the limits in featuring the boys he presented in his work, but it is important to recognize his selection of narratives was biased, based upon what he was looking for and therefore his reported studies skewed his results and conclusions. At the same time Shaw gave us a particularly optimistic view of the futures for many of these boys, who were likely to have no futures at all.

Subsequent chapters in this book take-up the individual narratives of troubled boys, who told their "own-stories" to an audience of appreciative male researchers, many of whom were graduate assistants at the time. While Shaw's published studies did much to promote his belief, his work was in keeping with liberal sociology of his time. The bonus given us through these oral histories is a better appreciation of the failures of the juvenile justice system which he work energetically to promote. The transcribed accounts of these boys lives including harsh portraits of their treatment by the juvenile justice system in whose care they were placed, give us considerably more to think about. And this research reveals much more about the role of gender socialization in the lives of incarcerated boys.

These transcriptions have rested in the archives of the Chicago Historical Society, now the Chicago History Museum, and have not seen the light of day for some time. Unearthing them again for me has been a particularly rewarding experience.

CHAPTER ONE

Jack-Roller Stories

At the beginning of the twentieth century the streets of Chicago were littered with destitute children. Dirty, unkempt and frequently traumatized they banded together in small groups for safety as well as for companionship. Few ever attended school. Most were malnourished and often sickly. Many who did survive the city winters sleeping under bridges and in doorways found their livelihoods in begging, prostitution, pick-pocketing, and more violent ventures.

For the most part these were offspring of newly arriving immigrant families who lived in destitute conditions, crowded into virtually uninhabitable tenements where the space was meager and air was putrid. Diphtheria, typhoid, cholera, smallpox, and yellow fever regularly ravished working-class neighborhoods. Families doubled and tripled-up to crowd single room apartments. Some families travelling west were known to abandon their children on Chicago's city streets. Chicago opened its first orphanage as a response to a cholera epidemic in 1849 that took the lives of many parents. But there were never enough beds. Black children abandoned to the streets were kept out of these facilities and it wasn't until the opening of black private orphanages in 1916 that some of these children were provided public shelter.

There was little in the way of social or health services for working class residents, and, as time progressed, those children abandoned to the streets would either perish or be picked up and sent away to work as free labor for room and board. Often they'd be sent to prison or county work houses or alms houses. In some instances these houses were farms built in the fashion of military barracks and jail cells and mingled the homeless poor with mental patients, nonviolent criminals, and tubercular patients. Those children considered more fortunate would go to the freshly built juvenile detention centers that opened in the rural areas.

Prior to 1900 many boys went to state prison and shared cells with older, more seasoned criminals. It was not unusual for a boy of eight to be locked-up in jail with a man three times his age who was serving a sentence for rape or murder. Sometimes boys were sent to work camps in adjacent states or indentured to farmers. Some less fortunate would be put up for public auction by the state and worked in the homes and factories of those who absorbed some of the expense of their maintenance. And while the twentieth century did not provide a clean break with these practices, in 1899 Chicago became the first American municipality to institute a juvenile court system—a major advance from the harsher treatment of such children in the past (Willrich 2003). These courts were viewed as a means to rescue children from a life of moral decrepitude and to remove them from the streets and perhaps from negligent parents. The city also experimented with a rudimentary foster care system, which was nearly a total failure and remains one today.

Those roaming the streets represented a burden that families could not carry, or did not want to carry. They were often regarded by parents as capable of fending for themselves. Because of family size, economic struggles, parental alcoholism, or perhaps the death of one or more parents as the result of rapidly spreading epidemics, many children were casteaway or abandoned. Often they would simply be locked out and not permitted back until they could provide for themselves and their families. They were extra mouths to feed, and many of them were behavioral problems as soon as they could walk. They frequently stole from their own parents and abused their siblings. Some were quite violent and many suffered severe psychological problems and frequently brain injuries from the beatings of a drunken parent or toxic environmental conditions to which their pregnant mothers were exposed. Others simply ran away from chronic physical and sexual abuse. The notion of protective services for children was just in its infancy.

For the most part children from poor families were inadequately diagnosed for contagious diseases. According to social researchers Joseph Ferrie and Werner Trosken (2008): "Before 1880, more than half of all deaths in the city occurred among children less than 5 years old, and the leading causes of death were diarrheal diseases—such as typhoid fever, cholera infantum, and dysentery—and respiratory diseases—such as tuberculosis, influenza, bronchitis, and pneumonia" (p. 1). Children who did not die directly from such diseases were left with weakened immune systems that lead to their deaths from less serious disorders.

Mothers living in poverty received little prenatal counseling or care.

Most immigrant women relied on midwives for childbirth assistance where the quality of help varied greatly. The consequences of parental alcoholism were not yet recognized for fetal abnormalities, including fetal alcohol syndrome, until 1973. And only decades after recognizing this disorder was the alcoholic father's role in genetic damage of the developing embryo understood. In the studies undertaken by Shaw of delinquent boys in the 1920s, there is ample evidence of alcohol abuse among many of these boys' parents, particularly their fathers.

Drinking and smoking, as means of coping with inordinate familial stress, contributed to possibly a variety of behavioral and health problems in children. It is more likely that children born into poor urban neighborhoods were disproportionately exposed to noxious chemicals such as lead and mercury that could wind-up affecting both cognitive functioning and physical development. They certainly resided in the most heavily polluted areas of the city.

The Treatment of Street Children

The abandonment of children was nothing new. It had long been characteristic of cities where a new born added nothing to the health and stability of the family, and might even be met with infanticide. Industrial capitalism promoted an acceleration of child desertion, especially in the poorest sectors of the city. Infanticide in many cases was viewed as resulting from accident or neglect (Adler 2006, pp. 200–235). This maltreatment and negligence also produced roving bands of young, often vicious, nocturnal scavengers seeking-out potential victims—people with money to spend. And the city being a place wherein the poor and rich walked in close proximity, uneasy propinquity gave rise to bourgeois social consciousness. Children were seen as both victims and victimizers.

In 1855 the Chicago Reform School opened in what was a former city operated poor house. It was touted as a progressive venture, and was an attempt to segregate young boys from older hardened criminals in the county jails in which they were typically incarcerated. It was run much like a military camp with students getting up at 5:45 AM, marching to class with the beat of a drum, and then drilling and toiling in industrial workshops for the remainder of the day. Here there would be much prayer and lots of required monk-like silence. Boys slept in hammocks in a large dormitory room. Those sent here were not only truants or runaways but also boys convicted of more serious crimes. Street children and truants mixed with young thieves and violent thugs overseen by corrupt and greedy officials. But by the 1870s, it had become a factory for the production of delinquents. After several scandals involving the abuse of children and the Great Fire that destroyed part of it in 1872, the school was forced to close its doors. Taking its place was a new Illinois State Reformatory at Pontiac.

The Reformatory was located in Pontiac in Livingston County: "A beautiful interior city of the State" (Fallows 1900, p. 141). This 276-acre facility, which was "intended to be a place of confinement for the education of boys who were homeless, reckless, and incorrigible and who had not been convicted of a crime," opened its door in January of 1893. However, it immediately began admitting boys between the ages of 10 and 21, who had been found guilty of criminal behavior—often violent sociopaths. That same year saw a much smaller reformatory for girls opened in Geneva, Illinois.

Often children were picked up from the streets and sent away for years. It was deemed much more humane by the new juvenile courts to make them wards of the state rather than to allow them to be products of bad parenting and to let them back on the street to victimize people. There was also concern that children were endangered by parental abuse and neglect. Boys and girls taken to court were denied *habeas corpus*. What they seemingly needed was fresh air, sun, religion, and discipline.

The Women's Club of Chicago, a relatively conservative organization of tradition-based middle class reformers, which worked to promote a new juvenile justice system, commented in an 1896 report:

> In all large cities one condition exists which is comparatively unknown in small communities, namely, numbers of children who, through the death, neglect, poverty, weakness or criminality of parents or guardians, do not attend school, have practically no home training or control, and through such neglect drift into criminality. There are hundreds of such children in Chicago and elsewhere throughout the State, growing up to constitute an ignorant and criminal class, dangerous to the welfare of the whole country [Clapp 1995].

With the help of the Women's Club of Chicago, Jane Addams, and the women of Hull House, the Illinois Juvenile Court Act was passed in 1899. It was the first juvenile court system in the world. Children under 12 could no longer be placed in jail; all those under 16 years of age would have hearings before sympathetic judges professionally attuned to domestic issues. The emphasis of the court would be on rehabilitation rather than punishment. Instead of going to jail incorrigible young offenders would be sent to reformatories where they would be schooled and hopefully trained to become model citizens. Hull House and other private social agencies would provide probation officers for boys and girls who were deemed neither violent nor dangerous. But the caseload for each officer was usually overwhelming.

As the twentieth century emerged and institutional reforms were taking place, there was a more optimistic sense that progressive social policy could address these seemingly intractable urban problems. It was believed that social science, especially psychology, social work and sociology, could protect the lives of vulnerable children living in poverty and help improve the quality of life in the city. Treatment rather than punishment seemed to be a more enlightened approach to girls and boys lost to the streets. Progressive reformers saw a need for amelioration—a much safer approach than those being put forth by radical socialist who would have required major structural changes and a redistribution of resources. Between 1899 and 1909, over 14,000 children were arrested in the Chicago streets—most of these were from immigrant homes (Breckinridge and Abbott 1912, p. 21).

Immigrant-Delinquent Connection

The promotion of a juvenile court was directly connected to the process of Americanizing newly arriving foreigners. Xenophobia in the late 1800s was as American as apple pie. Immigrants were looked upon as the source of most of the problems being experienced in the American cities including the loss of work, alcoholism, disease, prostitution and most other crimes. Despite a serious economic depression that swept the country in the late 1890s, assistance to these families primarily took the form of private charity. To allocate tax money to address issues of poverty, dilapidated housing and issues of public health was not seen as politically viable. The stigmatized immigrant was viewed as taking away jobs from those born here and attempting to introduce socialism to America and undermine American values. To support immigrants was seen as misguided and dangerous. While they provided needed cheap labor, they also became involved in workers' movements. Hull House and other groups worked to Americanize immigrants to encourage them to assimilate as quickly as possible. Still parents needed to work, and immigrants worked the longest hours at the most repugnant jobs.

Historian David Tanenhaus (2004) has suggested that the development of the new juvenile justice system was merely an extension of the

Americanization movement. There was considerable resistance on the part of some immigrant children to attend school. More boys than girls resisted. Public schools could be dangerous places for children of immigrants who often needed to learn a new language in order to keep up with the school work and were frequently viewed as outsiders and object of disdain. Immigrants looked different and smelled different. They were often shabbily or "inappropriately" dressed. There was considerable bullying and shaming not only from other students, but also from teachers. In many cases, immigrant children needed to work to help support the household.

For children who refused to go to public school, there were truant officers who would come to their homes or pick truants up from the street. It was seen as a way of keeping these youngsters out of trouble. Newly designed detention centers would come equipped with a school. One way or another, children would be Americanized.

Delinquency, Sociology and Reform

Into this era of juvenile justice reform there emerged new a type of sociology that hoped to better explain the reasons for street crime as well as the dynamics of it. It understood juvenile crime as the outcome of a rapidly changing society. At the Department of Sociology at the University of Chicago in the second decade of the 1900s, Ernest W. Burgess and Robert E. Park worked with a number of their graduate students to produce various studies on crime and juvenile delinquency. Some of these young men and women looked at how the streets of the city were being transformed by roving bands of boys and girls who had somehow "gone wrong." Unlike studies of the past, these focused on social problems, not individual pathologies. Delinquent children were viewed as a product of rapid social change, intense urbanization, and an inability of traditional immigrant parents to control their offspring as they adjusted to modern urban life in America. Sociologists looked at issues such as poverty, immigration, and home environment as opposed to innate racialist reasons for these difficulties. They often worked closely with Jane Addams of Hull House and other settlement houses and reform organizations.

The Chicago school of sociology, as it was later to be called, developed a cadre of well-trained social researchers and ethnographers who went out into the streets to study what was happening there. Although they saw themselves as social scientists rather than social reformers and activists, they were often funded by groups looking for ways to address problems of street crime and urban unrest. Many of these researchers developed important studies that would provide justification for implementing social reform.

Renowned for its more progressive theories of criminal behavior, which viewed delinquency as outcome of social disorganization that accompanied rapid urbanization, social migration and cultural instability, the Chicago school scholars rejected the then contemporary notion of delinquents as a human subspecies. Criminal behavior was viewed as a social product of intense social and economic transition. The delinquent was lost—detached from healthy familial systems of nurturance, discipline and socialization. They recognized what one of the central figures of sociology, Emile Durkheim, called *anomie*, but they rarely used this term.

Here is where old peasant cultures based on tradition and cooperation came into conflict with urban individualism, competition and autonomy. This is where those raised in small agrarian villages had to conform to the demands of urban industrial life. Traditional values could no longer hold people together. Although the Chicago school joined with various civic groups to promote local policy change directed at remedying the lives of individual actors, they frequently failed to recognize or speak to the structural problems of severe income inequality as the source of many of the urban ills they identified.

Between 1915 and 1933 graduate students under the guidance of Park and Burgess studied marginality in the city, and a number of these researchers looked at urban crime and juvenile urban crime in particular. The renowned American criminologist Edwin Sutherland earned his doctorate from the University of Chicago in 1913 and was influenced by an earlier cohort of Chicago professors including W.I. Thomas, Albion Small and George Herbert Mead. He took his first sociology course at Chicago with Charles Henderson—a part time sociology professor, university chaplain and social reformer. But under Park and Burgess the study of urban crime was to blossom. Students such as Walter Reckless studied urban vice, John Landesco looked at organized crime, Frederic Thrasher researched street gangs and Shaw and McKay examined juvenile delinquency. Chicago was a social laboratory and these graduate students were encouraged not only to collect data, but also to go out into the streets and speak with people—interview them. Their work had a humanizing influence on the public image of so-called street thugs, tramps and hoodlums. The narratives they collected elicited feelings of compassion and empathy in those who read their stories. This is where the Chicago school approach contributed to the more contemporary image of the complexity of the so-called social deviant. This is where fact met fiction in sensationalized tabloid of criminal biography (Salerno 2007).

The city of Chicago was a place where students could learn first-hand about the changes taking place in American cities. Many of these of young graduate students grew-up in rural areas and this was their first exposure to big city life. Yet, they saw aspects of themselves in the people they researched and interviewed.

Clifford Shaw and Juvenile Delinquency

Clifford Shaw came to Chicago in 1919 to pursue a doctorate in sociology. Born and raised on a small farm in Indiana, he found living accommodations off-campus in a run-down part of the city at a settlement house called House of Happiness. This facility catered to Polish and other Eastern European immigrants in its surrounding neighborhood. While still taking graduate courses at Chicago in 1921, he secured a part-time job as a parole officer for the Illinois State Training School for Boys at St. Charles, and between 1924 and 1926 he became a probation officer at the Cook County Juvenile Court. It was this work that made the theories he studied and data he collected come alive. He ingratiated himself with the boys he supervised and they in turn helped him better understand the phenomenon of juvenile crime on a personal level. Jon Snodgrass, who conducted an extensive review of the relationship between Shaw and his research partner and classmate at Chicago Henry McKay, quotes McKay as saying: "I believe he (Shaw) was at his best when interviewing juvenile delinquents.... I have never been sure whether he joined them or they joined him" (Snodgrass 1976, p. 8).

It was this ability to be assimilated into the lives of the boys he served and to be an advocate for them that brought him much closer to the material on juvenile crime than others who only studied it from afar. The sincerity by which he seemed to approach these young teens and pre-teens resulted in some powerful connections with them. They were reported to have significant trust in him. Unlike other criminologists, he was at home not simply collecting data, creating spot-maps and charts displaying trends in arrests and incarcerations, but perhaps most comfortable in speaking at length and empathically to boys whose lives had been ruptured and traumatized. He brought many of these boys into his home and, after his marriage, frequently introduced them to his wife and children. He showed them kindness, respect and trust.

His outstanding work was promoted and encouraged by both Robert Park and Ernest Burgess who eventually helped Shaw secure the position of Director of Research at the Institute for Juvenile Research in Chicago in 1926. This position was a creation of a research funds controlled in part by Burgess.

The Institute for Juvenile Research was originally founded as Chicago's Juvenile Psychopathic Institute in 1909 and was located at Jane Addam's Hull House. Initially the institute grew out of the juvenile court reform movement and was intended to provide psychiatric and social services to the young people brought into the juvenile courts. Its first director was Dr. William Healy, a young child psychiatrist, who later on testified at the Leopold and Loeb trial. Aside from providing psychiatric assessments of some of the children brought before the new court, he was also charged with doing research on factors contributing to juvenile delinquency. In 1917 the Institute for Juvenile Research was taken over by the State of Illinois and soon thereafter Healy left for a position in Boston's new juvenile court system. Healy had a long and distinguished professional career both as an advocate for young people and as a prolific scholar and author on the topic of juvenile delinquency. He helped to promote the writings of Freud in the United States (Snodgrass 1984).

But under Shaw's new direction a large number of research projects dealing with delinquency were initiated. Funding now emphasized more sociological interests. Henry R. McKay was hired shortly after Shaw's appointment to assist him with the program of research. Like Shaw, McKay also had come from a rural farm community to study sociology at the University of Chicago. And like Shaw he was a graduate assistant of Professor Ernest Burgess.

Throughout the mid and late 1920s, Shaw and McKay collaborated on numerous studies of delinquency in the city. They worked well together exhibiting complementary strengths. Where McKay focused more on statistics, Shaw was more connected to one-on-one interviews. Much of their joint work was to advance the importance of neighborhood and socio-ecological factors involved in the production of juvenile crime. And although they did not ignore the economic hardships and impoverishment of the neighborhoods they examined, they often failed to connect these findings to issues such as the need for resource redistribution and radical social and political reform. Inequality was viewed as a natural consequence of a free society. Instead they sought funding for programs of local amelioration.

Taking over from Healy, Shaw rejected the psychopathology model as an explanation of juvenile crime—a model halfheartedly put forth by Healy. As a sociologist Shaw assumed that most if not all the delinquents he studied were basically pummeled by the factors of their neighborhood environment. He and McKay believed that these were all "normal" children adjusting to specific familial and neighborhood challenges. And while this is for the most part true, they both failed to completely recognize that early childhood trauma and experiences of abuse often left indelible marks on children's psyches that translated into behavioral difficulties and feelings that they might carry around forever. This was something that Healy did recognize. The solutions Shaw and McKay proposed for addressing these problems were neighborhood action programs, recreation activities and the like. While offering some relief, this stance came under considerable criticism by some sociologists and activists. (See Bennett 1981, pp. 165–178.) Saul Alinsky, the renowned community organizer who at one time in his career worked for Shaw, referred to Institute for Juvenile Research's work as "making surveys of all those kids in cold water tenements—with rats nibbling their toes and nothing to eat—and then discovering the solution: camping trips and some shit they called character building" (Alinksy 1972, p. 68).

Shaw and McKay either ignored the profound impact of early trauma, including physical and sexual abuse, on lives of children interviewed or they simply assumed that the results of these early personal traumas could be managed through proper guidance and discipline. Today childhood trauma is seen as central to understanding conduct disorders in juveniles and its history appears ubiquitous in the so-called delinquent population accounting for such features as lack of empathy, impulsivity, anger, and acting out (Greenwald 2002).

Shaw and McKay viewed the problem of juvenile delinquency as emerging out of "social disorganization" or a lack of proper social control in communities. While personal trauma might have been experienced, there was no way they saw themselves or anyone else as capable of ameliorating it. The disorganizing social processes on the other hand were viewed as a consequence of ecological factors running their natural course. Through proper planning and public policy things of this nature could be addressed. Still, as Jon Snodgrass has pointed out, they saw the conditions that wreaked havoc with these neighborhoods—the economic exploitation and abuse of working class immigrants—as the "natural order" of things (Snodgrass 1976, p. 11). While they fought for funding to provide programs to address the delinquency of children in deteriorating housing and neighborhoods, radical social change was not their aim. One might raise challenges to a research institute that began with attempts to investigate the psychology of antisocial children being hijacked into the service of academic urban research and programs of civic education and surveillance.

The Jack-Roller and Other Stories

Clifford Shaw recognized that the interviews conducted by Healy of children coming before the juvenile courts produced rich descriptive material. It was not a major leap from these structured interviews to a more in-depth self-telling of events. He himself had conducted similar interviews when he worked as both a probations officer and a parole officer with the courts. He had already insinuated himself into the lives of some of these young boys and was listening to what they had to say about their families and friends—what they had to say about their homes and their neighborhoods. And few adults listened to them. But all of these narratives were filtered through Shaw's sociological perspective, as well as his own rural childhood experience.

While Shaw used interviews as preparation for collecting more detailed autobiographies from these troubled boys, this technique was not new. He used these narratives as additional sources of research material, but not primary data.

The stories of these boys were seen as interpretive. He never thought these stories were completely accurate recollections of events. Whether something was true or not, however, was not the point. It was the way the boy saw things; and so it was his version of the truth. Shaw saw this as in keeping with the perspective passed down by George Herbert Mead and W.I. Thomas referred to as "Thomas Theorem." This meant what was true for the first person story teller was how she or he perceived an incident and how that person acted in accordance with that understanding. So this perspective, which would later develop into what was called "symbolic interaction," became a characteristic of Chicago school research. W.I. Thomas and Dorothy Swaine (1928) had noted: "If a man perceives a situation as real, it is real in its consequences."

W.I. Thomas had also stressed the importance of personal documents, such as personal letters, in his own research. He himself used interviews with prostitutes and letters to the lovelorn column of newspapers as elements of his data in his work including *The Unadjusted Girl*, and later in *The Polish Peasant*. Also, it was Thomas who borrowed ethnographic methods from anthropology and applied them to studying city life in Chicago. *The Jack-Roller* was produced in keeping with this tradition.

The Jack-Roller was the story of one boy Shaw met in 1922 when he was a parole officer working with young delinquents released from the St. Charles Training School. But Healy had met this same boy several years before Shaw, and he interviewed him prior to Shaw's research project. In fact Healy met with the boy as he repeatedly was brought before the court. Between the age of six and eight the boy referred to in *The Jack-Roller* as Stanley had been picked up from the Chicago streets by the police 19 times. The times Healy encountered him, the boy was charged with things such as sleeping under a doorstep with a companion several blocks from his home, begging for food, eating out of a garbage can, sleeping in an alley, and stealing vegetables. Each time he would be brought back home he would run-away. He begged Healy and the judge not to send him back home. But the judge usually did. Healy described the child in his report as "undernourished and has exceedingly carious teeth. Home conditions are very bad" (in Shaw 1966, pp. 24–25). At age nine, after having been reprimanded to Parental School and the Detention Home, he was sent to the St. Charles School for the crime of petty theft.

Own(ed) Stories and *True* Confessions

Shaw first met the boy he would refer to as Stanley when he was working as a part-time parole officer with the Juvenile Courts. Stanley's real name was Michael Majer. He was the 14-year-old son of Polish immigrants and came from an exceedingly dysfunctional family residing in Back-of-the-Yards, Chicago. Stanley had been arrested for vagrancy, truancy and petty thievery on many occasions, but he saw in this young parole officer an authentic friendliness. Shaw and Stanley appeared to connect immediately. Shaw invited Stanley into his home. He took the boy to dinner, introduced him to his friends. Without judgment, he listened to him as he recounted his tales of childhood petty crime.

Upon Shaw's urging, Stanley began the writing project—recounting his personal experiences with crime. Shaw would later suggest he develop those recollections into a longer, autobiographical account—a life history in crime. These first-person narratives were a part of Shaw's research agenda developed while working with Ernest Burgess at the University of Chicago as well as with the Illinois Institute for Juvenile Justice. Both W.I. Thomas and Ernest Burgess had made much of autobiographical materials in their own work and encouraged their graduate student to do the same.

Personal confessions, or "street biographies," had been used by British journalists such as Henry Mayhew (1812–1887) a century earlier. In fact Mayhew is credited with helping to develop "oral history" methods with street children in London long before sociologists ever undertook this in America (Bennett 1981, p. 11). But Chicago was an exceptional place in the early 1920s. It was the new American metropolis with all of its vices and few of its virtues. While it emerged as the home for American organized crime, it was also the home of innovative and cutting-edge social research of the time as well as creative modern fiction (Cappetti 1993, Salerno 2007).

True crime confessions were becoming a significant component of pulp fiction of the 1920s and 1930s (Stott 1973); and there can be little doubt that both Shaw and his client "Stanley" had been exposed to this literature. Sitting in his cell Stanley may have read dime-novels and popular confession magazines, which had gained currency both outside and inside of prison. Crime fiction of the day was complimented by new social science research in criminology (Salerno 2007; Linder 1996; Bulmer 1984).

True crime was a significantly rich and variegated genre in the 1920s. While its genealogy in literature is frequently contested by literary scholars, most early twentieth crime stories were linked to city journalism and crime reporting. Therefore, true crime became a non-fiction sensationalistic account of criminal behavior, which often made celebrities of its subjects by revealing the extraordinary elements of their behavior as well as their human complexities.

William Roughead (1870–1952), an attorney in Scotland, became an important figure in converting murder and human tragedy into popular literature. His books, *The Evil That Men Do, In Queer Street, The Knave's Looking Glass, Roughs Walk Here* and others spanned a period of decades from pre–World War I to post–World War II. His influence on American crime writing was significant. Edmund Pearson (1880–1937) his American counterpart was to credit Roughead for inspiring his own interest in this type of fiction.

An important genus of true crime is the criminal and prisoner biography and autobiography. The interest in the life of the urban criminal gained importance as the wrongdoings of outlaws of the Old West was overshadowed by the newspaper descriptions of the diabolical nature of urban deviance. The city gangster took center stage as a figure who represented a proletarian defiance of the rich and powerful. He was in a sense the repository of nineteenth century populist masculinity. While many of the crime stories of the early twentieth century dealt with gruesome serial killings and maniacal ax murderers, post–World War I crime stories dealt with more esoteric criminal types.

Juvenile delinquency *per se* was represented at the close of the nineteenth century by a notorious boy of 14, Jesse Pomeroy, who was found guilty of the kidnapping and brutal murder of a four-year-old boy whose mutilated body was found in a deserted marsh outside of Boston. He later confessed using the same pocket knife for his murder of a ten-year-old girl and admitted to the abduction and torture of many more young children. Prior to his murder conviction Pomeroy served time for kidnapping and torturing boys and girls, some of whom he sexually abused and for which he had been incarcerated in a state reform school along with boys sent there for truancy. The press referred to him as "the boy fiend" because of the particularly brutal ways he murdered and tortured other children. But as the twentieth century approached, the Pomeroy case came to represent the unrestrained quality of young boys who increasingly roamed the city streets. Stories such as this one eventually became the material for movies and novels (Hawes 1971, pp. 3–11).

Just prior to the publication of Stanley's story, Eddie Guerin, a notorious Chicago bred Irishman and self-described "world class thief" (suspected of having engineered a heist of the Louvre's Mona Lisa), won notoriety for being the first man to escape Devil's Island Penal Colony. He later published his criminal confession as an autobiography (Guerin 1928). His publisher, John Murray in London, was renowned for having published the literary works of Lord Byron, Jane Austin and the writings of Arthur Conan Doyle. Guerin's own story gave him international fame as a bank robber in France where he, with the help of his girlfriend, Chicago May Duignan, supposedly absconded with thousands of francs that were never recovered. Other criminals were to follow his lead in recounting their own tales of danger and adventure.

The Jack-Roller is very important historical example of this particular form of narrative (Dearey, Petty, Thompson, et al. 2011). It served as a model that other prisoner-authors, including Nathan Leopold (of Leopold and Lobe), read and used as a guide to secure early release through writing their own contrite autobiography (Salerno 2007, p. 151).

For certain, Shaw was influenced by the criminal autobiography of Jack Black, *You Can't Win*, which was published in 1926. Black (whose real name is never given in his book) was a member of the hobo underworld, a burglar and a thief, who spent much of his life in prison. His book became a best seller and went on to influence the work of William S. Boroughs and others of the Beat Generation. In *The Jack-Roller*, Clifford Shaw (1966, pp. 112–113) gives an extensive description of Black's impressions of the hierarchy that characterizes the code of thieves. And this theme is picked up in Stanley's first person narrative.

In 1929, a University of Chicago student James T. Farrell published his first short story in a literary journal *Blues*. The story was entitled "Slob." At the encouragement of his English professors it was made into a novel and became the basis of proletarian fiction known as the Studs Lonigan trilogy. This work is a narrative of a sensitive and intelligent 16-year-old boy living in poverty and surrounded by racism and violence in Chicago's South Side. It was a coming of age story that depicted the struggles of a child of working class immigrants at a time when boyhood was defined by narrow-mindedness and cruelty. This story of boyhood gives the reader a remarkable insight into the making of a juvenile delinquent, perhaps because of the author's deeper understanding of this character and what it meant to be an insecure boy at that time living in the city.

Farrell, much like his contemporary Richard Wright whose novel *Native Son* (1940) became a classic in naturalism, was to capture the spirit of the times as the Great Depression swept into American cities. Both novelists vividly portrayed the spirit of the urban male delinquent, and depicted such criminal behavior as wedded to a sense of male aloneness and powerlessness. Unlike the Chicago school sociologists with whom both studied, and unlike Shaw's theory, their theory of delinquency had more to do with the structure of capitalism, not the deteriorating neighborhood. For both of these authors the degradation of the human spirit was seen as a product of a predatory market system and unbridled, unregulated material greed.

With the advent of the Great Depression violent crimes spiked in the cities. The disenfranchised now frequently romanticized hoodlums and began to hold them in greater esteem than their own politicians and members of the financial aristocracy. As the country began to veer to the left, labor unions gathered strength. Strikes and rioting of the unemployed became more common place. American liberalism stood its ground. It served as a shield against more radical programs of social justice aimed at the redistribution of wealth. As Bertolt Brecht wrote in 1928: "What's robbing a bank compared to founding a bank?" Street violence spiked but so did capitalistic greed and political corruption. Street criminals were only after the crumbs that millionaires ignored.

Liberal discourse on the making of juvenile delinquents also served the interests of the most powerful. The juvenile delinquent was seen as a boy who lost his way, someone the Boy Scouts might help convert to the straight and narrow. Boys were not born evil, but they were made evil by their parents and the neighborhoods in which they lived. *The Jack-Roller* supported this view. In reading Stanley's story the reader was expected to develop a sense of pity for the lowly criminal. Still Stanley was no urban folk hero; nor was he an Al Capone or Machine Gun Kelly. He was portrayed as a reluctant small-time hooligan who had been beaten down by the tides of urban life. He was not a dynamic criminal like Henry Tufts, a criminal whose autobiography was recorded and edited by Edmund Perason in the same way Shaw recorded, edited and published Stanley's story. Stanley came to represent Chicago school criminology. He was not a character readers could respect or fear like Jack Black, Eddie Guerin or Henry Tufts. Nor was he as radical or reflective as Studs Lonigan or Bigger Thomas. Stanley was a two-dimensional loser from whom society might learn some lessons about how boys became delinquents.

When *The Jack-Roller* was published in 1930, there was substantial sentiment that Stanley, a chronic truant, could never have written something so eloquent—so articulate—without considerable help. Nevertheless, Stanley's writing was good. Shaw swore that the only help he gave was in some editing for grammar and spelling. But we do know from Shaw's own personal archives that he substantially edited out excerpts if not whole chapters of Stanley's story. And while there is no reason to reject the contention that Stanley's words were his own, one must keep in mind that the boy wanted to please Shaw who in turn needed to produce a book that would hold the interest of social scientists and the general public.

Shaw provided a framework and context for the writing. He advised Stanley about his audience and how the book would be used. He helped to structure the book and to organize it (Denzin 1995; Brown 2007; Gelsthorpe 2007). Edwin Sutherland, the renowned criminologist challenged the book as more of a joint product of Shaw and Stanley in that the only story actually written for Shaw by the boy was included in the book's appendix. Much of the book was produced through Shaw's repeated series of requests for Stanley to amplify certain parts of his story and editing out other parts. Sutherland (1932, p. 135) suggested that the story was possibly shaped by "the interests and hypotheses of the investigator."

William Healy had used the term "own story" to describe his interviews with children who came before the court. Healy believed that a child's autobiographical account could reveal important information to the clinician, court officials and researchers. He put quotes around "own story" and used it as a descriptive category for personal case material. In this sense it was an innovative approach in criminology—a field which had been stuck in the pseudo-scientific approach of criminologists like Cesare Lombroso. Such criminologists viewed crime as something inherent in the person. Healy saw the personal recounting, the story told by the child, as a more scientific means of understanding the unique circumstances surrounding one's criminal career (Bennett 1981, pp. 112–113).

However, "own story" was popularized neither by Healy, nor by Shaw. A "boy's own" was associated with a variety of boy oriented papers and magazines published in Great Britain and the United States from the mid–1800s and well into the 1920s. *Boy's Own Paper, Boy's Own Magazine, Boy's Own Journal,* constituted a set of serials published for the edification and enjoyment of boys. They contained stories of boys' adventures, information about male heroes and were influential in shaping youthful masculinity. It had been a construct floating in the ether of sensationalistic story-telling and true confession romances for many decades. For Shaw, the concept of one's "own story" was a bit different from Healy's. Yes, it was a piece of the picture that could be supplemented and supported by more "objective" devices such as records, statistics and court reports. But theoretically it took on another meaning. It was Shaw's contention that the story told by the delinquent was just that—a personal recounting of events. While it might not be an objective, accurate accounting, it was the teller's subjective perception and as such it was crucial. If Stanley did not reveal something in his own story, what was left out was assumed not very significant for the boy.

Shaw appeared to believe that Stanley's behavior was a product of completely discernable, conscious forces, even if Stanley interpreted these forces differently from others. Therefore, there were never projective tests administered to ascertain hidden or repressed material. There was nothing of significance lurking in the unconscious and, even if something were there, nothing was to be done about it. Shaw was looking for a cohesive social narrative, and Stanley supplied it. He saw in this autobiography a self-reflection on a troubled life which could be turned around. Stanley's "own story" provided a narrative of recovery.

Stanley's opening in *The Jack-Roller* is preceded by Shaw's first three chapters, which introduce the reader to the importance of one's "own story" as a method of research, but also provide the data and sociological perspective that Shaw will later use in his analysis of Stanley's story. In fact Shaw annotates Stanley's account by frequently interjecting interpretive and informational commentary, which runs throughout the first person narrative. Stanley's "own story," which is obviously a collaborative effort, is treated as a morality tale that helps illustrate. There is no provision in Shaw's approach for what the boy *failed to say* in his interview or autobiography. There is no recognition that what Stanley omitted could be significant. There is little interpretation and no questioning of the laws themselves.

Shaw and McKay did not come to terms with events repressed by these children—experiences that these boys could easily fail to recognize because of their age or lack of interpersonal sophistication. Shaw's perspective was much more pragmatic and policy oriented. It was focused on the influence of bad neighborhoods. Therefore, the stories told to them or that they solicited were rather circumscribed.

In all the other stories recorded by Shaw and McKay not one boy spoke about being raped or sodomized by a sibling, parent, a relative, or a cell mate. Studies into sexual abuse and early trauma in the home have revealed that nearly 80 percent of children who have suffered sexual assault at first denied that it ever took place and very little reporting of abuse by the child has ever been voluntary (Bradley and Wood 1996). While some boys might portray themselves of victimizers of other boys, few portray themselves as victims. The need for boys to deny pain is essential to their gendered identity (Corbert 2009). Boys are rarely allowed to be victims. If a male child is sexually abused, it is seldom that he allows himself to recognize the abuse let alone come to terms with it. If they are abused, they are pathetic and can no longer be boys. While we will never know the extent of Stanley's sexual abuse (if it did occur), we are given some first person evidence of his physical and emotional abuse. This is something boys can more readily reveal.

Stanley's "Disowned Story": In Some Ways More Interesting

While the narrative of Stanley's life is not naively accepted by Shaw as an accurate accounting of what transpired and how it transpired, it is received by him as the boy's sense of what happened rather than the story he requested. What we don't have in Stanley's story is what Stanley didn't see or what he couldn't see, what he failed to report or could not access. While Stanley talks about sexual assaults that occurred in places of confinement, he doesn't personalize this experience.

Shaw saw the story-telling itself as therapeutic. It allowed the young person telling it to see himself or herself as a human being. It allowed the teller to come to terms with a personal life in crime. But did it really allow Stanley to come to confront more than a fantasy of his life in crime? It is obvious that there is much unreported or selectively reported in his or anyone's criminal autobiography. The book was intended to help secure his early release from prison.

While there is ample evidence of Stanley's inability to make a deep human connection with anyone throughout his story (except perhaps to Shaw himself), it is made more significant by the fact that he was able to be engaged by Shaw and co-construct an autobiography *with* him. Perhaps this points to Stanley's need for human recognition and appreciation. We are told by the sociologist and the boy himself that Stanley finds in Shaw a hero, a rescue figure. And it is clear that such idealization of a substitute caregiving figure was helped along by what psychoanalyst Hans Kohut refers to as mirroring, twinship, and idealization supplied by Shaw and badly needed by the boy to feel whole.

Stanley tells a tale of early abandonment. The loss of his mother at an early age resulting in the infliction of a wicked stepmother. This is in keeping with the fairy tale narrative structure. Nowhere in Stanley's life is there a close or intimate relationship with a woman, chum, sibling, or parent. When an elderly couple seeks to adopt him and shows him comforting love and welcomes him into their home, Stanley cannot reciprocate; he runs away. Some doubt might be raised as to the accuracy of the memory here that Stanley wanted to have, an offer and a denial. While his foster parents, who were apparently wealthy and cultured, bought him expensive clothes and accepted him as a son, Stanley tells the reader that he felt pitied and pined for the excitement of his life on the streets, which was his identity. We are never told that he felt loved, and can only wonder if he had ever experienced such a feeling in his life. Despite his siblings, despite his own wife, children, and grandchildren, he frequently winds-up friendless and alone. Without a more thorough rendering of Stanley's early parental relations, the cause of his ill-relatedness and dissociation remains shrouded.

Starting Down Grade

Stanley's story begins much like a dime novel. "Starting Down Grade" is the title of the chapter (chapter four) that launches his well-crafted, first person narrative. "To start out in life," writes Stanley, "everyone has his chances—some good, some very bad. Some are born with fortunes, beautiful homes, good and educated parents; while others are born in ignorance, poverty and crime" (Shaw 1966, p. 47).

The unfolding of the story begins soon after the death of Stanley's birth mother. He was four years old when she died and by the time he was five his father remarried a woman with seven children of her own. In the second paragraph he writes: "As far back as I can remember, my life was filled with sorrow and misery. The cause was my stepmother, who nagged me, beat me, insulted me, and drove me out of my own home" (Shaw, p. 47). We are treated in this chapter to a description of the boy's relationship with her that he claims to be abusive and the presence of an indifferent and often intoxicated father.

His first reported beating takes place in the kitchen as he "plays" with his cat in a nook behind the kitchen stove: "She pulled me out and beat me, striking me in the face and on the back with her hard and bony hand. That was the first time I ever knew fear" (p. 49). Stanley cites no reason for this action. Later she would "tie him to a chair" and beat him with a stick for being a bad influence on his brother. He frequently talks about going hungry while his step-siblings ate well.

The gentility and vulnerability that Stanley recounts for the reader asks us to believe that his play with this animal was nether vicious nor sadistic and that he was beaten for "no reason" by a woman who he perceived just hated him for being his father's son.

One never hears of his cat again or his attachment to it. Instead, he recounts how he was led into trouble by his stepbrother (a gang leader) and his stepbrother's friend Tony. We are soon regaled with his acts of risk-taking and thievery allegedly instigated by his stepbrother at the behest of his stepmother. Yet, there are numerous conflicting accounts about Stanley and his stepbrother William being sent out by his stepmother to steal. But whenever they are caught Stanley is beaten by her for stealing and being a bad influence on his stepbrother. He tells us his stepmother is cruel toward him, but she is frequently fetching him out of jail while his birth father is nowhere to be found. Nevertheless, thievery and the related excitement become addictive, and Stanley frequently heads down to the bright lights and human wreckage of West Madison Street before he is nine, and is taken in by its wondrous decadence.

The opening of Stanley's "own story" does not explain his beatings as a result of his behavior but rather he sees himself being physically punished for who he was, a boy without a mother to protect him, an unwanted or rejected child and just one more mouth to feed. There is little or no connection between any sense of "wrong doing" and the beating he received other than the irrationality and ill will of his step-mother. Stanley wants us to believe that he was "made bad" by this woman, a woman who didn't love him and loved only her own children.

In subsequent chapters of Stanley's autobiography we are treated to a life unfettered by family or friends. Nothing appears to weigh him down or hold him back. He is unencumbered by guilt. He ingratiates himself with strangers from whom he steals or finds it necessary to bludgeon. Those who want to take care of him, those who take him in, are seen as well-meaning fools to be pitied and are easily betrayed. Everyone gets what he deserves, including himself. How he passes his time while incarcerated is never revealed to us in any degree of detail, and this is where he spends most of his life. When he is outside the adventure begins. He engages in something he considers to be the lowest type of criminality, which is jack-rolling, but it's something he can do well. It requires misleading people, enticing them into corners, gaining their confidence and then physically hurting them and stealing from them. In a way this is a re-enactment of his childhood betrayal narrative. For him these betrayals frequently involve himself as an enticing sex object but instead of being a victim he becomes the sexual predator. He leads people on and bludgeons gay men who want him sexually.

We are given few insights into the psychic reasons for his antisocial behavior, and it's as though he doesn't know any better. Not that he is Alex DeLarge of *Clockwork Orange*. He seems far less violent. He does not confess to murder, though it's not difficult to see that he can easily find justification for taking another's life.

His autobiography is a fascinating and entertaining story of the coming of age of a delinquent. While we don't have evidence of Stanley having stolen from Shaw, we do know that he used Shaw to gain early release from prison, just as Shaw used him to make a name for himself as a criminologist. While the book is a fascinating account of Stanley's own story, it also has a powerful subtext that speaks to issues of gender, sexuality and power. These issues are explored here in subsequent chapters.

Who Owns the Story?

Making his life public might not have been his own idea, yet Stanley's story eventually made him the cause célèbre of hundreds of sociologists, psychologists, historians and thousands of scholars from all over the world. Critics of this type of ethnographic research, such as Norman Denzin (1992, p. 41), complain that Stanley was a creation of sociologists, a "textual production." For Denzin, "these accounts romanticize the subject. They turned Stanley into the sociological version of a screen hero." He was what they wanted him to be.

For Denzin everything is socially constructed and articulated in biased ways using culturally biased tools and subjectively developed interpretive models. All observation is interpretation that is subjectively processed. In fact, in reading *The Jack-Roller*, every reader comes away with a somewhat different story. While Stanley's words are inked onto paper, every reading of his words conjures different understandings over time.

If we are to ask whether or not Shaw put words into Stanley's mouth, the answer would have to be yes, but.... Once Shaw became a sympathetic listener to the young boy's story, the autobiographical tale took on a life of its own. The boy gave Shaw what he thought Shaw wanted to hear and Shaw heard what he wanted to hear. This is common to communication wherein there are disparities of power, and is especially frequent when boys (especially those incarcerated) are being questioned by men in authority (Pollack 1998). Stanley respected Shaw as much as he could respect anyone, and wanted Shaw to think well of him. Shaw was a caring older man who was there for Stanley when his father was not. There can be little doubt that his concern for Stanley was authentic. This form of transference provided a foundation for their relationship. Shaw became Stanley's collaborator and helped to write Stanley's story by listening to it in a particular way and interpreting it.

Jon Snodgrass has pointed to the exploitive nature of this work. The fact that Michael Majer was promised royalties from the book's subsequent printings and never received them, led both Snodgrass and Bennett to conclude that Majer's story was not only financially expropriated but in some ways distorted to serve the vested interests of a particular scholarly position (Bennett 1981, p. 233; Snodgrass 2015, pp. 5–7). However, while this was indeed Stanley's story, it was also a part of Shaw's "own story."

Chapter Two

Decoding *The Jack-Roller*

Originally published in 1930, *The Jack-Roller* has been revisited numerous times as a model of important qualitative social research. Today it remains a sociological classic. Despite various reviews of this work few have ventured to contextualize its story in terms of boyhood, gender, power and sexuality at the beginning of the twentieth century. And this is where much of its unique value resides (See Grant 2014, pp. 118–148).

The story of Stanley is a story typical of many boys from poor immigrant families who attempted to develop an identity of their own on the mean streets of the city in the 1920s. In some ways it has an association with the genre in literature referred to as *Bildungsroman* by Wilhelm Dilthey (1833–1911), the renowned German sociologist and philosopher. These were stories that primarily focused on boys entering young manhood or girls entering womanhood wherein we could get a glimpse into the youth's psychological and social development through a personal narrative of this person's life's experiences (Dilthey 1985). Rousseau's *Emile* (1762), Dickens' *Nickolas Nickleby* (1839), Flaubert's *Madame Bovary* (1857) and Henry James' *Roderick Hudson* (1877) stand as earlier examples of such coming of age stories.

Clifford Shaw's story-tellers recounted tales of personal development within a context of a life course. Most of these were boys who were neglected, abused or otherwise denied the protection of secure family life in early childhood. Often they were fatherless, or with absent or abusive fathers. The Juvenile Court system itself was intended to protect children who came before it, and not punish them. However, in its early stages of development the court reflected white middle class values. It saw as part of its charge the control and regulation of bad boys and viewed its goal as the production of normal young men. In this sense, it helped define what constituted both normal boyhood as well as manhood. Looking at *The*

Jack-Roller as a story of coming of age we can better glean the unique forces that helped to shape boyhood of that era. Not only do we see Stanley in terms of social class and immigrant life, but we also see him representing what it means to be a boy growing up on the dangerous streets of Chicago and encountering a new system of juvenile justice that was designed to put him on the road to "normalcy." Urban life posed certain challenges in developing a "natural male virility" that farm life or peasant life did not.

Early twentieth century psychologists often recommended that boys be treated as young male adults and be physically punished for disobedience. Girls, on the other hand, should be treated tenderly and with great affection. According to John B. Watson in his influential book *Psychological Care of Infant and Child* (1928), boys needed to be tough, control their feelings and resist asking for sympathy. There was great worry that boys were becoming too soft and girl-like. At the end of the nineteenth century Henry James' character Basil Ransom remarks in *The Bostonians* (1886, p. 343): "The whole generation is womanized; the masculine tone passing out of the world; it's a feminine, nervous, hysterical, chattering canting age." Fear of the growing feminization of American culture and its impact on boys was viewed as both dangerous and unnatural. In some respects this was a male reaction to the drive for women's suffrage and the feared loss of patriarchal power. It was also a very real reaction to the uncontrollable economic downturns that characterized cities at the opening of the twentieth century (Bederman 1995). Unemployed white males feared the loss of their jobs to immigrants and non-whites who flooded the job market putting their ability to earn a living in jeopardy and threatening their white privilege. And the beginning of the twentieth century witnessed a quadrupling of women in the paid work force as women began leaving home and moving in greater number into factory, office and retail work in large cities (Odem 1995, p. 21).

In the nineteenth century boys who were shy, emotionally sensitive or preferred playing with girls were frequently singled out as "sissies" or effeminate and made targets of school yard bullies. By the twentieth century doctors began to see these children as psychologically defective and categorized them as "sexual inverts" or homosexuals. They were supposedly in need of some sort of intervention. Thus effeminateness was married to the notion of sexual preference or "inversion." It was during this period that "the homosexual" became an identity as opposed to a sexual preference. Shortly before this "homosexual" was considered by mainstream sexologists as a type of sexual activity. According to William Byron

Forbush in his book *The Boy Problem*, published in 1902, "boys are nearly primitive man; they associate to hunt, fish roam, fight and to contest physical superiority with each other" (Forbush 2013, p. 46). The Boy Scouts of America was formed in 1910 in part to combat the demasculinization of boys, which was seen as becoming far too common.

A new masculinity was needed to debunk this perceived demasculinization, and to the challenge of waves of what many perceived as "brutish" male immigrants of darker complexions flooding American cities during and right after the First World War. To this end social commentators erected a new and more potent form of masculine normalcy. Psychiatrist Edward Strecker (1926) saw the normal boy as having "an appreciable love of power" a "dash of savagery" and "emotional virility." All of these were also traits of a proper jack-roller. And according to one prominent youth worker, Paul Hanly Furley (1926), boys unlike girls were literally hard-wired to join gangs and to be aggressive and violent.

Stanley's Gender Tale

Stanley's autobiography is an epic of gangster life—the emergence of the male urban delinquent. It is also a shift in perspective from the outside observer to the inside self-observed. It is a contribution to progressive era sociology in that it took into consideration the social environment. Mark Twain's *Huckleberry Finn*, published in 1885, was a classic portrayal of rural American boyhood as rambunctious, insensitive and intractable told in the first person. For some readers, it was an eyebrow-raising portrayal of what *white boyhood* was about. Even Clifford Shaw, born onto a Midwest farm, would recount his own boyhood "delinquencies" by recalling time he stole bolts from the local blacksmith shop to repair his toy wagon. The story ended with his denial and the blacksmith turning him upside down and shaking him until the bolts came out of his pockets (Snodgrass 1972, p. 130). But it was child's play compared to the behavior of non-white immigrant boys who were beginning to flood American cities at this time, stealing from the local grocer and having sex with virginal daughters. These new boys threatened the whiteness of cities and challenged the myth of a homogenous social order. These boys were often portrayed in the newspapers as idiots, animalistic hoodlums and spawns of the "dangerous classes." Their presence was thought to threaten street safety and even take jobs away from white adults.

They were for the most part considered a drain on a growing middle class. But Shaw offered some of these boys a chance to tell their stories. First person narration for a young person, gave the child a chance to express how he saw the world from a position of powerlessness, and oppression. In some ways it was an attempt to *even the playing field*.

The end of the First World War saw a proliferation of *True Story*, *True Confessions*, *True Detective*, *Real Confessions* and *True Crime* magazines, which ran a constant stream of first-person exposés. The male self and its construction was a particularly important theme in American literature during this period. It later formed much of the basis of hard-boiled fiction. The male was the loner, the alienated guy with "a loose screw." In 1917 the *Chicago Tribune* ran a story that claimed that World War I was responsible for "more bad boys." "The psychology of the war," lamented the *Tribune*, "[has] turned upon the Chicago boy to make him a more obnoxious individual. He likes to consider himself an American army to put to route some involuntary 'Germans.' He builds trenches in the back lawn and longs ardently for a gun, often getting it" (Nov. 9, p. 16). The same article noted that juvenile crime was up because of the dire economic conditions that the war had instigated. What it took to be a young man in an urban world was particularly informed by sex, danger and violence. Stanley fully understood the role of delinquent as it had been invented and portrayed in the popular culture.

With the help of Clifford Shaw, Stanley constructed a dark narrative of leaving home, growing up, merging into a life of crime and being reborn as a somewhat honest young man. Though he was not an exceptional boy, he wanted the reader to believe that he was. Stanley represents an entire cohort of young boys, children of immigrants, who first found asylum on the city streets and matured in the juvenile justice system. His time is marked by his many crimes and incarcerations. He goes from abusive home to street to jail to dubious respectability. He rides the rails, breaks into houses, rolls drunks, sells his body, and bludgeons strangers for their money. While he recognizes his own destructiveness, we never get a sense that he has much feeling or empathy for others. He remains a victim of circumstance. He is a loner who connects with companions only to satisfy his basic survival needs. He is often disingenuous and we as readers frequently don't believe him. He knows how to con, how to manipulate, and he boasts of this. But he has very little emotional sense of himself or others than what he projects onto them.

Stanley's environment is the seediest part of the Chicago, which adds to the drama. Shaw himself maps out where the boy grew up. The most formative years of his life were conditioned by what historians refer to as

Back-of-the-Yards. Stanley's neighborhood was dark from soot and smoke with a complete absence of trees, shrubbery and grass. Shaw notes: "It is one of the grimmest and most unattractive neighborhoods in the city, being almost completely surrounded by packing plants, stock yards, railroads, factories and waste lands ... [the] air in the neighborhood is smoky and always filled with a disagreeable odor from the stock yards" (Shaw, p. 34). Between 1924 and 1926, twenty-eight percent of males between the ages of 17 and 21 who lived there were charged with serious criminal offenses. It was a place where most nightmares rather than dreams came true.

To be a child of a poor immigrant family at the turn of the century was a challenge for any boy. To grow up in the Back-of-the-Yards was an even harsher sentence. The clash of cultures, the new and the old, took its toll on most children. But the butchery of the slaughter houses and stench of the stock yards invaded the very souls of children. Stanley lost his biological mother to tuberculosis at the age of four and tells the reader, "I never knew a real mother's affection." Just months after her death his father (who was never emotionally close to his remaining children) remarried another Polish-born woman with seven children of her own from two previous marriages. Stanley described her as "devoid of features." He saw her as emotionaly empty. There can be little doubt that Stanley grew-up in a household of abuse and neglect. That he would take away negative life lessons would not surprise any educated reader.

The absence of a father's love is even more obvious to the reader than the absence of a nurturing mother. Constant beatings were the order of the day for most male children who grew-up in immigrant households. And Stanley regales us with his specific domestic terrors. His father was arrested on more than one occasion for beating his wife and sending her to the hospital. The step-mother in turn beat her husband's children. Observers who came into the home saw the children as dirty, abused and malnourished and saw the father as a violent drunk. It was suggested on more than one occasion that the children be removed from the home for their own safety. But this was never done (Shaw 1966, p. 43).

Sex and violence were central to the lives of boys growing up in most poor sections of the city. Psychoanalyst Mechthild Bereswell (2007) contends that Stanley's inability to see his father as an important source of his emotional damage and the corresponding monopoly of blame he placed on his stepmother for having ruined his life, reveals the source of an important internal conflict related to his own masculinity. It also underlies a developing disdain for if not hatred of women, especially powerful women. Stanley remembers his birth mother as a gentle, loving woman who was beautiful and sickly. She was also passive and powerless. This was the feminine ideal of his time and stood in visible opposition to his stepmother, a person supposedly devoid of emotions, a woman more like a man in many ways (Shaw 1966, p. 47). A disdain for female power dominates his story.

Males and male companionship are driving forces in Stanley's early life. His need to be accepted by men runs through his narrative. Added to this is the obvious use of his sexuality throughout his story to lure gay men into traps so his jack-roller buddies could beat them and steal from them. It is Stanley's contention that these "perverts" got what they deserved. And one can only conjecture if he himself felt that the difficulties he experienced as a child (including the loss of his mother, emotional abandonment by this father and the brutal beatings by his step mother) were also well deserved.

Stanley's association with sex is surreptitiously imbedded in his narrative. His very early homosexual experiences (from age six on) testify to its importance in his life. We are told that he associated with boys who taught him how to masturbate and they would visit public baths where they'd sometimes pleasure one another (Gadd and Jefferson 2007). Not only are neighborhood children "inappropriate" toward him sexually in his most formative years and teach him "bad sexual habits" but as a small and frail boy he was subject to sexual assault throughout his many incarcerations. And while he greatly admired older convicts and sought their guidance, he felt they could not be trusted. He speaks negatively of those men who would approach him for sex, yet he found their gaze and desire of him rewarding. He had sex with a number of men for money. While he is frequently prideful, he is also self-loathing, and finds comfort in projecting his own weaknesses on to others, particularly women who seem to constantly betray him, or onto gay men whose perversions he adamantly detests.

He appears driven by an underlying fear that he is neither man enough nor worthy enough for love. His most vicious battles are fought defending what he perceives to be his manhood and fighting against what he sees as a betrayal by women in his life (including his birth mother's abandonment of him through her early death). His first marriage turned out to be a disaster in this regard (Snodgrass 1982). His wife, who became the primary source of family financial support, appeared to challenge his very sense of manhood. He was institutionalized for his violent outbursts that were often directed toward her.

There seemed to be no deep emotional connection with others in his life, little with parents and siblings, and practically none later with his wife and children. He had no best friends. His attachments remained relatively tentative and shallow, although his older brother George would frequently help him. He viewed Shaw's interest and respect for him as special and flattering. To open-up to others was to subject himself to hurt. Emotional distance was both a mark of his manhood and a means of self-protection. Shaw's children, who grew to know Stanley through his many visits to their home, spoke of him as deeply depressed (Personal interview with Bill Shaw). He frequently used gambling and the excitement of criminal behavior as ways to counteract this.

Boyhood on the Street

While some critics have emphasized the uniqueness of Stanley, Shaw certainly did not. Stanley's tale is similar in many ways to other boys who found themselves in similar situations. However, Shaw wanted to make his case study exemplary. He hoped to normalize Stanley as much as possible, so others might have empathy for him. He believed that boys who grew-up on the street would have to use many of the same methods to survive, especially in those times. For Shaw, it was social environment that created the boy jack-roller, not some intrinsic quality of the boy himself. And it should be remembered that Clifford Shaw was breaking with the traditional criminological perspective in this regard. It was his contention that delinquents were social products. This boy was not evil, he was troubled. And looking into his life was a way of locating the trouble's source. For Shaw the street was a cauldron of antisocial behavior and a laboratory for social research. Unlike Clifford Shaw, Stanley frequently alluded to his "disease" or "germ" of criminality that entered his brain (Shaw 1966, pp. 203–205).

Children who were domestically deserted and abused often found refuge with one another on the street. This was the basis of informal gang life. The street offered a place to hide and to find companionship and support. It was a place where one could eke out a livelihood through petty thievery, prostitution and often move into more violent and lucrative activities. Young boys were particularly drawn to the excitement of the seediest quarter of the city. It was a place of adventure where boys got high on adrenalin and testosterone. And Stanley was constantly drawn there:

The first place I went to was West Madison Street, the haven of rest for bums, prostitutes, degenerates, and the rest of the scum of the earth, who gather there to drift on to some other place. "Floaters" is a good name for them. But this place held lures for me. The lures and the irresistible call drew me on like a magnet, and I was always helpless before them [p. 93].

West Madison was a place where boys could forget about school; there they could gamble, roll dice and find easy victims. There were all night movies and vaudeville houses there as well as places to get cheap food. Each and every child from the street had been dealt a bad hand, and every one had a unique tale to tell. West Madison was a mecca for many of these young people. Shaw had faith in these children. He believed, rightly or wrongly, that each boy possessed an autobiography that was ripe with insight. This was the essence of his qualitative research. It was not making the child into a statistical unit, but respecting the originality and dignity of each life story, especially how the story was played out in the child's mind and how the child defied or understood his or her situation. William Healy, a psychiatrist who had worked with Stanley and other boys in the juvenile justice system, was not dismissive of intrapsychic forces. But while Shaw and other reformers emphasized the environment as having had a profound impact on these children, few sociologists ever discussed the broader socio-structural conditions of inequality that fostered these circumstances, nor had they much to say about free-wheeling capitalistic the system that supported it. It was as much taken for granted as was selling one's body in order to eat.

With the influx of poor black migrants from the South looking for work and an escape from racist persecution and the inflow of immigrants, particularly from Eastern Europe, enormous pressures were placed on housing, employment and other social and economic resources just before World War I. Chicago became the scene of one of America's bloodiest race riots in 1916, as well as violent labor disputes. But the city was not an exception. Throughout the United States American cities in the early twentieth century experienced sweeping waves of labor unrest and corporate and police violence directed against it. Blacks and young immigrants were often hired by companies as strike-breakers as unionized labor fought for better wages and healthier working conditions (Olzak 1989).

Stanley lived in a poor, predominantly Polish community. Polish immigration progressed rapidly in the first two decades of the twentieth century nearly a half million Polish immigrants had come to Chicago because of the political conditions in Europe. Germany, Russia and Austria ripped Poland apart and many Poles left Europe to escape war, harsh discrimination and economic oppression. But the American city was no oasis. These immigrants found themselves working long hours in horrid conditions in the meat packing industry bringing home barely enough money to feed their families. Alcoholism intensified as a major urban problem. By 1924, the United States imposed tight restrictions on the flow of Polish immigrants into the country. Like Italians and Jews, they were viewed as inferior human stock and classified as mentally inferior to Northern Europeans who were let in in larger numbers (Pula 1995).

Aside from selling newspapers, poor immigrant boys often found the selling of sexual favors to older men to be a way of sustaining themselves and their families in the 1920s and 1930s (Kaye 2003, p. 16). It was part of what Kerwin Kaye called "sexual pragmatism." If the boy's motives were "strictly financial" there could be no stigma or labeling as a "sexual invert" or homosexual. And the law did not hold underage boys responsible in any way for their "seduction." Jack-rollers took full advantage of this. Despised by other more elite criminal classes, small gangs of jack-rollers (who already were objects of disdain) could freely engage in bludgeoning gay men and robbing them of their money. For a gay man to complain of such victimization was equivalent to an admission of soliciting young boys for sex, and the punishment could be jail for either reckless endangerment, or sexually assaulting a minor. There were very few legal protections if the victim of a bludgeoning was seen by authorities as a "pervert" himself.

In their careful reading of Stanley's story, and combining this with the interviews Stanley gave Jon Snodgrass (1982) later in his life, David Gadd and Tony Jefferson (2007) conclude that there is considerable evidence that Stanley was sexually abused outside of his home both at St. Charles and very early on by older boys and men. They see Stanley's sexual development and almost certainly his early trauma of physical and sexual abuse being disregarded if not completely ignored by Shaw and Burgess who helped the young boy tell his story. Perhaps this was the only way boyhood could be explained by them at the time.

The Romance of Bad Boys and Street Rats

The feral nature of boys (especially poor boys) has a deep and colorful literary history (Kidd 2004). The relationship of young boys to untamed nature and urban savagery has been a central motif in Western film and fiction. It has a rich journalistic genealogy as well. Psychologists of the late nineteenth century often promoted the notion of male savagery. It was argued by at least one renowned adolescent psychologist that young middle class white boys needed to be encouraged to express violence and intense competition in order to dislodge their repressed innate savagery so as to eventually develop into mature "manly" men (Hall 1904). Throughout the early twentieth century, the bad boy became an important trope in a "coming of age" genre. *The Jack-Roller* fits well into this literary class. Kenneth Kidd (2004, p. 12) identifies "American bad boy books" as a subgenre of realism. He sees such books as primarily autobiographical memoirs, which depict a homosocial quest for self-survival in a rapidly urbanizing society. Such books illustrated the myths of male savagery, and promoted emerging theories of juvenile delinquency. In such narratives, the boy was typically seen as suffering from the loss of a mother's love, or worse, he was an orphan. He might also endure an absent or brutalizing father. Frequently, the result of this for such a boy was outwardly directed aggression, contempt for authority, treacherousness and risk-taking. These were valuable character traits for men in any capitalistic society. While many bad boy books attempted to normalize the savagery and violence young boys, particularly those growing up in the mid and late nineteenth century, there was an admission on part of the authors that the primitiveness and savagery was part of male evolutionary and social development. This was not seen as the case with women. In an evolutionary sense there were frequent references in boy literature to white boys emulating young Africans slave children or Native Americans (Kidd 2004, pp. 51–85).

But for the most part, these so-called delinquents were boys beaten down by poverty. In these fictionalized accounts, much like in *The Jack-Roller*, the narrator's young life is portrayed as a heroic tragedy. Troubled boys, who had just the right amount of aggression, could be saved. Better yet, with a small bit of help they could rescue themselves and lift themselves out of the deplorable conditions that made them into delinquents. *The Jack-Roller* was a heroic tale of overcoming odds through resilience, aggression, intelligence and strength. Horatio Alger's stories of boys overcoming poverty and hardship had become very popular in the 1920s as story-tellers found ways of exploiting the thousands of hungry street children surrounding them by making them into tragic characters and giving them happy endings. It was Alger, a defrocked minister accused of "improper behavior" with his young male parishioners, who found a fortune and considerable approbation in these imaginary fantastical tales in which he infused helpless young street boys with ennobling strengths, and gave them a type of judgment, motivation and intellect that allowed them to be fully responsible for their own lives. But for the most part the truth of these boys' existences was nothing to celebrate, noting to write a Disney musical about. These were unloved, filthy, abandoned, often dangerous children who had to escape the brutalization and instability of terror-filled proletarian domestic life. In the process they became what they needed to become to stay alive. And many of them did not survive. Shaw was to join the legion of "child savers" who could socially intervene to rescue troubled boys.

Saving Boys

The American Civil War orphaned tens of thousands of children many of whom made their way to large cities where some were eventually were placed into almshouses but many more filled the streets. Between 1854 and 1929 close to half a million abandoned or orphaned children were picked up as vagrants, packed onto "orphan trains" and sent to live in rural areas in the Midwest to get "support and guidance" from fostering farm families. Boys were particularly wanted on the farm. But just like in the cities from which they came, they were often exploited as sources of cheap manual labor. The authorities and child welfare experts viewed rural life and hard labor as far superior to life in the decadent city. It was in line with America's Calvinistic asceticism. And boys, who could be put to working on the farm, were particularly valuable to farmers. Perhaps here is where the bucolic myth of the value of the rural life for a boy was born. Most boys, however, were subject to unsanitary living conditions away from the main house, abusive practices including, beatings, isolation, rape and starvation. Many were kept out of school. Severe corporal punishment was the common practice on the farm. A good number ran away and hopped a freight and found their way back into lives of vice on the city streets, others became hobos.

The maltreatment of boys during this period was particularly egregious. There was a religious fervor that went along with harsh corporal punishment, which was believed to bring boys closer to God, and make them into men. Despite child-saving reforms that helped to institute a progressive Juvenile Court system in Chicago, the police at the time received greater discretionary power to use force to discipline boys in any way they saw fit including beatings (Walcott 2005). Boys who were judged to be "loitering" were often preemptively arrested. Children were often picked up by the police and charged with crimes they did not commit and for which the authorities had no legitimate suspects. It was not an uncommon practice for police to take bribes from parents in order to keep their children out of jail. Violence was regularly used by the police to regulate juvenile behavior (Walcott 2005, p. 121).

Social historian Stephen Robinson (2006) found that the rape of boys was common place in the early 1900s and largely went ignored until the late 1930s. Before this the laws were quite clear: *"boys cannot be raped."* Rape, according to American law, required forced sexual intercourse with a female (p. 357). Boys were seen as brutalized, but legally boys could not be sexually violated.

In fact boys' bodies have little place in the documented history of juvenile delinquency as opposed to bodies of young girls. "One is hard pressed to find mention of boys' sexuality—or the corporal dimension of their designation as delinquents—in the literature on boys and juvenile delinquency," notes historian Tamara Myers (2005): "This absence is in part explained by the fact that official documents from juvenile justice institutions, like annual reports, are silent on the issue of boys' sexuality." While Meyers is speaking primarily of her research on delinquent boys in early twentieth century Quebec, the same can be said for Chicago at that time. There was very little notice of sexual activities or abuse of boys in jails and detention centers prior to the 1930s, and such a paucity of references led many to mistakenly conclude that either little was going on, or that boys were capable of protecting themselves. Such phenomena was rarely explored by scholars. However, even with contemporary recognition of such problems and safeguards in place, current government studies reveal that 10 percent of young people in juvenile detention have been sexually abused even in their current holding facility during the year in which they were surveyed and 81 percent of these children were abused by a member of the staff of the facility in which they were housed (Beck 2013). It has been concluded that the vast majority of cases of sexual abuse go unreported for fear of more dire institutional or inmate reprisals. But studies also tell us that boys who have been physically or sexually abused and/or neglected at home prior to incarceration are nearly 60 times as likely to be arrested as juvenile offenders than those who were not (Widom and Maxfield 2001). This is phenomenon is as true for boys as it is girls.

Although Charles Dickens had given readers the model of the exploited child in his early nineteenth century Victorian stories, twentieth century

American and British writers frequently associated boyhood with innate ferocity and the pioneer, adventuring spirit. The untamed boy was viewed as a natural and healthy phenomenon. In the United States, more introverted and sensitive boys and boys who exhibited characteristics often associated with girls were viewed as having psychological and developmental problems. This was in line with a fear of feminization of boys through education and culture associated with the middle classes. Such boys were often described as "inverts" by sexologists like Kraft-Ebbing or Havelock Ellis. These were children who were physically boys on the outside, but who displayed characteristics frequently associated with femininity.

For many authors, America's loss of innocence was metaphorically depicted in the degradation of white childhood as a result of urbanization, the influx of dangerous immigrants from Asia, southern Europe and migrating black people from the South. This romance with American rural purity and whiteness and the demonization of disease-carrying immigrants and the filthy rabble of cities appeared to symbolize the corrupting moral influences of urbanization was having on the bucolic soul, especially the loss of innocence of young rural white girls who ventured away from their confined domestic lives. This was clearly expressed in novels like Theodore Dreiser's *Sister Carrie* and Steven Crain's *Maggie: A Girl of the Streets*. If the norm for boys was aggression (physical and sexual), the norm for girls was passivity and purity.

While men were still in charge and in positions of power, some male fictional characters were beginning to develop a heightened sense of self-reflection. Characters frequently were presented as alternatives to the brutishness of masculinity and lack of empathy associated with boyhood and masculinity. Charles Dickens' work depicted the vulnerable side of men and boys. And Oscar Wilde imbued many of his male figures with compassion and sensitivity. The dandy in fact took on a significant position in Wild's work and the work of Baudelaire. The development of conscience, deep thinking and introspection were hallmarks of male characters in Russian novels of Tolstoy, Dostoevsky and Gogol. Male vulnerability and sensitivity gained a secure place in European literature.

Boys in nineteenth century American literature displayed strength, rascality and unrestrained competitiveness. The sensitive male was an anomaly in boy stories of the mid–nineteenth-century; they were more European than American. While Charles Dickens allowed his boys to be seen as victims of capitalistic exploitation and adult abuse, many of his characters had the intelligence to understand some of the complexities of the issues confronting them and exhibited moral courage in the face of adversity. Orphaned chimney sweeps, and children confined to workhouses were not simply prey, but intelligent and complex figures who often struggled to free themselves from positions of abuse. But in the novels of the American author Thomas Baily Aldrich, boys assumed a rebellious and mischievous character. In American literature boys moved away from the victim position to become victimizers, ruffians and con-men. This was essentially American boyhood wherein not only was there a healthy disrespect for the law but a disdain for those who attempt to impose it, particularly upon the poor and landless. There was little respect for poor men who attempted to abide by it.

Boys were portrayed as rebels, fighting against restrictions placed upon them by adult society. Poor boys frequently identified with the disenfranchised and the outcastes and outlaws of the Old West. In games of cowboy and Indian, few wanted the Indian role because they knew how it would end. The American icon of chivalry was the lone vigilante who took the law into his own hands. The American materialistic dream was fighting the corrupt and powerful and winning. Boyhood in America was valued for its savagery, its cunning and its ability to withstand misfortune. Social Darwinism was infused into American economics and sociology. In fact, boys were conditioned to see inequality and poverty as weaknesses and to aspire to be in a position of dominance over others. This was part of the pioneer tradition of American exceptionalism. It was at the heart of industrial capitalism. Edger Rice Boroughs story of Tarzan was to become a popular tale of American masculinity. Published one year after the establishment of the Boy Scouts of America in 1910, *Tarzan of the Apes* was a story of the male conquest and dominance over nature, suggesting civilization through brute force.

The stories of the coming of age of American boys do not bestow upon boyhood the same innocence, frailty and sensitivity associated with girls. Boys in American stories rarely die of exposure, hunger or abuse. It is more likely that if a boy is abandoned, he is raised by wolves rather than devoured by them, or makes wolf-hide clothing for himself. American boys in nineteenth century novels are depicted as rugged, nasty, shrewd and cruel. Henry William Gibson in his classical comprehensive study on boyhood, described the young boy as "a little beast," and notes that "many things that make a difference to man and beast make no difference to him." In terms of sexuality, sex was seen as an innate drive that affected healthy boys and only perverted girls. For Freud a boy's sexuality and his aggression were primal instincts. Girls who were devalued for openly expressing their sexual desires were seen by psychoanalysts as suffering from hysteria and probably in need of vaginal massage. Boys had to subdue and repress their innate sexual aggression and lust for violence. However, if channeled appropriately, these forces could serve productive purposes. Sexual energy could be converted into aggressive energy that helped to define manliness.

Civilization was the outcome of repression and sublimation of sex on the part of males. Only males could bring about civilization by converting these innate drives into activities aimed at controlling and subduing the natural world, including women and animals. Girls were viewed as weak, emotionally dependent and sexually repressed. For most American writers and social theorists this masculinized notion of civilization was further limited by the color of one's skin. Only white males could impose the necessary rational form or order to tame society.

The innocent, unaffected American boy was viewed in the same light as other the primitives who needed to sublimate his innate aggression into something more acceptable like business. As Hanford M. Burr noted in his 1910 study of adolescent boys: "It is well for us to remember that the impulse which leads a man to ruthlessly crush a business or professional rival is in essence one with that which led the savage to fight to the death any possible rival with such weapons as he knew how to use. The moral quality of the impulses is identical, though the law distinguishes between them, and allows a place for one, and assigns the other to a prison" (Burr 1910, p. 109).

From the late nineteenth to early twentieth white males with intelligence and money became symbols of power and strength. Simultaneously, they took on emotionally repressed personas and a type of artificial refinement that announced their social standing but with which they were often uncomfortable. They built lavish homes and furnished them with luxurious imported furnishings. They hired gardeners, butlers and maids. They dressed in finely tailored suits and donned expensive silk hats. However, instead of poor boys desiring to emulate them, many saw in these men a particular type of weakened subspecies associated with their faux civility, a type of femininity or a refined and adulterated masculinity. For boys who lived in poverty, these were hats to throw snowballs at! This was not as Veblen perceived, symbols of aristocratic power, but rather symbols of weakness and effeminateness. Raw power vested in those who had nothing; the hungry peasants and the factory workers. The French Revolution epitomized a disdain for the pantywaist aristocracy.

By the beginning of the twentieth century, along with the rise of labor unions and political conflict, there was a surge in the growth of the police state and the institutionalization of schools to contain and control this savagery. The juvenile justice system was a part of the state machinery used to control the minds and bodies of poor children. There was a corresponding crack-down on those who were seen as threatening the newly entrenched aristocracy. Boyhood, particularly boyhood coupled with poverty, was dangerous.

These boys simply needed to be tamed by men working for the powerful. Perhaps discipline could be imposed through corporeal punishment at school or through having boys disciplined in the military or the Boy Scouts. Grants from wealthy families and religious institutions went to establish organizations of social and cultural control aimed at harnessing this energy.

Race and Delinquency

One difficulty with the liberal narratives put forth by Chicago school sociologists was their treatment or failure to address the powerful influences of race on developing notion of juvenile delinquency and the system of juvenile justice. While on one hand promoting the need for racial equality, professors at the University of Chicago made little effort to address racial segregation even in university housing, city schools, hospitals, beaches and prisons. In fact most white professors in the sociology department at the University of Chicago sent their children to the white-only Lab School that was the exemplar of liberal education designed by John Dewey. It wasn't until 1937 that the University's Quadrangle Club, which was the exclusive faculty dining room frequented by most prominent professors there, lifted its color ban. It had long been closed to Jews and women as well.

As previously noted, Hull House was primarily aimed at Americanizing poor immigrants from Europe who had poured into the city bringing with them their foreign ways. Separate settlements were opened for people of color from the South. But these were not given much importance since the desperate drive to promote assimilationist programs for immigrants overshadowed the plight of Black people. Black folk spoke English (Hansen 2011). However, there were few facilities that would admit young black boys and girls who were abandoned to the streets. The disappearance of black children often went unreported.

In his study, *Juvenile Justice in the Making,* historian David S. Tanenhaus notes that there was a significant recognition on the part of juvenile justice professions of the enormous difficulty finding adequate care for dependent and neglected children of color. Most social welfare institutions that were run through private and religious contributions could establish racial criteria as well as religious criteria for those they might serve. Most of these progressive community-based organizations refused to take in black children. Because of this abandoned black boys and girls, who grew in numbers in the 1920s, were sent to state institutions and correctional facilities which had gradually become more integrated (Tanenhaus 2004, pp. 36–38).

The Chicago Vice Commission's report, *The Social Evil in Chicago* published in 1911, and overseen by W.I. Thomas, Charles Henderson, Graham Taylor at the University of Chicago, along with William Healy, the renowned child psychiatrist, noted; "Negroes are much more liable to arrest than whites since police officers share in the general public opinion that 'Negroes are more criminal than whites,' and also feel that there is little risk of trouble in arresting Negroes, while greater care must be exercised in arresting whites" (Vice Commission of Chicago 1911, p. 345). According to the report the crime rate for young black men was exaggerated by the fact that there were fewer arrests for similar crimes for whites than blacks because it was far easier to arrest black youth. Accordingly, "fewer Negroes than whites escape prosecution." One criminal court judge told the commission: "Young white men are banding together in gangs and deliberately going out and holding people up, right and left, and shooting them down. I notice that there are few colored imitators of the white men, but the bad man of the city of Chicago at the present time is a young white man" (p. 345). Another judge noted: "I was astonished at the number of criminals involved in the sexual abuse of children. But I remember no case in which a colored defendant was charged with that crime" (347). Yet the Commission was to note: "The history of social evil in Chicago is intimately connected with the colored population" (p. 343).

Stanley observes of his time spent in Bridewell, the Chicago House of Detention, that "Niggers (were treated) no better than brutes." Accordingly, "here they were given the hardest work, the worst cells, and subjected to the most brutal punishment" (Shaw 1966, p. 157). He goes on to explain: "Everybody, especially the guards, are prejudiced against them" (Shaw 1966, p. 157). While professing to be sensitive to the disparity in the treatment of young black men, Stanley echoes many of the racist stereotypes of his time, seeing "niggers" as the lowest form of criminal and granting himself a status somewhat above his black counterparts.

As noted black children who resided in Chicago were not given the same access to juvenile courts or juvenile detention as their white counterparts and by and large were sent to regular adult prison or county jails for minor infractions of the law to be integrated into a population of adult serious criminals. It was not uncommon for a 7-year-old black child abandoned to the street to be taken through adult court and sent for an extended stay in Bridewell or other state run institutions while his white counterpart found his way into a juvenile detention center or foster care (Ward 2012, pp. 79–85). A Hull House study published in 1913 noted that despite the fact that young black male children constituted only 3 percent of Chicago's population, they constituted 12 percent of the adult jail population. They were subjected to harsher sentencing than white boys, and much harsher treatment once they were there.

The so-called "Black Belt" in Chicago (which came to be referred to as *Bronzeville* during the Chicago Black Renaissance) constituted an area of the city to which most black migrants from the South lived. Restrictive covenants and real estate steering prevented black people access to quality housing, clean water and fresh air. Close to 75 percent of the black population was relegated to the most dangerous and unhealthy part of the city and had little or no chance of leaving. Homes of African Americans infrequently located in middle class white neighborhoods were often bombed. Between July 1917 and March 1921 58 homes of black families were bombed (Drake and Cayton 1945, pp. 178–179). For the most part progressives who advocated for the rights of children in the courts did not include children of color in their appeals. The education of black children was relegated to overcrowded, dilapidated structures with a high proportion of unlicensed teachers and school buildings in the most dilapidated condition. The unavailability of recreational space for young African Americans was taken up in the report on the Chicago Riot in 1916 and seen as an issue connected to racial conflict.

The fact that Stanley was held up to represent the new stream of juvenile delinquents who emerged from immigrant families signified part of Shaw's blindness to the growing number of incarcerated boys of color, and the unique problems they confronted compared to Polish and Italian boys. In this sense, while *The Jack-Roller* represents an attempt by American sociologists and criminologists to develop a homogenizing sociological representation of juvenile delinquency by examining the life of this one boy and attempting to generalize from it, they failed to distinguish the dire plight of boys of color, or pay much attention to the issues confronting young white girls and girls of color. Race is hardly on the radar here, and perhaps this is because the notion of juvenile crime as a product of "cultural conflict" would then be more difficult to sustain.

Chicago School Research and Delinquency

The American portrayal of male juvenile delinquency has been infused with cultural stereotypes that are not expunged by the Chicago school research. While these scholars helped to dislodge the popular view of criminality being something that was innate, or inherent in one's genetic make-up connected to lower ordered human beings, their research and methods seemed to compliment and confirm the tabloid perspective as well as the perspective taken by the "child savers." They did not look at the psychological impact poverty and discrimination had on families and their offspring, nor did they condemn the abuses of labor or the exploitation of the poor. They sometimes agreed with the negative stereotypes of immigrants and the poor portrayed in the press and by so doing helped to perpetuate such portrayals. They failed to look at such things as alcoholism and family abuse head-on, and they eschewed recognizing changing sexual mores and attitudes among the younger generation.

But what they did accomplish was to help humanize the public image of troubled boys. *The Jack-Roller*, for all its faults, presented Stanley as a somewhat complex person with ideas and conclusions of his own based upon his unique experiences. Boys who were interviewed for their studies were each exceptional. And the interviewers were sympathetic, which itself was a means of eliciting a self-edited version of their lives. What was presented of these boys' life stories in Shaw's books was aimed at supporting such community based projects of social intervention and amelioration such as the Chicago Area Project, which was funded both privately by the economically advantaged and by local municipal government.

We are indebted to Shaw and McKay for their dedication to finding ways to intervene and assist white boys before they found their way into a dysfunctional corrections system that could only make things worse for most of them. Yet, it is difficult to say the potential risk of incarceration for the boys they did serve. While community organizing and organized recreation were positive answer to address the needs of poor children in poor communities, it was a very limited one. Politically, it appeared to be the safest avenue.

In examining some of these autobiographical accounts in greater detail, it might be possible for us to discern the much greater variety of challenges confronting these children that were either ignored or went unrecognized at that time. While ignoring many of these factors that led to juvenile incarceration did serve the interest of the theoretical approach adopted by Shaw and his colleagues, it also supported a biased if not conservative view of the urban world at that time.

Chapter Three

Shaw's Other Boys

The Jack-Roller took on a life of its own in scholarly sociological circles. While Stanley became the darling delinquent of sociologists, there appeared to be a considerable portion of his story that went untold or was masked from the reader. Jon Snodgrass recognized this and went back to find Stanley who became the subject of his important study, *The Jack-Roller at Seventy* (1982). This follow-up study provided evidence that *The Jack-Roller* might have been a misleading life narrative. Unlike Clifford Shaw's romantic portrayal of Stanley's life as redemptive wherein Stanley secured a job as a salesman and married the women of his dreams, the real Stanley was later arrested for a botched armed robbery attempt and eventually confined to a mental hospital for having threatened his wife with a knife. His life story was punctuated by fist fights, walking off his jobs, bouts of depression, gambling and more intense bipolar symptoms. These are revealed in Snodgrass's interviews with Stanley. There is a particular type of toxic masculinity exhibited here, wherein Stanley's anger and frustration are linked to his displays of closed-mindedness, racism, homophobia, and misogyny. His emotional inaccessibility, his black and white thinking are qualities not alien to Shaw's own understanding of manhood. Terry Kupers (2005) has recognized such qualities as disproportionately represented in American prisons and writes about it as a structural impediment to seeking mental health among such men.

Contained in Snodgrass's exploration of Stanley's later life is an abandonment narrative; a man who spent most of his aging years alone, without the support of family or friends; a tragic figure who could not ask for help as it might be perceived to be weakness. While he did remarry, his second marriage was also fraught with difficulties and ended in his physical abuse of his wife and her filing for divorce. His attachments seemed weak and plagued with insecurities. This was a volatile man, whose episodic explosions of anger were triggered by the slightest frustration. His brother George would help him out of jams and, in later years (after the death of Shaw), come to be his main support, the only person upon whom he could always depend.

Clifford Shaw's work on delinquency, however, is not built completely on the story of Stanley. Shaw's empirical research on youthful offenders constitutes a wealth of important insights and observations. Along with his research partner Henry McKay, he began to address important policy issues of their day (Shaw and McKay 1942). But the personal stories he and his staff collected on these young men helped to humanize the so-called juvenile delinquent and show the youthful offender as warranting both closer study and the possibility of a second chance. These tales were an antidote to the press portrayal of these boys as street monsters and a blight on society.

The personal narratives that were collected from boys incarcerated for violating the law reflected those qualities associated with most boys of that time but which went largely ignored by the tabloid press. Rage and insecurity were among these traits that for the most part were ignored in popular media. From Shaw's first person accounts, there could be no doubt that the lack of familial, religious, communal and educational support for these boys appeared to lead them to acts of desperation and criminality. If Shaw were psychologically trained he would have easily picked up on such self-destructiveness. But there was little here beyond a focus on social structure. A critical psychological piece was missing.

The Jack-Roller was followed by Shaw's *Natural History of a Delinquent Career* (1931) and *Brothers in Crime* (1938). In each of these books, Shaw had young boys provide portraits of their lives in crime as *life processes*, by which he meant the development of attitudes, habits and values over an extended period of time. But if this was his aim, one could say he fell a bit short of his goal. That boys of 15 or 16 could have a deep understanding of either themselves or the conditions that led them into lives of crime was an extremely optimistic position to hold, especially if anyone understood adolescent psychology. The chronology of a delinquent career is another matter. But even here, the boys themselves sometimes got even this chronology wrong. There can be little doubt that the history of criminal events and incarcerations had to be reviewed carefully by the editor to make the story coincide with the institutionally recorded events. We know today that family-based trauma, sexual, psychological, verbal or physical, have a profound impact on memory and how one experiences things. Prenatal care and nutrition also play major roles in the development of children's psychic lives, not simply their physical health. While this information was becoming clearer in the 1920s, it wasn't popularized until much later. And this factor was something that sociologists and criminologists of the time frequently overlooked.

The importance of memory is significant to this type of research (Thompson 2010). How one remembers, what one remembers and what one chooses to forget are significant factors that shape the personal autobiographical narrative. Since the 1980s autobiographical memory has become a focus of cognitive research. How one constructs a notion of self through relating a chronological series of episodes in one's life must be filtered through both idiosyncratic and social experiences that have shaped one's cognitive processing, and the way through which one maintains, recollects, fails to recollect, or edits memory. It is important to keep in mind that the notion of one's "own story" is never one's own in any real sense. It is a story that is always grounded in a socio-cultural environment and is intersubjectively constructed. Psychological organizing principles and what Bourdieu refers to as *habitus* play significant parts in what one experiences and how one perceives and interprets those experiences. One's sense of the past must be selective in order to develop a self-portrait in line with how one understands the world. Shaw's attempt to construct a "typical" delinquent was doomed to fail. But he continued to try.

The *Natural History of a Delinquent Career* (1931) is a series of successive excerpts from Sidney Blotzman's life in crime. Again, Shaw creates an alias to cloak the boy's true identity. By the time *Natural History* is published, there is evidence that Shaw learned from *Jack-Roller* certain key lessons. First, we are given greater testimony from Sidney's mother, father and brother about their relationship with him. We learn his friendships or group associations helped to foster and encourage his antisocial behavior. Sidney is portrayed as a severely abused and neglected young child looking for the approval of others.

He gained a sense of importance by associating with older boys who were dangerous and powerful. Secondly, Shaw makes sure to include in the body of the text extensive references to such things as court transcripts, newspaper accounts and social services reports. The presentation of Sidney is more controlled and choreographed by Shaw. Although the life of crime here is much more variegated and sensationalistic, Sidney's story becomes more of an indictment of the system of policing, corrections and the courts which he saw as culpable in producing criminality.

This book begins with Sidney's crime of auto theft, kidnapping and sexual assault as described in newspaper accounts and court records. In the press, Sidney Blotstein (a Jewish boy of immigrant parents) is labeled a "moron." The term "moron" is used not only to describe those who were mentally deficient at the time, but also to rapists in general. But terms like "moron" and "idiot" likewise served as a code for racism associated with the American eugenics movement that saw Jews, Pols, and Italians as mentally inferior groups. The early 1920s were witnessing a backlash to Eastern and Southern European immigration, particularly the immigration of Pols, Italians and Jews. The popularity of American anthropologist Madison Grant (1916) and the eugenics movement, labeled these immigrants as intellectually and physically inferior to their northern European counterparts (Leonard 2016).

As we read Sidney's personal retelling of his crime, we get a very different accounting of the story. We learn about the crime "in his own words." From records of institutional testing of his mental acuity as well as his retelling of a complex narrative, he seems far from a moron. In fact, he is well above average in intelligence, significantly more intelligent than Stanley, perhaps even Shaw himself. While we come to see him as a criminal who grows more callous with each crime, we also come to see with great clarity the misshapen social institutions that helped to make him this way.

Once again Shaw sets the story of this young boy in one of the most miserable, dank and poverty stricken neighborhoods in Chicago in which the chances of being sent to prison as a young man are far greater than the odds of graduating high school. As the tale unfolds we begin to understand the sources of this boy's complexity—a violent alcoholic father who provides little support for his family, an abused mother who loves him, but is seldom there for him.

Like Stanley, Sidney is an adequate story-teller. Vignettes are chronologically woven together with surface memories and no subplots. There is a lack of affect and nuance in these recountings which bleaches emotive color from these incidents. The reader is unlikely to identify with him or with other characters. The details presented are focused on criminal activities and how Sidney wound up in jail or was arrested. There are very few references to the world surrounding him, or non-criminal incidents in his life. In this way Shaw does the boy a disservice. Sidney read books, but with the rare exception of reading Karl Marx in his early adult years, we don't know what he reads or what he thinks about what he reads. We know he goes to cinema, but we do not know what films he has seen or what appeals to him or why. There are no references to people and public events to ground the reader in the times. Although he went to school, we really don't have much in the way of detail on how he got along with his teachers or classmates, or why he stopped going. Were there subjects he liked? How did he feel being in school with others, as a Jew? Was he a bully? Did he get bullied? There is never a reference to the music which he must have heard and liked or disliked. There is no space to explore popular culture of the time, his attitude toward his own Judaism. There are no sports. He neither plays at a sport nor cheers for a team. Although his story is set in the 1920s, it lacks references to the vibrant social world around him, a world of political and cultural change. The story is narrowly descriptive and clinically presented, which makes it uninteresting and inadequate.

Despite such omissions Sidney's memories reveal a human being, not the so-called moron presented in two-dimensional tabloid descriptions. Though we see him as growing more violent, perhaps even more sadistic than Stanley, we sense a greater intelligence here, a greater complexity. He is psychologically oriented, even analytical. He makes several escapes from detention facilities in variously creative ways. Unlike Stanley, he does not want to pin blame for his violence on his mother or his surroundings though he sees how they contributed to it. Like Stanley, he appears a loner. His life resonates with the prominent motif of the Chicago school studies, *alienation.* Still Sidney, unlike Stanley, has a sense of self-esteem. He seems much bolder when he has an audience of fellow delinquents to whom he needs to prove himself. While he starts out as a small time criminal, he increasingly becomes associated with more experienced and violent felons. He is a show off. He wants to make a name for himself and believes he can do this through crime. Like Henry Hill in *Goodfellas*, he looks up to mobsters as men to emulate. He longs to be respected by those on the FBI's most wanted list. This is in contrast to the contempt he carries for his own father.

We are told by Shaw that Sidney's delinquent career began at the age of seven, and we are introduced to a family with a weak, alcoholic father who physically abuses his wife and children, including Sidney. As in *The Jack-Roller*, the neighborhood is "one of the worst slums" in the city, with large accumulations of debris in the streets and alleys, deteriorating housing stock "unpainted, dilapidated wooden tenements, interspersed with warehouses, junk yards, factories" and with one of the highest rates of delinquency in Chicago. This is what Ernest Burgess referred to as a "zone in transition." We are told that this is an area with a vast assortment of immigrant groups the majority of whom were from eastern or southern

Europe, groups that researchers working with funds of the Rockefeller Foundation target as racially dangerous and inferior. There is significant population shifts in these neighborhoods as newly arriving groups displace older ones. Robert E. Park used the term "invasion and succession" and Shaw used the term "social disorganization" to describe family and community in collapse due in part to "cultural conflict" that he saw as intergenerational as well as intergroup.

Unlike Stanley, whose criminal career was made to seem limited to crimes like mugging and petty theft, Sidney's life was one that encompassed car thefts, sexual assault, shootings and violence. The *Harvard Law Review* (1931, p. 1325) remarked that the story here (as well as Stanley's story in *The Jack-Roller*) constituted "fairly typical reactions and attitudes" of such delinquents and went on to criticize the autobiographical narrator (Sidney) for his "borrowed" sociological "insights" which were "irritating" and seriously limited the book's scientific value. The reviewer went on to note that the story's focus was "ill caste in the mold of the author's (Shaw's) etiological concept—the delinquency area." Still, unlike Stanley's story, Sidney was not seen purely as a product of his impoverished environment. Like Stanley he was not motivated purely by basic survival needs. Many of his crimes were activities in which he engaged for his own amusement.

Sidney's home situation, while quite dysfunctional, had the presence of a loving but seemingly inept mother. He had an older brother who did not get into trouble and who supported his family by working, giving his income to his mother and becoming active in his synagogue. Sidney readily assumed the role of the "bad boy" or the "bad son" as a form of identification to distinguish himself from his older sibling who had gained most of his mother's attention. In a prolog to Sidney's story written by sociologist Ernest Burgess, greater attention was paid to the psychological complexity of Sidney given his above average intelligence and loving mother. Yet neither Burgess nor Shaw saw this sibling relationship as significant enough to warrant closer examination, nor as a central factor in the narrative guiding Sidney's recklessness and search for an identity as an outsider.

Sidney's desire to be a successful and respected criminal of some renown led him into taking greater and greater risks. He was by his own description "cocky and self-confident" and took "real pride" in his ability to steal (Shaw 1931, p. 228). Sidney was self-centered and hedonistic. He felt more alive when getting away with big robberies, even small thefts; and for these feelings he was willing to take significant punishment. Aside from this he had no desire to work for the little money employers would be willing to pay him. Crime would enable him to be potent and well respected.

In an attempt to provide us with a "natural history" of a delinquent career, Clifford Shaw again borrows heavily from the ecological modeling of his teachers Park and Burgess. And there can be little doubt that the framework he imposes upon Sidney is the one favored most by Shaw and the Chicago School. Even the term "natural history" evokes a sort of evolutionary framework, a kind of "survival of the fittest" metaphor. It is this struggle to construct a sociological framework that is free from psychology and economics, but which emphasizes the human ecological ordering (a "natural" ordering) of social events that eventually diminishes the value of this brand of urban sociology. Behind this classical approach rests "natural laws" of society that operate without human cognition at the helm. But Sidney's own narrative breaks him free of this framework. If Stanley's story was one of remorse and redemption, a boy who sees the light and goes straight, Sidney's constructs a more fatalistic tale. Instead of blaming his mother for helping to make him this way, he lays much of the blame at the feet of the institutions of social control, ranging from parental school to prison. Foreshadowing the argument put forth by Michel Foucault that such institutions are culpable in creating the conditions they were developed to remedy Sidney notes: "An ounce of reformation in a correctional school, sometimes causes a ton of deformation" (Shaw 1931, p. 185).

Both Sidney and Stanley came from immigrant families that experienced many of the hardships of poverty in the big city, the lack of formal education and a well-functioning home life. But these factors of "social disorganization" can be seen here as only part of the story. The other part was more psychodynamic. Both boys were not only products of poor environments, they developed very different perspectives on life. Family life was overtly dissimilar and there is a sociological failure to recognize the cultural and religious differences let alone the psychodynamic factors at play. Sidney was a quick learner, learning the ins and outs of criminal behavior, learning to be a "bad guy." "I wanted to be one tough guy," Sidney notes. For him and other boys of similar circumstances, being tough meant being a man, being able to defend oneself against the bullies, and secure a living through violence and intimidation in a world in which children ate from garbage cans, stole coal from the railroad tracks, and sometimes died in the streets from cold and starvation. He did not cast himself in the role of victim as did Stanley, but rather viewed himself as a predator. Both Stanley and Sidney came from environments with absent, alcoholic fathers. Both seemed to adopt a deep-seated misogyny that ran through the machismo culture of that era. Both abused women physically and developed complex rationalizations for their behavior. But Sidney, the seemingly more intelligent of the two according to public records, was considerably "more dangerous," more "hard boiled."

We have no sense in Sidney's story of his ability to be intimate with another person. Like with Stanley, we are never shown an expression of his love for anyone (man or woman), or anything resembling love. He always appears to be holding something back. This is so often the case in this story that the reader must sometimes wonder how honest he is being with himself, or us. Would he actually trust the interviewer with the truth? Sex is something he appears to engage in either for money, immediate gratification, or to intimidate another. It is never connected to his caring for another person. Even his gang memberships are short lived and fleeting. He uses the gang to advance his personal agenda. We detect no sense of authentic loyalty to any person or group.

Significantly absent in his story and the story of other boys who were interviewed is the role of alcohol or drugs. There is no mention of these boys smoking cigarettes, although we are told that the vast majority of those brought to juvenile court were smokers and smoking was nearly universal for those incarcerated at St. Charles School (Eadie and Eadie 1911, pp. 262–263). That many of them came from alcoholic families need not imply that they themselves had a propensity toward substance abuse. But the reader might be surprised at the complete absence of any significant role played by such substances in these criminal narratives. As early as 1918 the Chicago Tribune reported that experts estimated that 50 percent of all crime in Chicago could be attributed to narcotics (*Chicago Tribune*, Dec. 7, p. 17). World War I had a profound effect on the increase in drug use among young men. Certainly, drugs were not as vilified as alcohol before the war. Opium, morphine and cocaine addictions had been a problem among prostitutes for some time, but drug use gradually increased among young men, especially those who had seen the horrors of war in Europe once they returned. The prohibition against alcohol was soon joined by illegalization of other drugs, but these restrictions only helped to increase demand for them. The rate of crime associated with drug and alcohol sales on dark markets soared. Some of the IJR unpublished interviews give evidence that boys were involved with trafficking illegal alcohol after prohibition.

Paternal care of urban boys living in poverty was extremely limited if not absent. Boys had few male companions or role models to emulate. According to historian Robert Griswold (1993), much of the disciplining of children of the lower classes remained in the hands of mothers. The only lesson most of these boys would learn from the men they called fathers were erratic beatings and verbal abuse under the parental influence of alcohol and the umbrella of discipline. Fathering of poor boys in cities like New York or Chicago in the early 1900s was a challenge for those struggling to survive. In fact the processes of industrialization and urbanization produced a massive separation of fathers from domestic life.

Katherine Nickerman (1993), a researcher on population at Columbia University, found that between 1900 and 1940, urban underclass husbands began deserting families in increasing numbers if not permanently then for prolonged periods of time. Women, like Sidney's mother, became primary supports for their children and had to avail themselves of public assistance that was becoming more accessible at this time. Men were often demoralized by the conditions under which they worked, and the rate of alcohol addiction grew significantly among new immigrants. Drinking was done outside the home and men would frequently not come home until they were fully inebriated. "At the very least," notes Nickerman, "saloons were places for men to reclaim the drinking and sociability that had once been integrated into their working lives.... At the very least the saloon was a sphere into which domestic demands did not intrude, and saloon going may have signified resistance to the needs of wife and children" (p. 213).

Nickerson finds it likely from her analysis of the historical data that heavy drinking not only was a cause of domestic tension, but also a creation of domestic conflict and family dissolution as the family's meager resources were squandered on alcohol in order to escape the horrors of sobriety. Sidney's father was a good example of this. After disappearing he'd come home only to physically abuse his wife and children, and then depend on them for financial support even though they were receiving minimal public assistance. One day Sidney and his mother returned home to find that his father sold the decrepit furniture they still owed money on in order to engage in a drinking binge. We also see the same behavior on part of the father in Shaw's study of five brothers in *Brothers in Crime* (1938).

Parenting of the Poor Children in the Industrial American City

As the American birth rate began to fall in the late nineteenth century, and as labor unions were becoming more powerful, there was a decisive liberalization of immigration restrictions that had as a goal an influx of cheap unskilled workers. Between 1880 and 1920 23 million immigrants came to the United States. This migration into cities of poor foreign born ethnics put pressure on meager social resources and kept workers' salaries low. But by 1924 the reaction to the influx of eastern and southern European immigrants led to the passage of the Johnson-Reed Act, which tightened up this migration of all but northern Europeans. Discrimination against Jews and Pols is hardly touched upon in the work of Shaw or Burgess.

The abuse and exploitation of immigrant labor in the slaughter houses, meat packing plants and tanneries of Chicago, in which Sidney's father and other fathers of poor immigrant children found themselves needs to be understood here. While this was not the only place of employment for poor immigrants, it was a significant one at the turn of the century. Upton Sinclair's best selling novel, *The Jungle*, was not specifically aimed at uncovering the contamination of meat, the lack of food inspection, and the filthy conditions under which beef and pork were prepared for market; although it was successful in unveiling these practices and helping to usher in food inspection reform. It was more intended as a testament to the deplorable conditions under which Chicago immigrants were forced to work. Sinclair, a socialist, was to claim that his book gained popularity, "not because the public cared anything about the workers, but simply because the public did not want to eat tubercular beef" (Bloom 2002, pp. 50–51).

Not only did most male immigrants in the early twentieth century work in dark, noisy, freezing, unventilated buildings in the winter and hot sweltering conditions in the summers, they stood on their feet for most of the day, elbow to elbow. In the slaughter houses they were surrounded with the squeals, groans and cries of animals being killed and often stood boot deep in blood and intestines of the animals they eviscerated. The stench was overpowering. It was not unusual for workers to lose fingers or hands and find pieces of themselves in rendering vats. There was no medical insurance and this was the cost of having a job. Too many accidents could result in being fired. Workers' pay was barely enough to feed their families, and laborers were often fired soon before their pay check came and sometimes were never paid. Workers in the meatpacking industry were not unionized until the 1930s and the fathers of many of the boys who were interviewed by Shaw and his colleagues worked under these or similar conditions.

For the sons of such workers to desire to emulate their fathers was unlikely given these circumstances. Their father's seemingly had no future.

They seemed helplessly exploited and pathetic. Boys certainly did not want this for themselves. These men seemed defenseless, perhaps even emasculated. Unlike some immigrants who came from more urban areas in Europe and had modest skills and education and a familiarity with English, it was still a struggle but seemingly not as hopeless. These immigrants saw education as a way to advance. But peasants from Italy, Poland and other rural European areas had greater difficulty understanding its importance in terms of stratification. Most immigrants of this time did not view it as helpful and could not impress the value of education on their children since many looked upon it as a waste of time. They often were religious and prayed for change. Therefore, the only way many of these boys saw themselves as financially well off was through forms of theft, mimicking the robber barons like John Rockefellers, John Jacob Astor and the Andrew Carnegie, but on a much smaller scale. Risk taking was one of the few strategies learned from reading the newspapers. Jail did not appear to be much worse than the conditions under which they already lived and some even preferred it to home.

The absence of loving and nurturing fathers was common to most lower-class urban children in this era of barely regulated capitalism and labor exploitation. The pressure on uneducated immigrant men, particularly those who spoke little English and who were expected to provide for a family, could not be much greater. Alcoholism at the turn of the century was rampant among poor male immigrants, and often was a response to the personal degradation, noxious working conditions and the physical and psychological abuses suffered at the hands of greedy and conniving employers and overseers who cared little for their workers and treated them abusively. Their children suffered the consequences. The infant mortality rate in Chicago was one of the highest of all major American cities. Health surveys showed 91 deaths per 1,000 children from birth to five years of age in 1920. The death rate for black children was nearly twice this. Most of these deaths were in the poorest areas of cities. Most orphanages and foundling asylums were for white children only and run by non-profit religious organizations that were underfunded and could only serve a fraction of those who were abandoned to the streets. The orphanage and foundling hospitals were outlets for unwanted children or children parents could not afford to feed, clothe and house. But there were limited beds here in these mainly religiously run institutions. It was more likely that children of the urban poor would wind up dead or incarcerated rather than in orphanages. Foster parenting, a system dating back centuries, was often viewed as a way of simultaneously providing for abandoned children and giving families (frequently farm families) extra labor power. Surrogate "parents" were provided by correctional facilities, foster homes, poor houses, asylums and reformatories, all of which appeared to be exploitive and punitive.

The difficulties in raising children in the poorest quarters of any city at the turn of the century were daunting. Deteriorating housing stock, lack of potable water and sewers, unpaved roads and pollution were only a part of the problem. Overcrowding, lack of recreational facilities, health epidemics and poor education compounded these difficulties. American industrial cities like Chicago were unhealthy, even life-threatening and there was a stigma associated with paltry public assistance that required sanctimonious lectures by home-visiting social workers. Conditions were particularly harsh for immigrants who came from some of the poorest enclaves of peasant society in Europe. Many had never lived in a city before, or even visited one. It was observed by Sophonsiba Breckenridge and Edith Abbott (1912) that the vast majority of children hauled into juvenile court in Chicago between 1899 and 1909 were children of immigrants. Seventy-four percent of the parents of delinquent boys and 67 percent of the delinquent girls were from places outside the United States. The authors of this 1912 report on delinquent children concludes: "Not only is it true that a disproportionately large number of these parents are immigrants but many of them are immigrants who did not come to this country when they were young, and it is obvious that the difficulty of adjustment confronting members of the foreign group is greater for those who come over comparatively late in life than for those who come over in early childhood" (p. 62).

While Breckenridge and Abbott make much of the cultural conflict between the old European generation and their new egoistic and individualistic children, the notion that cultural marginalization produced inordinate numbers of delinquent children was in line with programs to Americanize these people and provide assistance so that they could better fit into the American working class. For most affluent Americans there was danger in this ethnic heterogeneity. Reformers ranging from Jane Adams to Jacob Riis saw the hazard inherent in such diversity mixed with extreme poverty and labor unrest.

But the inability of parents to monitor and even care for their children was due for the most part to the structure of industrial capitalism. It wasn't until the 1930s that the 12–14 hour day, six day a week job was put to rest in many American cities. This type of labor was far different from that which existed in the countries from where these new immigrants came. People who had resources at their disposal, those from the evolving middle class were in a better position to address parenting and child training needs as important familial functions. However, for the economically and culturally marginalized immigrants who resided in the worst part of the city avoidance of starvation was their top priority. Mothers of poor immigrant families took jobs as domestic workers or nannies or took in piece work into their homes. Nannies were drawn away from their own children in order to care for children of the more affluent. It was only in the early part of the twentieth century that urban reformers began addressing some of the most difficult problems confronting parents of small children of these newly arriving families. Part of this reform was a movement to assimilate children who were viewed as not having been raised properly by their parents.

With a belief in the power of education to help remedy the delinquency issues in urban society, reformers who had won battles to restrict child labor now turned to getting children off the street and into schools so they could be Americanized. It was the public school wherein for many of these reformers, parents' "indifference" to the welfare and education of their children was a major cause of the growing delinquency problem in the early 1900s. Truancy laws enacted toward the end of the nineteenth century were intended to accomplish two social goals: protect children from neglect and to insure school attendance and deal with the growing number of dangerous and unsightly children roaming city streets. They hoped that with the opening of juvenile and family courts, children would be able to get the guidance and help they needed and to eventually be assimilated.

The Chicago Asylum and Reform School was originally established in 1855 as a socially motivated idea to segregate young children under 16 years of age from hardened adult criminals in the Illinois prison system. It would be a place for abandoned and troubled youngsters as well as truants and those who were arrested for more serious offenses. Its purpose was to prepare boys for an employable trade, to reform young people rather than punish them. If inmates here were found incorrigible, they could be sent to Bridewell Prison Farm also referred to as the Chicago House of Corrections. However, within a matter of years Chicago Reform School became a notorious hot bed of violent deviants. Like Bridewell itself in time it took on all of the characteristics of a penitentiary for youthful offenders. Eventually, it was taken over by the State of Illinois and moved to the town of Pontiac. By the early 1900s, Bridewell was to become a maximum security prison for adults and young people alike but with the younger inmates segregated in the compound into separate facilities.

But children who often roamed the streets of Chicago, who did not attend school, who were not violent, presented another kind of problem. New institutions needed to be designed to control, Americanize and rehabilitate them. A softer type of system of reform was necessary, which offered schooling and adult guidance.

Sidney Goes to Parental School

The Chicago Parental School, a progressive era response to truancy, opened its doors in 1902. It originally supplemented the Chicago Reform School but eventually took its place is a as an institution that dealt with young children whose parents felt they could not control. Unlike the Chicago Reform School or other reformatories, children were placed here who were not guilty of serious or violent crimes. It was part of the attempt in juvenile justice reform to bring reform to a juvenile justice system in the early twentieth century, to provide an alternative environment for children who needed greater parental supervision and otherwise could have been incarcerated alongside hardened inmates, which they had been up until the close of the nineteenth century. Children between the ages of seven and 14 were not attending public school regularly would be brought here and placed under the quasi-military control of surrogate parents who imposed a strict and often abusive discipline to ensure compliance. Boys wore uniforms and would sleep in cottages in dormitory cots and be awakened at five in the morning to be lined-up and ordered to drill for hours before and after attending classes. Food was meager. It was to be supplied at the expense of each inmate's parents, so if there was poverty in the child's home food was minimal at the school. For the first decade or two the facility presented itself as a model of training and discipline. But it was there that Sidney experienced his first encounter with institutionalized violence and sexual abuse.

Oftentimes older boys or inmates were put in charge of disciplining fellow students. During his incarceration here at age nine a "raw-boned" anti–Semitic boy appointed by house parents put Sidney through a horrific ordeal forcing him to submit to him sexually and also compelling him to acquiesce to humiliating and physically excruciating exercises wherein darning needles dug into his chest if he were not able to complete physical tasks successfully. This was all done under the supervision of adults.

All of the children interviewed in Shaw's books, Stanley, Sidney and the Martin brothers whose criminal activities were outlined in *Brothers in Crime* (1938), were alumni from the same Chicago Parental School. Among all of them Sidney speaks out most vehemently against his incarceration and experiences there. It is he who indicts the progressive era's attempts at providing boys with order and discipline. "Tell me one prison whose sole object was not vengeance! Tell me one good thing that ever came out of prison ... tell of one man whose reaction to prison influences were not hatred and bitterness" (p. 186).

While the Chicago Parental School was designed to foster a more stable, familial environment for children who were neglected and or abused by their parents at home, this school was to eventually come under the scrutiny of those in authority who discovered this institution to be even more abusive than the environments from which the boys originally came. In 1923, the description provided by Sidney in *Natural History of a Delinquent Career* was substantiated in the press coverage of legal action filed against the school by a local alderman (See Chicago Daily *Tribune*, July 22 to August 21, 1923). The administrators of the institution were summoned to testify in court and charged with acts of violence against young boys who often were guilty of nothing more serious than skipping school. As it came to light in court hearings, acts of violence and torture of boys were common. One 12-year-old boy, around whom an investigation was launched, was found dead hanging from a pipe in an iron cage used for isolating boys. The boy was said to have hung himself with his bed sheets while in solitary confinement. But there were suspicious circumstances that pointed to a cover-up.

A teacher from the Parental School testified that he could no longer live as a witness to the savage beating of young boys by house parents or those older children who assisted them in the abuse. "At times I heard terrible crying and pleadings at night when boys were being beaten in adjacent collages and have had to shut my window to keep the noise out." When asked by the school defense attorney why he didn't say anything earlier to the superintendent, he said that he had done so several times but the superintendent called him a "traitor" and threatened to fire him. In fact, according to one teacher the head of the school inflicted many of the punishments himself or ordered others to perform them.

Small children were beaten with rubber hoses, one young boy was kicked in the stomach by the superintendent's assistant when he tried to run away. Another boy was punched in his face by his teacher for being disrespectful. When boys were captured for attempting to flee the facility, they would frequently be brought into a neighboring cottage by orders of the superintendent and the boys there would be instructed to beat them mercilessly, which they did. Then each recaptured boy escapee would be thrown into a tiny steel isolation cage, solitary confinement, where he would remain for days or weeks with only stale bread and milk two times each day. There was no access to anything outside the cage. No water would be given to boys in isolation. In the cage there would be a bucket in which the boy would relieve himself but it would be left for days without being emptied. It was found that more than a quarter of the cows on the school's property that provided the milk for the facility were contaminated with tuberculosis.

Boys at this facility were emaciated and were given only to coffee and stale bread. Many boys fell ill but were forced into rigorous and abusive exercise programs that would last several hours at a stretch. A former cook at the school testified that there would be frequently deliveries of contaminated meat which school officials knew about, but would feed it to the boys anyway after heavily seasoning it. Former inmates of the school testified to sexual abuse they witnessed.

Sidney personally experienced what he called "squattings" as punishment and being dunked in a tub of ice cold water by other boys or cottage officers. Often there would be "punishment parties" for minor rule infractions and things like failures to win drilling or marching competitions. Cold baths were typical while Sidney was there. He recalls the following when he was returned to the facility after "escaping" to seek food and refuge in his home.

> It was January and very cold. The windows where the room with the bathtub were opened wide. The lady and man officer both held me in the tub after it was filled to the top. The coldness made me gasp and my lungs didn't have a bit of air in them when they pushed my head under water I swallowed a lot of water and became unconscious. The family officers thought I was merely pretending at first because they only dunked me two or three times when I became unconscious. He carried me up to the cage [Shaw 1931, p. 104].

This court action against the Chicago Parental School by local politicians shown a spotlight on the abuses taking place under the guise of reform and rehabilitation. While this particular case led to modest reforms in the system and the replacement of key personnel at the school, it was to be one in a long series of action against this facility and others like it in years to come.

The important similarities in Shaw's first two books of crime autobiography deal with social environment and observed the ineffectiveness of established juvenile justice facilities to bring about change in either boy's life. If there was change, it was certainly to the detriment of the young boy and the society in which he lived. The facilities toughened the boys, taught them to be better criminals and infused each with anger resulting from punishment and dehumanizing incarceration. The public facilities and institutions that reformers designed to protect these boys and serve the interest of society took on roles of leading characters in these boys personal stories: Reform School, the State Reformatory, Parental School, St. Charles, Pontiac and the like. These institutions became the true means of Americanizing children of immigrants. It was here where they would learn what it meant to be American.

Brothers in Crime

By the time one gets to reading *Brothers in Crime* (1938), the third volume in Shaw's trilogy of personal confessions and prison autobiographical narratives, we already have an idea where we are going with five unique but similar "own story" recollections. These last were the so-called "Martin boys."

The earlier books suggest that boys like Stanley and Sidney, surrounded by blight and domestic violence, found themselves forming alliances with other boys and learning the "ways of the streets" from their examples. The small gangs or groups they associated with were often fledging bands that had short life spans. Neither boy was ever a part of a long-term cohesive group of criminals specializing in particularly skilled lawless behavior.

In his book *Brothers in Crime* (1938), Clifford Shaw, Henry McKay and James McDonald collect the life stories of five brothers from the same family whose criminal activities were connected to their associations as siblings and shared experiences. Here we have an "all in the family" type of criminality. The very fact that five of the brothers in one family would develop antisocial characteristics is presented as evidence of the power of the social environment to produce delinquency. The primary aim of this study, according to its authors, was to "suggest the relationship between delinquency and the culture conflicts which often confront the immigrant family in the physically deteriorated and socially disorganized communities in large American cities" (p. x).

This trope of cultural conflict was extensively used by Chicago school sociologists and had been creatively borrowed from the French sociologist Emile Durkheim. It was Durkheim's contention that large, heterogeneous cities were "naturally" breeding grounds for crime and social deviance. With urban ethnic, racial and economic diversity came what he referred to as "anomie" or a loss of a unified moral code of behavior. This loss of "collective conscience" promoted an ethos of egoistic self-interest that was unconstrained by homogeneous ethical and religious standards. But when this notion of "anomie" was applied to ethnically diverse groups that controlled centers of power and wealth, it became difficult to make this case and distinguish the top as motivated by ethnic values. Therefore, "environmental factors" such as run-down neighborhoods were a close secondary conditioning factor. It must have been the polluted air people were breathing or the dilapidated housing in which they lived.

The perceived need for mechanisms of social control, the fear of crowds, particularly the dangerous "rabble" and the belief in the inherent destructiveness of all humans were ideological elements underlying such a trope. Those in power saw those without it as a dangerous classes who needed to be fastened to the wheels of production through training and discipline. There was little questioning about the morality and efficacy of laws defining criminal behavior. Most of the laws were designed to protect the propertied classes from those without property. The arrest of a child for begging on the street or stealing an apple or a piece of coal would set into motion a costly series of actions designed to isolate, reform and punish in the name of private property, but resulted instead in the production of a "criminal class." The violence of the wealthy was hidden behind laws that justified and supported it. The creation of a police class, taken from the same "rabble" as the criminal class, were to be paid to keep the wealthy safe. In such occupations the police could take out their own displaced rage on their neighbors. Police, teachers and social workers were given access to debt in order to keep them in a different sort of prison.

An exerted effort was made by Shaw and company to tell us that it was not the values or lack of values of immigrants that was the source of blame, but rather the neighborhoods in which they lived. In other words, it was a neighborhood populated with poor people. But not all immigrants were dysfunctional, it was the wretched neighborhood in which they lived that created this antisocial behavior; a dilapidated neighborhood filled with foreigners who could not control their children or didn't know how to properly exercise control. In this particular story about the Martins it was the mother's half-brother who came to America earlier and became successful enough to send for his sister and her family. We learn that the Martin boys' mother and father came in steerage and were quarantined at Ellis Island and took a train to Chicago. Their first month's rent was paid by this uncle who disappeared from the narrative once they arrived in the city. This relative lived in a better part of the city, owned a multifamily dwelling and had a regular job and an intact marriage. We are advised by the author that no others from that family stem ever had encounters with the criminal justice system.

Racism and Inequality

As previously noted, the progressive reform of juvenile justice was not particularly aimed at boys of color. In 1900, the first year the Juvenile Court began to function in Chicago, the city had not yet experienced the first massive wave of African American migrants from the South. However, there is ample evidence that children of color at that time stood a much greater chance of being incarcerated for activities for which white boys would have been released. It should be remembered that cities at the turn of the century were not immune from Jim Crow laws. Discrimination in employment, housing and education were grounded in racist ideology. So was the Chicago police department.

It needs to be remembered that children of immigrants were always more suspect by white authorities. Unlike white middle class and even working class neighborhoods wherein there were better schools and more experienced teachers, the truancy rate among children of Eastern and Southern Europe was significantly higher and therefore these communities were regularly under greater surveillance. Though not quite as severe, this was also true in Chicago's Black Belt. Between 1910 and 1920 the African American population of the city jumped from 44,000 to nearly 110,000.

Programs designed to Americanize immigrants had to include reform schools and elements of the juvenile justice system. Settlement houses would provide the means through which these peoples would learn English and good manners. Such foreigners and their rebellious adolescents, who learned they were better than their foreign-born parents, needed to be assimilated into a culture of cleanliness, hard work, moral fortitude, competition and religious piety. However, the urban environment was a major obstacle to overcome in this regard.

As noted previously, settlement houses like Hull House, excluded black people from their residential programs. While this was not chiefly due to the racial prejudices of these progressives, there was certainly a great deal of prejudice and discrimination among their clientele. Very little was done to discourage racial biases and stereotypes that often plagued immigrants who saw themselves as better than this group of Americans. And little was done to insure that the Americanization curriculum included a graphic history of the importance of racism in the nation's development. In the early 1900s, most American history texts used in public schools presented a view of slavery primarily from the slave owner's position, glossing over the racism underlying slavery in the South. A most popular text by Henry Steel Commager and Samuel Elliott Morison, *The Growth of the American Republic* (1930) drew on earlier sources that failed to present the horrific conditions that characterized American slavery (Zimmerman 2002, pp. 110–111).

Men and boys of color, who had migrated from the south with their families, found themselves deep in poverty in Chicago due to racial barriers to union jobs, the worst housing available, poor quality schools and a lack of recreational programs. Even middle class black Chicagoans who had once resided in better parts of the city were forced into the deteriorating Black Belt through a combination of violent bombings and real estate steering practices. The Chicago Race Riots were preceded by dozens of bombings of homes of newly arriving African American families from the South as well as real estate agents who sold or rented them homes. In fact the riot took place when two young black boys were stoned for swimming in the river considered by whites as their racially exclusive enclave. Police refusing to arrest the white culprits who allegedly threw the stones killing one boy instead arrested a black man who witnessed the event. This led to days of racial unrest.

Many African American boys arriving from the south were labeled as mentally defective by Chicago's educational and social welfare systems. If arrested, they'd more likely be sent off to adult prisons rather than juvenile institutions that were developed to serve the needs of their white male counterparts. We do not see young black males significantly represented in Shaw's studies of juvenile delinquents. Nor does Shaw attempt to provide community services for these young people as he did for immigrant classes. This lack of particular attention to this cohort of young men who suffered the same and even worse levels of poverty as immigrant groups but also whose families experienced centuries of disenfranchisement, dehumanization, violence and racial persecution in the South speaks to a glaring weakness in his studies. It is an omission that resulted in a failure to predict the urban distress of African American families in major cities and how this distress would translate into illness, addiction, incarceration and the highest school drop-out rates of young males in the nation. To focus almost exclusively on European boys, while young African Americans were disproportionately arrested and incarcerated reflects a particular bias in juvenile delinquency research of this era. We will take up this research omission in the next chapter, along with others.

The failure of the Chicago School, the reluctance of Park and Burgess to take a moral stand and speak out strongly against racial discrimination and persecution of blacks and immigrants, represents a major weakness in their contribution to sociology. While some progressive voices in the department like that of Louis Wirth decried racist practices, he too was silenced by funding that was intended to promote control over racial conflict and that relegated solutions to the area of urban planning. This issue of race and the reluctance of these scholars to address discriminatory practices eventually led to future riots and a long history of discrimination in Chicago's housing, education, justice and correctional systems that are evident today.

The next chapter examines the biases built into the ethnographies that have come to represent a progressive approach to juvenile justice. As funding funneled into juvenile delinquency research through the Rockefeller Foundation and other funding sources seeking to keep a lid on racial violence and to avoid controversy of exploring the messy side of juvenile crime, the conclusions drawn by Shaw and his academic colleagues were sanitized and presented as set of interesting life stories wherein the physical neighborhood was to represent a wider variety of social dysfunctions and dynamic changes sweeping the nation. Not only was there a failure to recognize the psychodynamic elements underlying juvenile crime but also an attempt avoid the structural and personal difficulties that boys encountered in both living in cities and in just being boys. Instead these men provided their readers, most particularly their funding sources, with a highly deterministic view juvenile delinquency that could be addressed through funding after school programs and community workers.

CHAPTER FOUR

Exclusions of Convenience

Just as there was a barrier to women joining the sociology faculty at the University of Chicago, so there was a status division between the studies of male and female delinquents. The system of white patriarchy that dominated the sociology department (most academic departments generally) discouraged the advancement of both women and African American scholars there. Not only were these groups denied access to prestigious faculty positions and some heavily subsidized research directorships, but women were frequently discouraged from pursuing doctorates in sociology (Deegan 1978; 1985; 1990; Salerno 2013). While the university was open to accepting women and African American students when most institutions of higher education refused, no woman was hired as a potential tenured faculty member in the sociology department until the 1950s. Women were given little status there despite their enormous contributions to sociological research. Young women academics (like female journalists) were also discouraged from working with young male delinquents. Generally, women were not encouraged to interview boys for Shaw's studies although they did serve as typists, and edited transcripts. Just as there was a sexual division of labor in the sociology department at the university, there was also an implied gender division in terms of the matters researchers were seen as capable of studying. But men such as W.I. Thomas (1923) or Paul Cressey (1932) did not feel dissuaded from interviewing young female delinquents for their own research studies, which were by and large funded by women.

While the women associated with Hull House were successful in their efforts to develop a system of juvenile courts in Chicago, the courts were designed primarily to serve a male population. Male judges were seen as the best qualified to assess these cases. From its inception the juvenile court focused overwhelmingly on troubled boys who were viewed as considerably more dangerous to society than girls. But its mandated objective here was to control and reform rather than to punish. Legal scholar Cynthia Godsoe (2014) notes that girls predominantly entered the courts for reasons of sexual misconduct or moral violations. This would include premarital sexual relations, not simply prostitution. It would be typical for the parents of girls to bring their daughters to court in an attempt to intimidate them or gain better control over their sex lives. Girls who "acted-out" sexually were sent away with the hope of restraining them. Boys, however, were rarely brought in on matters having to do with sex. In the first few years of its existence (1899–1902) 3,546 boys went through juvenile court compared to only 451 girls (Breckinridge and Abbott 1912, p. 21). Between 1899 and 1909, 31.4 percent of the girls were brought in on "immorality" charges compared to 1.6 percent of the boys (p. 36); and girls were charged with "incorrigibility" at twice the rate of boys (p. 36).

Sophonisba Breckinridge and Edith Abbott (1912) note that for girls the term "incorrigible" is often "much the same as those plainly described as immoral" and so they note that "more than eighty percent of the delinquent girls are brought into court because their virtue is in peril, if it has not been already lost" (pp. 37–38). This is not true for boys whose virtues were never in peril (since they were probably viewed as having no virtue to be lost) and whose offenses that brought them to the court were overwhelming theft and destruction of private property. We are not given any real sense of sexual misconduct on their part or a clear meaning of "immorality" for boys either, perhaps with the exception of rape. Euphemistic slogans that the authors of the Vice Commission Report applied to young females engaged in so-called "unsupervised recreation," such as "hundreds of young girls are annually started on the road to ruin" (p. 158n), were never applied to boys in the same fashion.

But even the notions of "sexual misconduct" and "immorality" are confounded by the very use of these terms as applied to many of these young female offenders. In her study of 131 delinquent girls held in the Juvenile Detention Home in Chicago in 1917, June Purcell-Guild, who had served as superintendent of that facility, noted that only 31 of these girls were being held for non-sexual offenses such as larceny. While 81 of these young women claimed to have engaged in consensual intercourse, only 19 claimed to have been raped. Purcell-Guild found that a number of these girls were raped by members of their own households, relatives, employers, and boarders. For many, these incidents led to further incidents of sexual misconduct on the part of those who were victimized. She found that the families of many of these girls contributed both directly and indirectly to their sexual abuse. Mothers, some of whom were prostitutes, recruited their daughters into selling their bodies (Purcell-Guild 1919). Lisa Pasko (2010, p. 1102) confirms that between 1904 and 1927, nearly 70 percent of the young women who were institutionalized were victims of incest.

That girls bodies could be used as a source of income by destitute families is a strategy that plays out around the world even today. In the zealous strivings of progressives to save children by outlawing child labor, there simultaneously emerged what the tabloid press called "white slavery." While prostitution was legal in most states in the early twentieth century, many young girls "disappeared" and were feared to have been ensnared or kidnapped by swarthy immigrants or black men who kept them hostage in brothels in seedy parts of cities like Chicago or San Francisco. It was feared that girls (white girls of course) were swept off the streets and enslaved as prostitutes in lumber camps in Oregon.

The disappearance of young runaway girls from homes was seen as abductions, or reported as such despite the real likelihood of domestic sexual abuse in a large number of these cases. This is not to say that sex trafficking never took place in the American city. There is evidence of it, but it overwhelmingly affected newly arriving immigrants and young girls of color. But according to some feminist historians, much of the fear of "white slavery" actually centered on women becoming sexually promiscuous, independent and recognizing power in their sexual autonomy (Gordon 1986; Odem 1995; Meyerowitz 1993). Girls age 14, 15 and 16 constituted the largest number of morals cases to come before juvenile court.

For most states in the beginning of the twentieth century the age of consent for girls was 10 or 12 years of age. By 1920, however, it jumped to age 16 and even 18 in some states due to efforts made by some progressive women's groups. The reformatories that emerged for girls housed a very different population than those for boys with a very different focus on treatment.

The interesting findings from the Purcell-Guild interviews is that large numbers of the girls she spoke to and who were incarcerated for acts of immorality were consigned to the court by "well meaning" parents who sought to insure the moral integrity of their daughters. Many of these girls were "medically examined" and found *never* to have had vaginal intercourse. In one case of "immorality" brought into court a girl slept on the floor of a male friend's bedroom for several nights but claimed that nothing improper had occurred, which was "confirmed by a physician's examination" at the facility in which she was incarcerated. Another 14-year-old girl "admitted she was boy crazy and kissed boys frequently." She was also medically examined and proven to be "uninjured" (Purcell-Guild 1919, p. 447). In some instances the moral incredulity of the researcher/interviewer jumps off the page: "Girl after girl said she loved to dance or she 'was crazy about dancing,' or used other extravagant terms in replying to the question: Do you dance? ... It is to be regretted that a lack of time forbade a more detailed inquiry of each girl concerning dances and dancing. It is clear, however, that dancing plays an important part in contributing to girl delinquency" (Purcell-Guild 1919, p. 456).

Purcell-Guild goes on to tell us that "a very large number of these girls who had had relations with one or two men seemed to feel that if a man were their 'steady' that was sufficient reasons for relations." She concluded, "Some of these girls were naturally unmoral rather than immoral. Their attitude probably might have been a 'distorted' result of the prenuptial customs of some European countries" (p. 469). The notion of these young girls' *unrestrained sexual nature* runs through this piece. Again the majority of the girls in the study were between 15 and 18 years of age. It has been suggested that the knowledge of sexual trauma by the authorities in the cases of most of these girls had little bearing on their treatment as juvenile offenders (Pasko 2010, p. 1107).

Sociologist Dana Britton (2003, p. 3) asserts:

> Ideas about gender have shaped prisons, both literally and figuratively, from their very appearance as institutions of social control. Nineteenth century reformers made women's presumed inherent difference the primary basis for their case for separate institutions for women, run exclusively by female staff. In a similar way ideas about gendered bodies played a similar role in the architecture and styles of discipline advocated for early men's prisons.

The same might be said for gender and the *meaning* of delinquency. While Shaw did include token interviews with females (two) and one African American boy, most of the interviews that are now housed at the Chicago History Museum Research Center, a total of 133, are life histories of young males who were children of European parents (Stockton 1983; Leslie 2011).

Just as Freud had little sense of what guided women's behavior, the same might be said of Shaw and most of the leading criminologists of his time. To quote Meda Chesney-Lind (1989, p. 8): "The extensive focus on male delinquency and the inattention to the role played by patriarchal arrangements in the generation of adolescent delinquency and conformity has rendered the major delinquency theories fundamentally inadequate to the task of explaining female behavior. There is, in short, an urgent need to rethink current models in light of girls' situation in patriarchal society."

The question of heterosexuality, homosexuality, bisexuality and transgender or transsexuality were rarely considered in the institutions that incarcerated girls. In fact, the latter two terms were not developed until the mid–1960s. Since women were staffing these facilities there was an assumption that any girl who exhibited "aberrant" attitudes about sex was mentally disturbed. Aside from this there was an assumption that since incarcerated girls were not subject to male staff, any incidents of sexual abuse while incarcerated were deranged fantasies of disturbed minds, not unlike some of the girls' claims of sexual abuse at home. Few complaints were taken seriously.

Drug Addicts: Janet and *The Fantastic Lodge*

The decision to separate drug users from other delinquents was Shaw's choice. In the late 1800s drug use, particularly morphine addiction, was most typically associated with medical doctors injecting middle and upper class women with the drug to dull the pain of perceived "female troubles" (Mara Kiere 1998). When the first "drug epidemic" was announced in the United States in the 1890s, women constituted two-thirds of all addicts. While the media focused its most scathing criticism on the poor immigrants and prostitutes who used drugs, particularly those who smoked opium, there was less concern about those in the upper classes.

The Vice Commission Report on Chicago in 1911 entitled *The Social Evil in Chicago*, which was primarily a product of sociologists at the University of Chicago and progressive social workers associated with Hull House, dealt with inadequate controls over the morals of poor young women. It recognized the wide use of drugs among this group and even advocated a ban against women entering a saloon unless accompanied by a man as well as the availability of over-the-counter opiates by restricting what pharmacies could sell and to whom. It was only later that drugs began to be seen in a wider social context. Certainly, many progressives at this time perceived crime including prostitution to be more frequently associated with alcohol and saloons. Heroin, marketed by Beyer Aspirin, was used as a cough suppressant up until 1910. It wasn't until 1925 that it was outlawed in the United States.

Opium dens, which were frequently confined in Chicago to its small Chinese immigrant community in the late 1800s, were the first to feel the heavy restrictions placed on drugs. As a city "wide open" to alcohol and saloons, this challenge appeared connected to growing anti–Asian sentiment. But by the early 1900s, the then legal drug cocaine was targeted for restrictions by women's temperance groups. Some of the women associated with Hull House began to see addiction as a health problem, not only in prostitutes but in young men. Cocaine came under particular attack. Like alcohol, cocaine was seen as a cause of family disorder. A study at Hull House in 1904 found that the increasing use of this drug among teenage boys as well as some of their parents in Chicago's Near West Side was contributing to growing delinquency and family disorganization there. While cocaine laws were enacted, by the 1920s marijuana, not cocaine, was becoming a more popular drug. It had been introduced to the city by Mexican immigrants who had come north after the Mexican Revolution of 1910 and by the time the Volstead Act was passed to outlaw alcohol in 1919 it gained greater popularity nationally.

Cities like New York and Chicago experienced a spike in drug use particularly in poor neighborhoods in the early 1900s. Joseph Spellane (1998) has shown the history of the underground drug market's movement from Chicago's Levee district (four blocks between 18th and 22nd Street in the South Loop area), which was an active vice area of the city into neighborhoods of the Black Belt. As they did with prostitution, city officials and police authorities made a purposeful decision to confine and restrict illicit drugs, dance halls and gambling to the area with the highest concentrations of African Americans. Opiates, including heroin, were frequently use by sex workers there, and eventually made their way into the "sporting world" or "cabaret culture" of some slum neighborhoods, which became entertainment centers for middle class and affluent whites seeking late night adventures.

Marijuana had a certain cache among the hip cabaret and dance hall set and heroin was frequently used in the jazz and blues clubs of the South Side by the 1920s. Although the first U.S. federal drug law, the Harrison Narcotics Act, was passed in 1914, the illegalization of many recreational drugs did not occur until the late 1920s. But marijuana remained legal. The anti-marijuana propaganda that developed in the 1930s was both a product of xenophobia associated with Mexican immigrants and sensationalism of the tabloid press. The control of marijuana remained a local issue and it was not controlled nationally until 1937. Drug use (especially addiction) was primarily seen by progressive criminologists such as Clifford Shaw as a consequence of deeply rooted mental problems more than associated with juvenile delinquency and the social environment. It was viewed as an issue apart from juvenile delinquency

The use of many recreational drugs was not viewed as a major national problem until alcohol was again legalized and then again after World War II. Much of this opposition to drugs emerged from the old centers of prohibition reform, including religious organizations. But there was opposition from the alcohol lobby as well which saw drugs like marijuana competing for a share of its protected market (Tracy and Acker 2004). Drug users were seen as separate from the population that Shaw wanted to examine—children of immigrant families. Still, his focus on immigrants as the source of criminal behavior did not serve this group well. Drugs, women and young black males did not factor in significantly to his assessment of juvenile delinquency. Under the direction of one of his staff members, Solomin Korbrin, the Institute for Juvenile Research did conduct nearly 80 interviews with drug users, the vast majority of whom were young African Americans. Real understanding of the use of drugs in black communities was never undertaken. Drugs were associated with African Americans and therefore received low priority for research and high priority for arrests (Covington 2007). The drug interviews were funded through NIH grants and were nowhere as extensive as the interviews conducted with the children of immigrants. For the most part these studies remained unpublished and never saw the light of day. While they are referred to in Korbrin's work, they were never dealt with in any effective way by Shaw.

One of the autobiographical stories that Shaw's staff did collect and eventually was published, was an account of a young Caucasian female drug user in her early twenties, they called Janet. The interview was conducted by Howard Becker who studied sociology at the University of Chicago in the early 1950s. Becker had ready access to marijuana users and the drug itself because of his work as a jazz musician, which brought him into contact with many casual users and hardened heroin addicts.

Rather than looking at deviant phenomena as a product of social disorganization Becker's focus was more on estrangement, and the power of labels. He had studied with Ernest Burgess, Herbert Blumer and Everett Hughes at the University Chicago and was a classmate of Erving Goffman. He was 23 years old at the time he was hired by Korbrin who was collecting background materials from drug offenders.

Becker was more influenced by the renowned criminologist Edwin Sutherland who was rather suspect of Shaw's work. He was also influenced by the work of Alfred Lindesmith, who studied drug addiction at the University of Chicago under the supervision of Herbert Blumer and Sutherland. These interactionists had a very different approach to crime and deviant behavior than did Shaw, Burgess, and those associated with Hull

House and the Chicago Area Project. Lindesmith had conducted over 50 interviews himself with opiate addicts for a paper he published in 1937. He rejected the popular notion that drug addiction was a mental disorder and therefore primarily a medical issue. While he saw such drug use as associated with many of the same factors that Shaw associated with delinquency, such as poor neighborhoods, he emphasized ritualistic elements of addiction and many more psychodynamic and communal factors underlying it. The tabloid notion of the drug user as someone who lost his or her mind, depicted in films like *Reefer Madness* (1936), missed the important social and psychological factors underlying addiction.

Howard Becker's studies of deviance were exceedingly more theoretical than Shaw's work on juvenile delinquents. Becker, like his classmate Erving Goffman, described deviance not so much a product of "disorganization" as Shaw had described juvenile delinquency, but rather as a product of classification and alternative social organization. This type of understanding has been associated with what sociologists referred to at the time as labeling theory. It is more focused on issues of power, perception and treatment. When one reads his interview with Janet, one can get a fuller understanding of Janet as a complete person. Janet's story is much more compelling than Stanley's "own story" on many levels. Since Janet was older than Stanley and underwent psychoanalysis, it became obvious that she was considerably more attuned to her own feelings.

Becker was introduced to his subject Janet Clark (whose real name was Marilyn Bishop) in 1951 as the girlfriend of a fellow club musician, a mutual friend. There was no obvious power differential nor class distinction as there was between Shaw and Stanley or even Shaw and Sidney. She was 21 and he was 23. She would visit Becker and his wife at their home once each week for about six months. They would socialize a bit, talk about mutual friends and record her answers to pertinent questions and personal reflections on Becker's tape machine.

The way in which Becker conducted his interviews with Janet revealed considerably more about his subject than Stanley's story revealed about himself. John Dollard (1935) in his study of life histories points to the weakness inherent in Stanley's story in *The Jack-Roller*. In an attempt not to interfere with his tale of a life in crime, Dollard charges that Shaw prevented Stanley from doing "a much better job of presenting himself." For Dollard, "the virtue of non-interference is at best a negative one" (p. 186). Thus, the life history of Stanley in "an enigmatic document with many situations inadequately defined and with many interrogations that beg further light from the writer." Stanley's life is comprised of a series of acts or events which were listed for him by Shaw as a means to instigate and organize the boy's story, but Stanley was left on his own to tell his story.

By contrast *The Fantastic Lodge* (Janet's story) becomes a powerful autobiographical statement of a heroin addict, containing some of the same lyrical elements found in Jack London's work or in the writings of Nelson Algren and Jack Kerouac. There is a mature self-refection here. The gentle almost undecipherable guidance received from Becker and the authentic language of a female addict that Janet uses kept the story reading much like a novel.

There is a depth to her story and personal insights about herself and others that was never achieved in the stories Shaw had collected from boys. Their narratives appear clinical and more emotionally empty by contrast. In Janet's story, there was a rich sensitivity to the world around her, to the people with whom she interacted and the culture and subculture of which she became a part. There is above all an attention to detail that gives it a particularly naturalistic sensibility. We are given access to her emotional highs and lows as we enter into her world. Here we get a deeper sense of womanhood of the era in which she is writing and a closer proximity to the powerful roles played by family, gender and sexuality in a seemingly honest and unadulterated presentation. We read about her poverty, her desperation, her having to give up her baby and of her depression. She is not writing her story to help free herself from institutional incarceration, or satisfy the unspoken need of an outside authority who will judge her, but rather she shares her life story with a friend. And Becker does not inhibit, he listens and encourages her.

Those familiar with Janet tell us that she frequently carried this manuscript around with her in a shopping bag attempting to keep it safe (Bennett 1981, p. 219). It was one of her most valued possessions. Attached to her book manuscript were her hopes of escaping the life in which she found herself mired. We know from her life story of her tragic losses and the abuses she suffered as a young child and later as a young woman. We know that she wanted to be a writer and she took pride in having produced a life story that captured her life's tragic experiences with humor, grace and eloquence. While Becker understood the value of the manuscript and wanted to see it published, Clifford Shaw had other ideas. The irony here is that Janet was denied her rights to her "own story" by Shaw and the Institute for Juvenile Research as both campaigned to block the book's publication. In her book *Telling Women's Lives*, sociologist Judy Long notes: "The course of negotiations provides a history of attempts to limit, contain or neutralize the threat of Janet's differentness. The charge of 'atypicality' was central to Clifford Shaw's campaign to block the publication of *The Lodge*.

Shaw's counter proposal were four other life histories (all male) that in his opinion illuminated addiction better than did Janet's" (Long 1998, p. 98). Whether or not this reflected Shaw's fear that the world he thought he knew so well was changing around him is not known. But it was. Becker's work was a sign of a new generation of sociologists who understood there were no axiomatic causes of deviance.

While Janet, with the help of sociologist Helen Hughes, eventually convinced Shaw to turn the rights to her life story back to her, the University of Chicago Press refused publication for fear of law suits. Shaw died in 1957 and Janet died of a drug overdose in 1959. The book was finally published in 1961 by Houghton Mifflin in Boston, with the help of sociologist David Riesman, author of *The Lonely Crowd*, who was a friend and colleague of Helen Hughes, an expert on social movements. The repression of the story of the female delinquent by the forces of promoting the notion of one's "own story" is drenched with scholarly irony.

The Exclusion of Black Boys

It is worth reemphasizing how young African American males were overlooked by Shaw as well. By the late 1920s, young black males constituted a quarter of the population of St. Charles School alone (Moses 1936, p. 17). Despite the rapidly growing incarceration rates among African Americans compared to whites in Chicago and other major cities, most of the programs designed to "save" boys were directed toward young white boys who were children of immigrants. Shaw's interviews did not capture the experiences of black youth whose parents were escaping racism in the South, nor those of Mexican Americans and Asians who were also immigrants. While a graduate student at the University of Chicago, Edward Jackson Baur who worked closely with anthropologist Robert Redfield conducted interviews with Mexican-American boy delinquents in South Chicago, none of his life histories of these young men were ever published (Baur 1933). The result is interviews overwhelmingly conducted by older white males of European descent interviewing younger males from European families under the direction of an older white males with foundation monies coming primarily from rich white men of European backgrounds. There is an obvious insensitivity to race bias here, sexism and heterocentricity. That young black boys or men might have been less likely to confide their life histories to white males in authority, this might be grounded in the history of black oppression. We know for sure they were treated differently from those boys of European descent. The IJR interviews must be considered ethnically and culturally biased at least to this extent.

From the late 1800s into the twentieth century close to 90 percent of the black population was relegated to residing in what was called "the Black Belt." Despite massive black migration from the South during World War I and the bitter aftermath of Chicago's 1916 race riot, the topic of nonwhite delinquents was hardly examined. For the most part this had to do with racial segregation. Most of the organizations developed to deal with troubled boys were in fact segregated and restricted to white boys while increasing crime rates in the black community went unaddressed. Even after the establishment of the juvenile courts, African American children were not always directed to these courts by the authorities. And nonwhite boys were more frequently assigned to county jail rather than facilities designed to exclusively serve juveniles. The city's YMCA building erected in 1893 was restricted to young white men only. The intent was to cater to the needs of young white boys from immigrant families. A facility to service the needs of young black men was erected south of the Loop in 1916.

Since its founding in 1852 the YMCA remained a segregated institution until after World War II and did little to encourage racial tolerance and integration (Mjagkij 2003). Much like the segregation that took place in the YMCA, the Boy Scouts was racially restricted and segregated until the 1970s. Though the Boy Scouts of America was founded in 1911, the first "Negro Boys Troop" was not officially recognized by the Boy Scouts Council until 1916. Shaw himself hardly entered into the Black Belt and the Chicago Area Project had little to do with young black men until the 1960s. The Jim Crow policies of segregated facilities were to have a significant influence on the spike in black juvenile delinquency by the mid twentieth century. But little of this made its way into either the popular press or the history books.

Mostly those who studied at the University of Chicago, including many black scholars, followed the path of Chicago school theorists. Earl Moses, who researched delinquency in the Black Belt for his master's thesis in 1932, subscribed to the Shaw thesis: "The abnormally high increase in juvenile delinquency among Negroes in proportion to the total Negro population in Chicago is due largely to the settling of Negro migrant families in areas of deterioration and disorganization. The Negro delinquent, therefore, to a great extent is the product of settlement in disorganized areas where delinquent patterns of behavior prevail" (Moses 1936, p. 221). There is no mention of racist policies and poor educational resources.

While the city was well aware of racial segregation and race tension relative to public facilities which led to the 1916 race riot, twenty years later, in 1938, social workers were still concerned that the lack of adequate recreational space in the black community. It was believed that this need for recreational space was forcing black kids in South Chicago to use those parks typically occupied by whites. In an effort to thwart white reaction to this invasion they asked Shaw to have CAP hire a black youth worker to work with youth on the South Side. However, Shaw refused to get involved. As social policy historian Julia Grant (2014, p. 167) noted: "CAP largely opted to leave the community to fend for itself." Shaw and the CAP organization basically denied support to black youth on the South Side until after Shaw's retirement from IJR and CAP.

Nevertheless, Shaw can be seen as a progressive. In an attempt to refute the argument of those establishment figures claiming that race and genetic make-up were significant factors determining criminal behavior in children of color, Shaw took a strong stand. However, he and his research colleagues overlooked the powerful influence that racism had on the psychological development and behavior of young people who were stigmatized for the color of their skin or treated harshly and with prejudice not only by the educational and the juvenile justice systems, but also by an economic system that exploited African Americans workers, a realty system that limited access of African Americans to decent housing and a *de facto* segregated recreational system that limited to black youth to less than adequate outlets for after school activities. By accepting racism as normal and ignoring its power in undermining young lives, we have a lack of adequate policy analysis and weak social science. This was not only true for young African Americans, but also for young immigrants who were subject to racism themselves.

In 1921, the city of Chicago hosted one of the largest Klu Klux Klan rallies in American history. Nearly 12,000 hooded members assembled on a farm just outside of the city line to recruit another three thousand new members. The farm was owned by Charles Weeghman, a renown Chicago businessman and sponsor of what became known as Wrigley Field. Weeghman owned the Chicago Cubs between 1916 and 1918. In 1923, an assemblage of 25,000 Klan supporters gathered at Grant Park to witness the initiation of 4,650 new members (Grossman 2016).

We have the word of Clifford Shaw that he collected information on over 400 incarcerated boys, including their autobiographies that were either written out by each boy himself or recorded by a stenographer paid by Shaw. But those files available from the archives of the Institute for Juvenile

Research, which he headed at the time, contain fewer than half that number of subjects. It is likely that files could have been shared with other researchers at the time. Nevertheless, his research was indeed extensive. Why some of these boys made it into his books while others did not might help to explain by Shaw's objective. Very little of his attention was given to young black males who had become a sizable portion of those incarcerated by the 1920s. There was nearly no discussion of racism. It wasn't until the 1940s that federal funds specifically aimed at studying poor black urban youth became available that the IJR and CAP entered the picture.

Race Prejudice and the Chicago School

The Chicago world of researchers on juvenile delinquency was a relatively homogeneous community of white middle class professionals. Many of the settlement house people as well as government bureaucrats and consultants were connected to the University of Chicago's sociology department. Most espoused what might be seen today as conservative political positions. Their lack of interest in youth of color was clear.

Although Robert E. Park was renowned for his focus on race relations, his experiences in this regard were minimal before he came to the university and included chiefly his work as a secretary for Booker T. Washington, a political adversary of W.E.B. Du Bois. Park's personal antipathy for the likes of DuBois, the first black man to receive a Ph.D. in sociology from Harvard, and Park's belief that change in racial attitudes was an evolutionary process, and would come about in "due time" was disconcerting to many of his graduate students particularly African Americans who were less tolerant of racism than he.

It was his sincere belief that patience and research would solve the race problem, not political and social activism. He called for tolerance "on both sides." Like Washington, Park felt that African Americans needed to be patient and would most benefit from vocational training. Chicago had a near monopoly on urban sociology. It published journals and received considerable finding from the Social Science Research Council which represented its interests. In his brilliant analysis of racial politics and scholarship in the first two decades of the twentieth century, sociologist Aldon D. Morris (2015, p. 141) has concluded: "Given the entire record, this conclusion is inescapable: Park and the Chicago school locked Du Bois out of the intellectual fraternity of sociology by systematically ignoring his scholarship."

Park assumed the directorship position of the Urban League in Chicago in 1916 even though there were several local Negro leaders who might have helped speed up the process for achieving equal rights. Under his leadership the Urban League helped find housing and jobs for African American migrants from the South. The League helped to conduct systematic assessments of problems encountered in Chicago by the many black people who became homeless because of bombings of their homes and it uncovered issues of police brutality aimed nearly exclusively at black youth (Strickland 2001, pp. 56–83). And as the League came under attack by some members of the business community for encouraging blacks to migrate to Chicago, it defended itself by calling upon black people not to come to Chicago.

Robert Park mentored brilliant graduate students of color, but still could not envision any of them as occupying positions on the University of Chicago faculty at that time. He believed paternalistically that they would better serve their own interests and the interest of their race by joining the faculty at predominantly black colleges. Oliver C. Cox (1965), a radical Trinidadian scholar who completed a doctorate both in sociology and economics at the University of Chicago soon after Park's departure, noted:

> At the University of Chicago ... three great sociologists, Ellsworth Faris, William Ogborn and Robert E. Park dominated the department. I have become convinced by my personal association and study of these men, that they were profound liberals in the sense in which that term is currently defined by direct-action leaders. They were men possessed of praiseworthy attitudes toward Negroes but still strongly opposed to any definition of them as fully equal to whites; they were willing to do many things *for* Negroes but sternly opposed to Negroes taking such initiative as would move them along faster than the proper pace; and they would rather turn conservative than tolerate independent thinking or acting Negroes [pp. 11–12].

When Chicago sociologists described young males they near exclusively meant straight white boys. And when they used the term "juvenile delinquent," they were mostly referring to white boys as well. Black gangs had only a minor place in Thrasher's book *The Gang* (1927). For the most part black youth were invisible in these early studies. It was Du Bois' study *The Philadelphia Negro* commissioned by the University of Pennsylvania and published in 1899 wherein urban African Americans were studied statistically for the first time and interviewed personally by DuBois himself. This was nearly 15 years before Robert Park came to Chicago. DuBois' work revealed African Americans being arrested for less cause and receiving harsher punishments than whites. He noted that in 1850, although constituting only 5 percent of the city's population, blacks represented 39 percent of those serving time in county prison (1899, p. 239). The disproportionate representation of black boys and girls being incarcerated with adults in county jail was recognized by the leaders of Hull House as late as 1914. But almost nothing was done to address this issue. Geoff Ward (2012), a professor of criminology, notes:

> Beyond the racial politics of whiteness, the histories give little account of nonwhite youths and communities who had stakes in the emergence of American juvenile justice. The omission of race on historical work on juvenile justice mirrors the exclusion of nonwhites in the earliest practices of juvenile justice. White adults controlled juvenile justice systems and those systems were typically reserved for white youths, denying nonwhite youths and adults equal recognition, opportunity and influence [pp. 2–3].

St. Clair Drake and Horace Cayton's classic study of Chicago's Black Belt, *Black Metropolis* (1945), revealed that in 1930, 20 percent of boys hauled before the juvenile courts were African Americans who were basically engaged in crimes like purse snatching. A much higher percentage of them were sent to jail than whites. It wasn't until the Great Depression that the "youth problem" was "discovered" in the Black Belt by white society (Drake and Cayton 1945, p 589). The neglect of boys of color and the unique problems they encountered in the city after migrating from the South is not given consideration by Shaw and the Park-Burgess department. E. Franklin Frasier's studies as well as Charles Johnson's study of the black experience before him were written to support the theoretical propositions being formulated in that department that turned a blind-eye to the issue of racism and its impact on the black community. While it is certain they recognized it, it is also true that they took little action aside from studying its social dynamics.

If we desire to find realistic autobiographical descriptions of young black men who grew-up in poverty in the Black Belt and suffered its consequences, it would make more sense to turn to the writings of people like Richard Wright. Wright's two most widely read works, *Native Son* (1940), his story of Bigger Thompson who grew up in poverty on the streets of South Chicago and *Black Boy-American Hunger* (1945) his own memoir of growing-up in that same city are portrayals of urban black life and the struggle to retain one's humanity in the face of racist culture. But they are also important portrayals of boyhood and manhood and what it means to be denied human dignity, something boys of color could recognize. These books are far less about bad neighborhoods and more about reflection and the corrosive impact of American racism on the young male psyche. They are also about coming of age and the struggle for respect and manhood in the face of racist emasculation. Anyone familiar with these two works appreciates their complementarity, and cannot help but wonder if the violent Bigger Thompson is simply Wright's fictionalized alter-ego. There is little to compare to these stories as vivid portrayals of the black urban proletarian landscape.

The Exclusion of Gay Boys

The position of homosexuality in the tales of delinquency Shaw chose to publish is not clear except to say it is nearly invisible. For Shaw, young boys were often victims of "sexual perverts." Tamara Meyers in her study of the early years of juvenile detention in Quebec has noted in this regard: "One is hard pressed to find mention of boys sexuality—or the corporeal dimension of their designation of delinquents—in the literature on boys and juvenile delinquency. This absence is in part explained by the fact that official documents from juvenile justice institutions, like annual reports, are silent on the issue of boys' sexuality. Similarly newspaper accounts ignored this aspect of boys' lives" (Meyers 2005, p. 384).

The same must be said for boys brought before the juvenile courts in Chicago as compared to their female counterparts. Boys were given special consideration by the courts and the institutions to which they were assigned. Any act of homosexuality was viewed as an injury to society, and especially to the elevated position of masculinity. But such acts could often be hidden by boys. Boys picked up for prostitution, though few in number, could point a finger at the "degenerate" older man who forced him to have sex. Boys were typically seen as victims in such cases. However, a "fairy" or "invert" was another matter altogether since it was a set of effeminate behaviors that could be classified as non-male. The institutional emphasis was on rugged masculinity to counter feared feminization of boys that would make them into "pansies." National figures including Teddy Roosevelt spoke out against these tendencies undermining manhood (Bederman 1996). The performance of "tough boy" was frequently over the top. The grizzled violent cowboy, the hard-assed detective, the vicious gangster, the callous robber baron were cinematic, tabloid and literary role models.

It is unlikely that a boy in a juvenile detention center at this time would identify as anything other than heterosexual considering that homoerotic activity in the detention center was fairly commonplace and guards frequently turned their backs on such activity anyway. Any reported sexual assault by a fellow inmate or guard would damage one's masculinity and threaten one's boyhood. The small fraction of reported sexual assaults in

St. Charles or even the County Jail could not possibly approach the actual number of violent incidents against boys. However, to be a penetrated victim, or to behave in a feminine or "sissy" manner would readily bring physical abuse and ridicule from inmates and guards alike. Sexual abuse and rape were commonly overlooked by detention center authorities. In fact in such an environment the overt abuse of "fairies" (physically or sexually) could bolster one's reputation as a man.

In the early twentieth century in the United States views on homosexuality were shaped by Richard von Kraft-Ebing and Havelock Ellis, both of whom were medical doctors and viewed same sex attraction as a psychiatric and physiological disorder. Both Kraft-Ebing and Ellis used the term "invert" to describe those effeminate gay men and masculine women. They assumed that gender was biologically given rather than constructed and saw it as connected to sexual object of choice. For them and those they influenced "these people" were born into the wrong bodies with "souls" of one sex and bodies of the other. There was no clear distinction between homosexuality and effeminateness. Gender and sex were to be in "natural" alignment. A female soul encased in a male body would naturally be attracted to men sexually.

For Shaw and the sociologists at the Institute for Juvenile Research, anything other than heterosexual genital intercourse was considered an aberration and a disorder reflecting on a boy's character. Any consideration of "inverts" or gay boys in their studies would have led them afar from their "poor environment" and cultural conflict hypothesis. Citing the most recent statistics, sociologists and social workers have estimated that well over half of the children living on the streets today identify with some LGBTQ category. Large numbers of these homeless children have been sexually abused, have runaway or have been exiled from their homes by their parents. Given that definitions of masculinity in the early 1900s were considerably more narrow than they are today, there was far less consideration that masculinity could be performed in a variety of ways, or that sexual behavior could be detached from gender expectations. Masculinity in the 1920s, especially for adolescent boys, required insensitivity, toughness and something referred to as manliness. In fact, racism, misogyny and even homophobia itself were certain signs of manliness in this era. While many of the boys interviewed by Shaw probably had same-sex intercourse, they did not identify as "homosexuals," "fairies," or "inverts." For the most part they saw themselves as sexual predators and not victims. As Stanley noted in his story, he learned about sex at an early age sometimes through mutual masturbation with his jack-roller friends. He also used sex to lure homosexuals into vulnerable situations. He tells his reader that he found such behavior "disgusting" but also described it as "exciting." He expresses regular disdain for "pansies" and "fairies."

But a "homosexual subculture" was developing as part of an urban transition during the time Shaw was conducting his interviews. Gender performance and sexual preference did not abide by strict societal rules despite the sexual repression of the day. By the 1920s it was becoming clear that rigid codes of gender and sexual behavior were being challenged. At first such challenges were very much an underground phenomenon. Authorities sought to impose stricter moral codes as a means of forestalling the "social disorganization" that was feared as a result. In 1911 the Levee area, which constituted the red light district in Chicago was closed down by moral reformers and constant police raids. In the Levee prostitutes, both gay and straight, mingled in the evenings and frequently celebrated their talents in saloons, molly houses, music clubs and resorts.

Alongside of brothels that often included young males for their homosexual clients were *boy houses* catering to pederasts; and near Dearborn and Randolph were a wide variety of clubs catering to "perversions of every sort" including female impersonators, midget sex shows and bondage venues (dela Croix 2012, p. 21). But in the 1920s an emerging queer culture began to be recognized and accepted as part of the artistic and bohemian fabric of some neighborhoods. With the Levee District closed down, there was a cultural transition in the definition of vice itself, and a migration of counter cultural groups into other parts of the city. Lesbian women and gay men became vital to the development of Tower Town and parts of the Black Belt. But dance halls, speakeasies, gambling joints, and sex clubs also found safety in transitioning areas around the Water Tower that were hospitable and encouraging of difference. This space, frequently referred to as "Hobohemia" because of its intermingling of hobos, political radicals, artists, intellectuals, and outcasts of every sort gave birth to a vibrant nightlife and an energized cultural scene.

With the help of his graduate students Ernest Burgess made modest inroads into Tower Town where bohemians and lesbians established tearooms, coffee houses and salons. There was an openness there and greater acceptance of sexual difference as well as political radicalism. While some scholarly interest in homosexuality at the University of Chicago can be traced back to case studies done in 1910, Ernest Burgess' students began exploring the night life of Tower Town in the 1920s and 30s as well as "black-and-tan" clubs in the Black Belt—now more commonly known as Brownsville (Heap 2009). They conducted research, took photographs (including photos of female impersonators in various clubs), wrote papers and reported back to class. These areas of the city became popular "slumming" destinations for nighttime excursions of more affluent urbanites. They also became home to such renowned institutions such as the Dill Pickle Club and provided fertile soil for the Chicago Black Renaissance.

Female impersonator clubs had become a big part of an underground entertainment industry in Chicago in the early 1900s. Drag balls, which took place every New Year's Eve beginning in the last decade of the nineteenth century, were well attended events that traversed racial lines. Whether or not most men in drag or cross dressing women who imitated men were other than heterosexual transvestites was not the point, nor was their race. Performances were exaggerated and showy. Gender was recognized as a performance well before the notion of transgender or queer was in use, well before scholars like Erving Goffman or Judith Butler identified it as such. In Brownsville in particular, female impersonators had become a respectable part of entertainment and night life by the 1920s.

If this was happening, where were the sociological papers reporting on it? American Studies scholar Chad Heap discovered a treasure trove of unpublished documents on the gay and queer experience in Chicago in the Burgess Archives of the University of Chicago Library. Much of the ethnographic studies dated back into the 1920s and 1930s. But the University of Chicago was reluctant to publish anything that might tarnish its image with the conservative media and funding sources. Given the avalanche of bad publicity following W.I. Thomas' 1918 "sex scandal" (being found in a hotel room by federal agents with a married woman not his spouse) and his dismissal from the University of Chicago, and given William Randolph Hurst's newspaper attacks on supposed communists and "sexual degenerates" "hiding out" at the university and corrupting young minds, the university feared for its reputation. W.I. Thomas had been one of the first American sociologists to deal with issues of sex and gender as early as 1907. He went on record with his controversial opposition to monogamy and the institution of marriage and spoke out for women's rights and control over their own bodies. Despite the case against him being dismissed in court, the sensationalistic attacks by the *Tribune* of his arrest (where reporters were present in the hotel) and his expulsion from the University because of it had a significant chilling effect on this type of scholarship.

Thomas published a series of articles and books on topics ranging from free love to issues of women's equality. Although originally influenced by theories of innate racial difference, as had been anthropologist Franz

Boas, Thomas and Boas were among the first social scientists who came to reject these ideas. Thomas' book *The Unadjusted Girl* was published in 1923, contained letters, newspaper accounts and personal interviews with young prostitutes, many of whom were from immigrant families, but also references to lesbianism. The book was originally contracted with the University of Chicago Press, but because of the notoriety of the sex scandal, it was eventually published by Little, Brown, in Boston. The university press even reneged on publishing his greatest work, *The Polish Peasant in Europe and America*, which he co-authored with Florian Znaniecki even though they had issued a contract for that work to Thomas. Paul Cressey who was a graduate student in the department and who was supervised by Burgess, went into the field to investigate clubs where lonely men paid ten cents for tickets to dance with women to live music often performed by racially integrated bands. His thesis was published as *The Taxi Dance Hall*; but he feared that it was this book and his interviews with young women in the dance halls that kept him from an academic career (Salerno 2007, pp. 39–42).

While most early studies of vice and prostitution only minimally concerned "degenerate boys," Frederic Thrasher in his study of gangs in Chicago covered the topic of male sexuality with some degree of depth and candor. In a chapter entitled "Sex in the Gang" he tells the reader that he found young adolescent boys' attitude toward girls to be hostile and scornful. Such gang members frequently referred to girls as "sissies" and worked to deflect any attraction to them. He quotes a gang member's description of his gang leader: "The leader of our gang was what is usually termed a 'hard rock.' He was the leader because he was the 'hardest' and because he had a strip clipped off through the hair on his head so that he might show the girls how little he cared for what they thought of his looks" (Thrasher 1927, p. 156). *Hard* and *cold* were commonly used descriptors of tough males who joined gangs. In an interview with a 15-year-old boy where Thrasher asked if he liked girls, the boy responded: "Naw. I never love no girls. I don't want to monkey around wit' girls. Dey gives me troubles. I kill de girls" (p. 156).

Male cohesion and gender exclusivity became particularly evident in most youth gangs where girls were viewed as threatening member loyalty. Thrasher notes: "Among gangs of younger adolescents, there is a definite indifference and often hostility to girls as such, although sex interests may be evident in various types of autoerotic activity." He goes on to note that in older adolescent gangs girls may become gang members in a purely "sexual capacity" (Thrasher 1927, p. 155). On the other hand, he describes occasions wherein a girl will abandon what are conventionally regarded as feminine traits and take the role of a boy in a gang to be seen by others as manly. Such "boys" often assume a dual role of thug and sweetheart and perhaps might even assume the position of gang leader (Thrasher 1927, p. 169).

Looking back on the Shaw interviews with boys, it becomes apparent that this particular oversight and others raises doubt as to the conclusions and validity of Shaw's overall findings that geographic neighborhood is a factor determining crime. This is nothing new. Correlation between poverty and crime was presented most vividly by American political economist Henry George in his book *Progress and Poverty* (1879). Shaw's work looks at neighborhoods as cauldrons of deviant behavior, places that determined rates of delinquency (Shaw and McKay 1942). His "life stories" did not support his thesis. While these interviews were valuable, they were also limited by the researcher's scope and training—by his restricted way of approaching and understanding his subjects. The interviews he saw worthy of publishing were stories he hoped might lead to the early release of these boys back into society. Those which reflected badly on the interviewee were rejected. They would not support his hypothesis nor would they help gain early release for those boys he personally believed had potential to develop their lives. But in doing so, he failed to take notice of important variables that were shaping the future of juvenile delinquency. The stories were collected to reflect a particularly narrow theoretical focus that had outlived its usefulness. Still, had these studies not been done, the world of scholarly ethnography would have been poorer for it.

CHAPTER FIVE

Inclusions of Convenience

If there were whole categories of young people excluded from these delinquency studies for the convenience of presenting a coherent and narrow set of sociological research findings, then there were also inclusions of commonalities that would further distort research findings.

The availability of boys at the Saint Charles School, for which Clifford Shaw had worked as a probation officer for boys between 1924 and 1926, was important to his study. His contact with these boys allowed him an inside advantage over other researchers. But beyond this access, it was the boys with whom he worked and whose confidence and trust he secured in that process that gave him access to still other boys. Despite the over one hundred narratives or stories he and his staff collected from these boys there is considerably redundancy in their narratives. This is because a large number of these boys not only knew each other from Saint Charles or other juvenile reform institutions, they in fact worked together in criminal activities, came from the same neighborhood or were frequently arrested together. Often they were part of informal gangs. Some were even related to one another. In fact the collection of oral histories represents at least six sets of brothers. While the overall number of stories he collected might appear to be large, the content of these biographies are therefore quite similar. Finding unique perspectives from within this collection that differ radically from those Shaw published is a challenge. In this sense his research was focused.

In examining these manuscripts one finds common phrases used by these boys, and see their personal "justifications" as similar. Stylistically we find the detached manner in which their stories are told. This corresponds to John Bowlby's study of male delinquents in which he found a high proportion of what he termed "affectionless" delinquents. Bowlby (1944, p. 24) notes in this regard: "In addition to stealing, the majority of these children truanted and wandered. This wandering is particularly characteristic as a symptom of this same indifference to home ties, which is the hallmark of this group."

Recollections of boys here are frequently redundant, reporting the same criminal offenses. It is as though some of these stories were exchanged with friends and focused on the same story elements before they were told to the interviewer or story collector. We learn much about burglaries, car thefts, petty thievery from sidewalk vendors, truancy and of course jack-rolling. We learn about A&P break-ins, but do not learn about arson, prostitution, vicious assaults on individuals or animal abuse. Criminal activities appear limited and restrictive. His sample is primarily a snowball sample, which calls into question the representativeness of such cases. Asking boys who are incarcerated to identify other boys they know also raises ethical as well as methodological questions. This makes it a challenge to veer from the hackneyed jack-roller story. But a close review of these collected materials allows one to find differences which do not get reported.

Gang or Network

In going through these manuscripts one can't help but notice that the individual boys presented to us by Shaw were really part of neighborhood networks. As Gregory Zimmerman and Carter Rees (2014) have noted, peer networks form the basis of most urban delinquency. These are not gangs in any traditional sense; for the most part such groups are not well organized, not very sophisticated and often very loosely connected and coordinated. While these boys did associate with one another, perhaps even formed a club or two, they lacked some of the elements that Shaw's contemporary, Frederic Thrasher, suggested constituted gangs. We don't make out a sense of clear leadership from these stories or an organizational hierarchy or organizational traditions. We don't have people whose role it is to obviously give orders through threat of violence or others who take orders under a system of gang duress. We have no tales of gang initiation. Here in this type of crime, we have almost an *ad hoc* whimsical approach to criminal activity. "Let's go rob a drug store today," is said in a way reminiscent to Mickey Rooney in his 1940s movies with Judy Garland where he says, "Hey kids, let's put on a show in the ol' barn!"

We might have a specific place where boys hang out (an abandoned barn or a garage), perhaps even individual connections to neighborhood fences who will purchase their stolen goods, but we don't have a sophisticated system wherein which boys are dictated to by older more established criminals and protected by them. For the most part these boys are on their own. We don't have gangs here that threaten people from the neighborhood who might call the police on them. Aside from raping and bullying and stealing cars, most of these boys portray themselves as mischief makers. They reflect an accepted pattern of lower working class boyhood at the turn of the last century. However, it looks as though there is really not much hope for any of them entering the middle class unless they were to join the police. Most are damaged; some beyond repair.

Most of these boys are in jail because they are not highly skilled criminals and not motivated to do much else. They fear the cops more than they seem to fear other gangs. They are not among the brightest in their neighborhoods. While they don't like being confined to institutions, they see their arrests and imprisonments as inevitable. There is a fatalism that connects them. *It's who they are.* They fear becoming like their parents, but like their parents they view themselves as rather powerless ... except when it comes to small time thievery. In some ways, this sense of powerless is often a recapitulation of their parents' trauma. Such trauma seems to have made domestic life more turbulent and unreliable than lives of crime. They do not speak of a better future because they can't envision one.

Most of the families from which these boys came were not able to deal emotionally with major life transitions themselves, or perhaps one would say disruptions. This has little to do with intergenerational cultural conflict and more to do with these families emigrating from a place where they were surrounded by people they knew, and a culture with which they were familiar, to a place in which they were surrounded by strangers. Immigrants often went from an extended family to a place in which they were completely on their own. Many were incapable of speaking the language of their new environs. They were seen by some as "parasites" and people who overcrowded the neighborhood, large families in small spaces; people who were dirty and threatened working class jobs. They came as strangers and outsiders to cities like Chicago or New York—cities that were loud, dangerous, polluted, and they often came from rural areas. Yes, they were unfamiliar with their new culture, but there wasn't much of one to become familiar with at this time.

Masculine Memory and Narration

Masculine memory and narrative are overly represented here. Social scientists are now assessing the importance of how one tells his or her story.

As we now know, all memory is reconstructed, not merely information stored in our brains to which we later have access (Bartlett 1932). As one tells a story, one is both inventing it and presenting to the listener or reader the way in which she or he makes sense of things at that point in time. Autobiographical narratives are very much connected to one's self-perception (Fivush 2007). One's self-narrative is an expression of one's personal identity. What is found in these personal stories appears to be a lack of coherence which researchers have found most common in narratives of young boys. Girls tend to tell longer stories, more elaborate tales which frequently reach beyond their personal immediate experience. Boys stories tend to be more episodic (Tulving 1983).

How the stories were told and to whom they were told is of considerable significance. Since these were stories collected by men and told to men by young males, there is an immediate transferential dynamic of masculinity. The age of these boys is important in this regard. Older men tend to hear boys from a masculinist perspective and elicit autobiographical accounts that boys perceive they may want to hear or might be interested in hearing. These are stories which might elevate the boys potency, status or standing. Violence for most of the boys is not something to be hidden here, particularly if it's violence against another boy or man. Such a narrative element gives us insight into the meaning of boyhood and confirms the psychoanalytic notion of rebellion against male authority. This trope runs through all of these tales. Had these stories been told to a woman or recorded by one, particularly an older women, these oral histories could have been quite different. But since they were not, we cannot know this for sure. How one tells a story, to whom it is told, and under what circumstances is of critical importance here.

Overall masculine memory, or memories of boys and men as opposed to girls and women, tend to be far less inclusive and more linear. In part this has to do with socialization of boys to be less attentive to detail and affect. Less communication at an early age with one's mother can help slow down cognitive development. Language is quite different in that the use of it by girls tends to reflect more nuance. Education also becomes a factor in communicative ability. Plus there are significant differences in the type of memories of boys and girls. Female memory tends to be more comprehensive and masculine memory is more fragmented (Schulster 1995). These boyhood memories are far less processed by the story teller. Certainly age has something to do with this, but this can also be a function of one's social class and level of emotional sophistication.

These boys have structured their memories according to their limited understanding of the social world and their place in it. Although most of these boys are articulate, they are limited by the cultural, economic, educational and familial constraints. They do not necessarily experience themselves as marginalized, but they do understand that they have very limited options.

Pity the Poor Immigrant

The immigrant experience was an important motif in Chicago school sociology. In 1900 immigrants and their children accounted for nearly 80 percent of the city's population. The vast majority of immigrants entering cities like Chicago or New York had barely enough resources to keep themselves and their families alive. Many of the immigrants who came to the shores of America looking for a better life had experienced family disruption and a lack of religious and ethnic supports once they arrived in the city. Immigration had a profound effect on the development of sociology at the University of Chicago. Both W.I. Thomas and Robert E. Park characterized what was happening to the immigrant family as social disorganization for the first generation of arrivals and what Thomas labeled "personal demoralization" for their children (Thomas, Park and Miller 1921). Once the social fabric tore for newly arriving immigrants, according to these studies, so did adherence to law.

Yet, for these researchers it was not the immigrant who was the source of crime, but rather it was a result of inadequate social cohesion and institutional structures required to service their needs. In fact the study of immigrants, ethnic enclaves or "natural areas" of the city became an investigation into antisocial behavior that immigration and the corresponding social disorganization produced. The focus of this research was on natural "ecological processes" of conflict, racial and ethnic antagonism, or cultural and racial clashes that would with time lead to assimilation into the dominant Anglo-American culture. This was the aim of sociology and social work of the time. This structural determinism was to remain an important part of American sociology, as was this Spencerian orientation (Schwendinger and Schwendinger 1974).

However, there was considerable impetus for politicians to blame economic difficulties and high crime rates in cities on the influx of immigrants. Despite the data revealing a much higher crime rate among those born in the United States compared to their recent immigrant counterparts, measures directed against immigration proved to be quite popular.

As noted earlier, immigrants were plentiful. And the incarceration rates among the children of immigrants was extremely high. Whether or not Shaw and McKay sought out children of immigrants to present in their published work is unknown. But their work did see a connection between immigration and juvenile crime. In this regard they noted:

> [Most] of the delinquents in Chicago have been produced, in turn, by the newest large immigrant or migrant groups in the city. During the first decades of this century a large proportion of the delinquents were the children of German or Irish immigrants. Thirty years later a large portion of the offenders were the children of Polish and Italian immigrants who replaced the German and Irish in the inner-city areas [Shaw and McKay 1942, p. 374].

Edwin Sutherland, a leading figure in Chicago school criminology, likewise saw immigrants associated with crime through no fault of their own: "They have a feeling of being lost; they are frequently exploited and treated brutally by the police, native-born and other immigrants.... It is not surprising that they give way to their natural impulses and commit crimes" (Sutherland 1924, p. 132).

These themes of marginality, isolation and alienation became major tropes in Chicago school sociology. In all of the ecological theories, there appeared to be a natural flow of a new immigrant group replacing an older one in these "natural areas" of the city through a process Robert Park referred to as the "invasion and succession." This was in keeping with Chicago school's focused on Americanization and assimilation into Anglo-American culture of these various immigrant groups. But African Americans were another matter.

Whiteness and Delinquency

Ecological patterns of "invasion and succession" of immigrant groups did not describe the phenomenon of population movement out of the Black Belt. There was no place for African Americans to move. In fact, due to bombings of their homes, restrictive covenants and the like, many middle class black people were forced from communities that had previously been more integrated. In the Black Belt African Americans did not find themselves isolated, alone and surrounded by cultural strangers with customs and practices different from their own except for some regional differences. However, there was little physical mobility for this group as a whole which corresponded to their lack of social mobility. There was no place for African Americans to move, no ebb and flow. Race and racism kept them from moving out and moving on as did newly arriving immigrants.

Invasion and succession did not take place for this group since Chicago had become one of the most segregated cities in the United States. But the Black Belt was not natural. Also, the arrest rates here were much higher for black juvenile delinquents than for whites. By 1930 21.7 percent of all boys brought before juvenile court were black (Drake and Cayton 1945, p. 204). The treatment of black youth was much harsher. Shaw's work paid little attention to the rate of juvenile crime in this area, which was accelerating greater than that in immigrant enclaves by the late 1920s. Through the efforts of politicians and the police, vice was relegated to this area. It was contained here. Not only were young boys and girls of color treated differently by the police, they were viewed differently by white journalists and sociologists. They were viewed as "less than." There were also increasing numbers of Mexican youth and Asians. But we see none in these studies.

Crime in the non-white community did not fit into the Chicago school models which emphasized cultural conflict, social disorganization and intergenerational conflict. The urban black church was a stabilizing force in African American communities. Still, white control over access to unions and well-paying jobs economically devastated this section of the city. Education was of poor quality here. The health care system hardly existed. Drake and Cayton (1945, p. 204) noted that the tuberculous rate was five times greater there than it was for white sections of the city; and Chicago had the highest Negro death rate for tuberculous than any other city in the United States as blacks occupied the most densely overpopulated neighborhoods.

One can argue that white boys were over-represented in Shaw's interviews because they were more likely to confirm his theoretical assumptions. That the American public would have been more sympathetic to the plight of whites than to boys of color is another possible motivation.

Narrow Range of Topics in a Very Small World

Given the limited sampling, the range of topics is quite narrow. Had the interviews been conducted in accordance with the overall make-up of the delinquent population of the time, there might have been a fuller and perhaps a richer range of stories. But this narrowness is related to neighborhoods, family, history of truancy, arrests, criminal activities and experiences of incarceration in the same facilities.

While these stories vary slightly, they have autobiographical figures who have little sense of themselves and have less interest in finding out. We know they are writing these stories because they have been asked to do so. Perhaps they were even paid something. There might even be an early release for incarceration involved. But one can be pretty sure if it were not for Shaw and his research, they would have never recorded these stories.

These figures have little sense of others except as victimizers or victims. This is the lens through which they see the world. This is how they've seemingly been brought up, both as victims and victimizers. These are all small-time hoods who appear to be activated by criminal activity. Some might even be sociopathic. There is hardly a trace of guilt or a bad conscience. They mostly tend to be insensitive to the pain they cause others. Not much thought goes into what they do or why they do it. There is little consideration of where life might take them. They know it's back to jail.

The limited dimensionality of these characters, however, is what makes them interesting. They don't steal what they like, they steal because it's a way to make some money so they can go out to a restaurant or take in a movie. They do not speak of materialistic goals or ambitions. There is nothing to aspire to here except, perhaps, being a big-time hood who is respected by other hoods. We learn more about the institutions in which they were incarcerated than about them. While there is a very narrow range of topics, this is because these boys live in a very small world after all. A small, small world!

CHAPTER SIX

Introduction to the Institute for Juvenile Research Oral Histories

Over the past twenty years, oral history has gained considerable status and currency in the field of qualitative social research. Autobiographical accounts of the lives of social actors can shed considerable light on how individuals experienced their world. Historians such as Lynn Abrams (2010) have noted that these life stories are critically important especially for those marginalized groups who lack a voice of their own, voices that will now be heard. But Gayatri Spivak (1988) has raised a cautionary point in her concern for disenfranchised groups around the world still not having a voice of their own. Asking "who speaks for the subaltern," she raises a concern about academic researchers speaking for groups that have been colonized by powerful first world nations. There frequently is a danger in scholars attempting to speak for people who have been denied the ability to have their voices heard. And it is not uncommon for researchers who have the "best interests" of the groups for which they advocate to impose upon them a particular world view, which is in fact alien to them.

The series of oral histories that follows were products of extensive interviews conducted by researchers of young boys who came from a different strata of society, and were not necessarily sensitive to the differences in how they, as opposed to these boys, made sense of things. These boys had encounters with the police the moment they reached school age and in some cases even before. Most were truants, which put them immediately in a class of outlaws at the ripe old age of five or six. While, according to progressives, mandatory education was intended to help children secure what they needed to enhance their opportunities in capitalistic society, in these cases it made criminals of them and proceeded to remove these children from the homes of parents who were neglecting their education by placing them in reformatories and parental schools.

The histories presented here were originally collected by staff at the Illinois Institute for Juvenile Justice, a private organization funded through a variety of sources both public and private. Referred to in previous chapters as the IJR, the research division was comprised primarily of graduates trained in the University of Chicago's sociology department. Clifford Shaw was responsible for coordinating this work. Shaw's credentials as a sociologist and his experience in the juvenile court system put him in an advantageous position to explore the lives of young boys who were sent away for their crimes.

However, the methodology for collecting these stories, who to include and who to exclude, what methods to employ to collect these oral histories were never matter of great concern nor were the frequently recorded. And so those of us who are now interested in presenting them cannot tell you who collected them individually or how it was done. We have some sketchy ideas but a solid research protocol laid down by Shaw. We have no formally written directions that were uniformly applied to each interviewee. And this would have been helpful. The controversy that Shaw ran into, and that some oral historians still experience, is the issue of methodologies. How were the boys selected and approached? What questions were specifically asked? Were they uniformly asked? What instructions were given or even suggested? Some of these stories were collected over the course of weeks, others months, and still others over the course of years.

The histories are in no way uniform in length or depth. Some were written in long hand while others were recorded and transcribed. Some had an interviewer more involved or less involved in the process of collection. While the methods of oral history collection were not as scrutinized at the time as they are now, important objections were raised by sociologists like John Dollard (1935), who were attempting to address just this issue.

I have selected a few stories that have been housed in the archives of the Chicago Historical Museum, which is where the files of the defunct IJR now reside. Where Shaw gained some renown for those interviews with the boys he published in his books, including *The Jack-Roller*, the stories presented here were not offered by him to the public then. One can probably make sense of his decision not to publish these at the time. They would have been considerably more disturbing to the general public than reading them today. It was Shaw's aim to help rehabilitate these boys and not to condemn their behaviors.

After reading *The Jack-Roller*, one could walk away feeling bad for

Stanley and what he went through as a child. One applauds Shaw when he later tells of Stanley's rehabilitation. But if one were to then read Jon Snodgrass' interview with Stanley when he reached the age of seventy, a sympathetic person can easily lose the hopeful feelings for Stanley that Shaw helped to encourage.

In these autobiographical accounts of boys here were few incidents of rehabilitation. One cannot be sure, but the research of tracking down the life stories of these boys would be a considerable challenge. Snodgrass (1982) must be credited for his dedicated work of finding Stanley. These stories here are rather disturbing and contain significantly more violence than what Shaw published in his studies. Nevertheless, I found them to be more typical. While the names of boys and the people with whom they interacted have been changed here to protect the privacy of those involved, I have not edited their grammar nor the boy's use of profanity or slang. Neither have I edited the near maddening redunancy that makes these narratives more into a laundry list of crimes rather than human autobiographies.

The experiences lived by some of these boys were far worse than what Stanley or some other boys who would up in Shaw's published studies experienced. I believe that reading them now gives evidence to the importance of Eve Kosofsky Sedgwick's notion of "male homosocial desire" and the role it plays in male juvenile crime (1985). Here we see that even though there are no formal gangs in these stories, there are tight networks of male friends united around those "deviant" elements of late nineteenth century masculinity that are central to their criminal performances and social connectedness.

While we cannot avoid recognizing family dysfunctionality in these stories, the importance of this is dwarfed by the dysfunctional characteristics of those institutions designed to help these boys—rehabilitative institutions that instead promoted anti-social behavior. We therefore begin with a story of one boy's incarceration. Please keep in mind these stories were lifted directly from autobiographical manuscripts and contain each boy's original language complete with grammatical and typing errors as well as redundancies. The only edits here were done in an attempt to hide each boy's identity.

THE LONE WOLF

I WAS BORN IN A SMALL TOWN south of Chicago with a population of about ten or fifteen thousand on the third day of August 1909. I do not remember my mother, but I have often studied several photographs just taken before her marriage to my father. She was reputed to have a very kind disposition; and as far as I can tell her picture seems to uphold this statement.

Her mother and father were farmers on a small scale. In the family there were three boys and two girls, my mother being their first child. My mother was a pure-blooded German, her maiden name being Heziker. I have never been able to ascertain whether she had any theological belief or not, but I suppose she was something like her brothers and sisters—without any kind of belief.

My father was born and raised somewhere in southern Illinois. He was a descendent of a Welch farmer, and there were eight children, five boys and three girls; they had a pretty hard time of it. My father tiring of the fearful drudge of farm life where the only pay was the food he ate and a pair of overalls and a new blue denim jumper about every six months, decided to run away from home and try elsewhere. His first job was kitchen's helper or dishwasher in a lumber camp in Little Rock, Arkansas. It was during his stay there that he met my mother. Of their courtship I know nothing, as I could never at any time get him to talk about her.

Not liking to have my mother around a lumber camp, he brought her back to Marion where they were married. They rented a modest four room bungalow on the outskirts of the town. About a year after they were married I was born. Everything went smoothly for a while, until my mother seemed to have something wrong with her lungs. Things went from bad to worse and my father lost his position. My mother got worse, so dad took her to a doctor who told him she was suffering from tuberculosis. There being no work in Marion and my mother needing a doctor's care, my father decided to go back to Little Rock leaving my mother and me in the care of one of my aunts.

It was while my father was away that mother's case became critical; but he couldn't leave his job for it was taking all he made to keep a roof over her head. Shortly after this, my mother died. She was buried in a little sandy waste called Plymouth about two miles east of Marion. The ceremonies were brief, with only a few near relatives as mourners and pallbearers. I've often wondered why dad wasn't there; maybe he couldn't come, although he turned up about two months later. After my mother's death I was taken in by an aunt on my father's side, she being a widow with one child of her own, a girl about 12 years my senior.

Aunt Kate was a strict Methodist, but the kindest and most generous woman I've ever met. When I was about four years old my father showed up at my aunt's. My aunt told him he could live there with her until he could get a job. Instead of trying to get a job he started borrowing money from my aunt, and as soon as he's gets the money off her he'd go to buy liquor and get drunk. He would then proceed to come home and take his spite out on me. Coming home one day drunker than usual he gave me a cuff along the ear knocking me on the floor. My aunt seeing this bit of brutality ordered him to leave at once.

Everything was again going smoothly with my aunt taking the place of my mother as only she knew how; in fact I don't believe my mother could have done more. Every night she would make me say a prayer, when I would get up she would sit down and I would put my head on her lap and say some prayer after she had said it. She would say a line, then I would repeat it after her. It was the same at meals. Although, as I said before, she was a strict woman, those were the happiest days of my life.

My father, after leaving my aunt's, became entangled with another man's wife. I will give you a little incident so as to give you a glimpse of her character. Her and my father were arrested, the woman was put to dusting the windows, etc., in the courthouse. Her husband hearing of her predicament rushed to the jail promising to get her released if she would come home and behave herself. Martha (that being the woman's given name) promptly gave him her word to come home and be a faithful wife if he would only get her out of the mess she had made. True to his word her husband has her out in less than an hour. But Martha had no intentions of going back to live with Cal (that being her husband's name). So telling him to give her some money as she wanted to do some shopping, she told him she would be home later. And Cal unsuspecting fellow that he was gives her the money. As soon as Cal is out of sight Martha rushes to the jail and springs dad out. After which they run away together. Cal at once begins proceedings for a divorce on the grounds of desertion. He won the case without a struggle which was what Martha and dad were praying for. Not long after this dad and Martha were married in the court which ruled that Cal should get their only child which was a girl and about five years my junior.

Shortly after their marriage, my father decides to take me away from my aunt and have me live with him. And that was the beginning of the end of my happiness, since the day I was taking away from my aunt's care I haven't known for months complete happiness. There was a dreadful scene when my father informed my aunt of these plans, and hasty words were branded back-and-forth. In the end my aunt told my father never to speak to her again, and she meant it, as fourteen years have passed and they haven't spoken to each other to this day.

Martha not being able to keep her own child took an intense dislike to me. And she nagged my father so much, that he tried to get a new trial which he did but the case was hopeless from the beginning. From that day forward I was doomed. She has done told several relatives that if she couldn't keep her own child she'd be damned if she'd keep anyone else's brats. Then started in what has always been a nightmare of continual nagging and whippings for imaginary offenses. Naturally you would wonder why my father didn't interfere. One reason was he really never knew what I went through.

I suppose you can see this state of affairs couldn't last long. So I took to running away from home but I could never get very far until I was brought back and given a severe beaten by my father, and as soon as he was at work I would get another one from her. Once at about the age of eight I got as far as a little town about six miles south of West Frankfort where we were living at the time. Johnson City is the name of the town. I met a young man and his son, showing him the marks on my back I pleaded with him to let me work around his place for my board. We will call this man Mr. X as I have forgotten his name. Mr. X became very angry on seeing the welts and cuts on my back and was all for going before the magistrate to have me put in some orphan asylum. He finally gave up this idea when he saw how badly it scared me, and at least told me I could live with him if no one interfered he would raise me as if I was one of his own sons.

But this new found happiness wasn't to last long. One day someone saw me and trailed me to where I was staying, and then sent word to dad telling him where I was at. I had been there for about a month when Uncle Ed showed up saying my father had sent him to get me. At first Mr. X wouldn't give me up, but when Uncle Ed mention the police Mr. X decided it was best to give me up. But he told Uncle Ed to see if he couldn't put dad wise as to how things were around the house with me. And also telling him how my back was cut from being whipped by rosebush switches with my shirt off (and every time she would hit there would be from four to five stickers or thorns in my back). My uncle took me back home and gave a distorted account of the interview with Mr. X after which I was given another whipping and sent to bed. The next day dad bought a 30 foot dog chain and two padlocks, taking the padlock and chain I was chained to a bed for something like a month and a half. One padlock snapped the chain around my leg, the other was to fasten it to the bed. And there I stayed day and night, day in and day out at the mercy of my stepmother's evil temper for six long weeks. That is one of the most harmful things that was ever done to me. That chain and lock started me on my downfall, for I resolved never to stay at home again as long as I lived.

The same day the chain was taken off I ran away again; this time I went to Benton where I was picked up by the officers and put in the county jail until my parents could be sent word. Although I gave the name of Lester Vincent my stepmother found out. She was in the town of Benton by the next train; there she immediately went to the states attorney and the judge telling them that although I had a good home I was always running away and pilfering through her personal belongings and that she thought that if I was sent to some kind of school maybe I would come out a better boy. The upshot was I got sixteen months in Saint Charles. In other words I was railroaded on a woman's word to satisfy her revenge.

When I say I was sentenced to Saint Charles I am not telling the exact truth. I was merely told that I was going there. I never saw a judge or a court of any kind. Whether a child has the same right to a fair hearing before an impartial judge I have never been able to ascertain. Although I went to Saint Charles three times, I was never taken before a judge nor did I have any kind of hearing. Although everyone talks of the justice of the courts and as far as they know they might be right but if a man has the right of the fair hearing, then why put a child with the most formative period of his life before him in a place where instead of correcting his moral attitude it utterly corrupts?

To get back to the main subject, I was taken to Saint Charles by a man that I shall hate to my dying day. He is one of the cruelest person's I ever met. Although it has been many years ago I remember the scene as if it happened yesterday. I was taken from the bullpen where I was confined with some other man on a bright and sunny morning. Taking me down to his office the sheriff snapped a pair of handcuffs on my wrists, on me a child not yet 10 years old. Although I promised not to run away or give any trouble it was of no avail. I remember I started crying and an old woman who cooked at the jail coming up to the sheriff and asking him to take the cuffs off. He said something to the effect that she was paid to cook, and not to run the sheriff's office.

On arriving at Saint Charles I was taken to what is known as the receiving cottage, where my clothes and personal belongings were taken from me. After a good bath I was given new underwear, a hickory shirt with blue and white stripes, and a pair of blue denim overalls without a bib and made in the institution tailor shop. Next, my hair was clipped off to prevent lice or other vermin in case there were any on my person. Although this may be humiliating to some it is a good idea and should be carried out in all the institutions where a larger body of inmates are confined. The next morning I was taken to the hospital where I was vaccinated, and given a physical examination by a very competent doctor and nurse.

After I was in the receiving cottage about one week Mr. Dolly a sort of major domo or what is known as the detail officer came to the receiving cottage and assigned me and about twenty other fellows to a cottage where we would remain the rest of our stay there. I was assigned to cottage K now known as Harding cottage. The house officer for this cottage was a young lieutenant by the name of Dixon. Mr. Dixon was a just man to the best of my knowledge. Although he was harsh and stern and sometimes almost cruel, I think he believed the punishment he meted out was a just reward to the offender. Although men of more brains and experience then I govern that institution, there is a practice that I think should be abolished and that is putting inmates in charge of inmates with full power to punish as they see fit. The captain and lieutenant had something of the same power as some of the old medieval monarchs with the possible exception of death. I will give here an example of where murder was committed to my certain knowledge, but if I was to bring this before a court of justice I might be able to prove the statement and I might not.

Anyway there were several boys in the cottage with weak kidneys, and as far as I know Roy Houston was the worst case of this kind. Almost every morning his bed would be found wet. At this time we had in this cottage a colored fellow by the name of Walker Bryant. This fellow had no morals and was really an outrage to mankind. And this fellow was captain, but more of him later. It was the duty of the captain each morning to give the boys who wet their bed a cold shower and to see that the water ran on your kidneys. But Bryant had different ideas as to how and where the water should run. Instead of letting the water run on their kidneys he would make the victim stand upright with his head under the deadly stream of cold water. To anyone who is never tried this, get a shower with the small spray with a fairly heavy pressure of water and stand under the shower of cold water for about fifteen minutes never once removing your head from the water. You will then get the idea of the torture I am talking about.

One morning after war he wet the bed for about a week straight Bryant decided he would cure Houston once and for all; whether the water was colder than usual or if Bryant kept him under longer than usual I do not know. Anyway Houston couldn't stand it and jerked his head out of the water pretty often. This infuriated Bryant so much that after Roy was dressed he took him into what is known as the drill room, and there started punishing him in the favorite punishment used by house officers and inmate officers. This punishment is known as squats and is done in this manner. First place your hands in back of your neck interlocking the fingers, put your heels together and squat down until the hunches touch the heels then come back up to a standing position always keeping hands behind the neck. Keep repeating this movement; the rate of speed is usually timed by a tick of a clock, one tick you got down and the next tick you come up.

I am not railing at punishment; the school couldn't be run without it. But it should be administered by older heads with some experience with children. To get back to Roy Houston, he was squatted until detail time that morning. Of course he was taken off of the squats to go to work, everyone believing the incident to be closed. It wasn't until that night that the tragedy occurred. After we had all said the Lord's Prayer, Bryant called Houston and two other lads to the back of the dormitory, giving the other boys a punch in the stomach that knocked the wind out of them. Houston seeing the treatment meted out to the two other lads and probably fearing physical pain, threw his arm to ward off the blow. That was Roy's undoing and is what I believe to have caused his death. I believe Bryant was insane with rage for a few minutes, taking a rag used for scrubbing the floor he tied Roy's hands to a row of pipes running around the dormitory for heat in place of radiators. I was standing only two beds away so you can see this is not hearsay but the absolute truth. There were some sixty or seventy inmates there and you probably wonder why the other fellows didn't interfere. A little thing maybe, and it's hard to believe, but every fellow in that place refused to raise a hand. What I am trying to bring out is instead of trying to make a man of them, they break your spirit and rule through fear.

After Roy was tied to these pipes, Bryant hit him three terrific punches in the regions of the stomach and heart. Roy sank down with a curious rattle in his throat the likes of which I have never heard repeated. Bryant taking Roy's unconscious body threw it in the bed and pulling the blankets around him he threw a pillow on his face. Bryant after watching Roy's bed for a while and seeing no movement jerked the pillow from his face. Roy was still unconscious. Bryant finally became alarmed by Roy's quietness. Going to what is known as a lookout window where the house officer may look from his rooms into the dormitory Bryant rapped on this window and signaled that the officer is needed. Mr. Dixon unlocked the door and asked Briant what the trouble was. Bryant told Mr. Dixon that Roy Houston was sick. Going to Roy's bed Mr. Dixon looked at his body, noting a welt running across his face. He then he ask Bryant how they came to be there. Briant told Mr. Dixon he didn't know and hadn't noticed until then.

Four boys were detailed to take Roy down to the basement and give him a bath after which they were to take him to the hospital. The event that happened after this I wouldn't swear to it as I have only the words of another inmate. Although why he should enlarge on anything of this nature I can't see, so I believe it to be true; but I can offer no proof. After giving him a bath he was put in a blanket with four boys carrying him one at each corner. There is a campus about a block long over which they had to carry his body. The boys carrying Roy thinking he was pulling what is known as a fake, decided to take some fun. So they started throwing him up-and-down in the blanket. When they reached the hospital Roy was dead. I am not saying that Bryant really meant to kill him. But he was capable of it, and the remarks he made that night shows how little he cared.

And now comes the part I have never been able to understand, the doctor's verdict was heart trouble. Maybe there was something wrong with his heart. I know he would eat anything under the sun; for myself I have seen him eat garden worms. But that don't alter my convictions at all. A boy by the name of Stephens or Stevens (I do not know for sure which way his name is spelled), this boy told Mr. Dixon the story but Mr. Dixon would not or didn't want to believe it.

I was in Saint Charles three times but I find I can't write as though I were. It seems to me as if I should write it just as if I was there only twice although the first time I was there was a very short length of time, not over three months at the most. Maybe my short stay there needs some explaining. Shortly after going there I wrote my father telling him where I was and asking him to come and see me. Dad came and before he left home he sold something to get enough money to get me out. After he was there it took him just three days to get me out. There was long distance telephoning to the judge and state's attorney and long conferences in Colonel Adam's office. Although I do not know the nature of these conferences I firmly believe money passed hands. I cannot prove this and it's no use writing about a man long dead but that is an example of the crookedness that abounds in an institution of that kind. The superintendent at that time (and still may be that it is still that way I am not sure) needed only the judge or states attorney's word and he could turn out any inmate he desired to. I never suspected this until the last time I was sent there. And it was then that I first suspected the truth of my first release. For one thing I do know dad sold a team of horses wagon and two seats or harness and I don't think that was all, but even so it wouldn't have took that much money to make the trip. And I know that dad seemed awful short of money after we reached home.

The food was something terrible, half cooked, and not near enough

Six. Institute for Juvenile Research Oral Histories 121

for growing boys. I will give you a short illustration of some of the meals served there. You were given one cup of milk, after you had drunk this milk you were given one cup of coffee, tea, or coco which ever it happened to be, two slices of bread and a little square of breakfast brand half cooked of which half was in lumps; break this open and you'd find it had not even been wet less cooked. Sometimes this made your breakfast! For dinner, say, there was a stew and baked potatoes; a spoonful of the stew which would turn into a kind of grease as soon as it got cold, and it was put in your plate with one potato with the peeling still on and it would be placed in the center of this grease, three slices of bread about 1 inch thickness and all of the water you wanted to drink was what was known as dinner. Our supper was the only meal we really got any enjoyment out of and that was composed of beans and three or four prunes. Beans were served between four and five nights a week. And that all times you must eat everything put before you. It was of no use to complain that you weren't getting enough to eat. You were simply told you got as much as the rest, so why holler? I won't say all cottages were alike, I don't know.

This was the way things were run under Adams' is rule. I believe this mode of feeding was first started during the world war at which time I suppose it was necessary to feed kind of light but there is a limit to everything and this I firmly believe was carried beyond reason. And I am also pretty sure the state was allowing enough money so that each and every inmate was well fed. Where did this extra money go? Colonel Adams' death was a time of rejoicing to the inmates. I don't suppose that is a nice thing to say but it is the truth. And I for one rejoiced as much as the rest.

Colonel Frank D. Whip then took the office of superintendent left vacant by did the decease of Colonel Adams. Colonel Whip is one of the finest and whitest man I ever knew. On taking charge he had all of the boys stay after the show Saturday night, to give us a little talk, and shake us each by the hand and wish us well. There were no radical changes in the first six months outside an order for all officers to stop corporal punishment at once. And a few minor changes in the grounds. There were some officers there who didn't believe he meant that first order. But realization came too late and they lost their positions.

He used to buy boxes of candy and go among the boys, "his boys" as he used to call them, giving each one an equal amount. You may get the idea that Colonel Whip was a weak man, but he wasn't, if the occasion arose he could be as stern as the sternest judge. Although Colonel Whip brought the food up to a level where we were eating almost as we would at home, he never I'm sure understood the power of his lieutenants.

After the order prohibiting the use of corporal punishment the house officers simply had the inmate officers do it for them.

Now comes to vital and most important questions of all. Although they have their churches there both Catholic and Protestant, and both were under wonderful hands (the Protestants especially), the services were conducted by a woman by the name of Helma Sutherland who was in reality the fairy godmother to the orphans, and boys whose parents had forsaken them.

The real point is the morals of the institution were something unthinkable. How the practice of prostituting the body first started I have no idea. Whipping and brutality did not stop.

It was right after I was assigned to what is known as the dressing room, a place were clothes are kept and mended. It was my job to sew buttons on the shirts, overalls, uniforms or anything in that line, and also darn socks. There was never a boy to my knowledge who could do all the work, and if that work wasn't done the captain would make you squat and maybe beat you so bad till you could hardly sleep on account of the bruises on your body.

As I said before it was while trying to hold down this job that I had my first experience of a boy prostituting his body. The captain came to me one day saying if I gave him what he wanted he wouldn't beat me anymore, and would give me someone to help with the work. I refused (who wouldn't) but if I had known what was in store for me I would have yielded then and there. And I would have saved myself some of the cruelest punishment I have ever known. From that day forward my life became a hell on earth. For days on end I was beaten for the most trivial offence. My lips nine tenths of the time were swollen sometimes my eyes would be black and every bone in my body aching. This was kept up for about two weeks, when again he came to me with his proposal. I was beaten and there is no use denying it. Don't judge me too hard for who can say, the day may come when the position will be the same for you. I yielded and then came a more terrible punishment. My conscience hurt for some while it is true, but not for long. I was beaten no more for a while and I had plenty of help ... also just for a while.

The captain was always on the lookout for some new boy. The point is a boy came in to whom he took a liking as far as it is possible for him to like anyone. My help was taken away and the old round of squats and beatings started all over again. It is mostly the same in all cottages, the captains use this power for this purpose and sometimes worse even then prostitution. And these officers are supposed to set a good example for the other boys. If a captain has had any kind of intercourse with the boy and he catches him with another boy doing the same thing he did, he'll probably squat him and make off as though he were giving him a terrible punishment, when in reality he is merely making a show to deceive the other inmates. But let him catch someone he never had anything of that nature with, he probably would report him to the house officer. The house officer will give him from one to three demerits, a demerit is one month lost good time. His hair is then shaved off and the boy is then put on punishment for an indefinite length of time besides the punishment the captain metes out to him. In a short space of time it is all over the institution as well as the cottage. Maybe you can understand the humiliation of this.

Once a boy has been seduced it takes something out of this life and from then on he is an easy prey to anyone. There may be a few exceptions to this but as a majority it holds good. Especially if it once becomes known. If it is never know there may be a chance. The punishment by humiliation went out of date in the 18th century yet it is still being carried on in a different way, but not the less brutal for all that. I have been asked time and time again if there is any joy in this act. I will try and give you as truthful an answer as possible.

Before coming to puberty there is no pleasure, in most cases there will be pain until one is used to this practice. After puberty is a different question and a hard one to answer. At times there is a curious thrill, before you commit the act your blood will be racing and your breath will be short and uneven. At times you will get the final thrill, after which your strength seems to have been sapped but only a second or so. Yet on the other hand you may commit this act without the slightest thrill at all.

The school at Saint Charles as far as educational purposes are concerned is a pretty fair imitation of any other school. The majority of teachers are as a rule women of fairly good moral character, but there are that few that are not of such good character. I will give a short illustration of what I mean. There was a teacher whom we will call Miss B. Miss B was caught in the teachers' lavatory with a captain of a cottage. That night Miss B left the institution. Not long afterwards she was back teaching school again. The idea of this I can't understand. A few months after this four boys working in the A.C. were found in her room, three were under her bed and one in the bed with her.

I wish to relate one more incident that happened during my second stay there. There was a young French boy whom I will call number four as that was his clothes number. The incident I am about to relate happened on Saturday afternoon as we were taking a bath. Bryant took number four from the bathroom into the fruit room. There Bryant tried to have intercourse with him. Upon number four's refusal Bryant called two boys in to help him, and throwing number four to the ground he pissed in his mouth.

I will now pass on my third stay there. I was placed in cottage F now known as Jefferson cottage. The house officers were Mr. and Mrs. Lunn. Upon entering this cottage I was placed in the employees' dining room as a waiter. This job is considered one of the best positions in the institution. The woman in charge was a married woman by the name of Mrs. P, her husband working at that time in the powerhouse. It was here I met a boy by the name of Willard S. I will not give the rest of his name as he is now a chef in a leading hotel of Rockford, Illinois. Willard had what is known as a drag with the inmate officers. He soon became friends of a sort. Pretty soon Willard started making up to me telling me he would keep me from squats and having to drill. I accepted his proposal and true to his word for whatever it was in his power to do so he always kept me from punishment.

I was with Willard when I got my first thrill. I will now try to explain; all I know is that I soon came to look forward to our meeting. Although this happened once or twice and sometimes as much as three times a day I would never get tired. This may have been a case of homosexual love I couldn't say but I do know that I had the same feelings only once in my checkered career. I ran away from the dining room on the night in the middle of the fall 1924 or 1923, but was brought back immediately. I of course lost my job and was put on punishment for two weeks. After that I was assigned to the laundry to work. I was put in the ironing room under a very kind woman by the name of Miss Abel. After the time we became very good friends, and every Monday she would bring me delicacies from the table. Every Saturday I would go up to her room and scrub. After which she would always give me something.

In the spring of 1925 I was released for the third time. I was paroled to my father but my step mother wouldn't let things be, so I ran away once more after being home for only three days. I went to see my aunt Kate. It was the first time we had met since my father had taken me from her home so many years before. And Kate invited me to stay with her as long as I wished. She was keeping boarders at this time. And I was given a room with a young man who ran a barbershop. We both had to use the same dresser and it was while looking through a drawer that I came upon a gun a wild idea came to me that here was the key to my independence.

Taking the gun and putting it in my shirt, I told my aunt I was going to see an uncle of mine who lived in Harrisburg. She never suspected anything and told me to come back when I was ready and I would always be welcome. Going to a matinee I sat through the whole show trying to pass the time away, as I didn't want to try my luck in the daytime as I was a green horn at the racket and still am. When the show was over I found it still too late for my purpose so deciding to stroll around for a while until it got dark, I started walking out along the highway, becoming thirsty I stopped at a farmhouse to ask for a drink.

No one answered my knocking. I remembered something I had heard not long before to the effect that most of the farmers were richer than most people gave them credit for being. Going around to the back door I found it was hooked by a small latch. Breaking this I entered and found it to be poorer than the outside had given reason for me to believe. The only thing of value was a signet ring of hammered gold. Putting this on my finger I started to take my departure when I heard the owner's footsteps. Hastening to the back door I tried to slip out unseen, but I was too late for he was almost to the door. Jumping into the yard I pulled the gun and told him to stop or I would shoot. Seeing that I was in earnest he threw both hands up telling me not to shoot. Somehow we fell into conversation. How this was done I do not understand. Finally he spied the ring. He asked me to give it back as it was a keep sake, and he told me if I gave it back he would never say no more about it. I gave him the ring as I wouldn't of known what to do with it if I did keep it. I started back to Marion and it was while going back that I was arrested.

I was taken to the county jail where I was put in with a gang of other men, my bond being set at $20,000. This was an enormous amount to me and I was unable to get it filled. The next morning I was taken before what is known as the "kangaroo" court. This court is comprised of inmates and is for the benefit of prisoners of poor means. I was fined $10 for breaking and entering without the consent of the inmates. Only having between four and five dollars I was unable to pay my fine. So I was put to washing pans and scrubbing floors and flunking for prisoners who had paid their fine in full. Here I met a fellow who had served time in Leavenworth Penitentiary. He being the judge, he had me exempted from all work because I was so young and shouldn't have to pay as much as the men, that's the excuse he gave the court; but to me, he told the real reason. He wanted me to be his "kid" and if I was he would look out for me. Needless to say I became his kid. It was then I got my first introduction to what is known as the tongue bath, and there I rebelled, but catching me by the arm he twisted it until I thought it would break. The pain became so intense that at last I complied. And as God is my witness if we ever met again I shall get my revenge. That was my first and last experience of that kind and a dirtier practice I've never known.

Breakfast, dinner, and supper were the same a—a spoon of apricots, a spoon of gravy and a spoon of potatoes and two slices of bread. This never varied; it was always the same. I became sick and the doctor advised sending me to a sanitarium in East Saint Louis, but one day the boys were joking about blocking the doors, so they wouldn't close. In a spirit of bravado I told them I could block every door in that section with a wet blanket and some tobacco tins. Well I jammed those doors and it was a week before they would work.

The first ones to say I couldn't do this were the first to tell the sheriff I had. The sheriff transferred me to another floor and there locked me in a cell by myself. There was no face bowl in the cell neither was there any drinking water; if I wanted to wash my face I would pass a towel through the bars to some inmate who would wet it and pass it back. If I wanted to drink, someone would have to hold a cup against the bars while I drank. The sheriff told me I would stay there until I plead guilty or until I was released, for by jamming those doors I jammed my chances for going to the sanitarium. The odds were against me but I done what anyone else in my circumstances would have done, but I held out two weeks before finally pleading guilty to midnight robbery while armed with a deadly weapon.

I was sentenced to sixteen months in Saint Charles School for Boys. The parole officer, a very fine man, objected it in the name of the school telling his honor judge D.W. Hartwell that they wouldn't take me back anymore. The judge told him it was none of his business what he did he knew his duty and meant to carry it out. That night the papers stated I was sentence for the fourth time to Saint Charles for sixteen months. And I never knew until the night I was taken from jail that I wasn't going to Saint Charles but rather to the Illinois State Reformatory with a sentence of five to twenty years.

At the time I committed this crime I was only fifteen years of age. I may have been young in years but I believe even at that young age I knew more of the seamy side of life than most men do at 50. I entered the reformatory on November 7, 1925. I was put in an emergency cell for two days, it being Saturday afternoon when I arrived. Monday morning I was taken to the Receiving and Discharging department where I was given the number of 5152. My picture was then taken, my hair clipped off. I was then given the regular prison uniform. I was then taken to the hospital. Arriving at the hospital I was interviewed by a Dr. Marshall one of the crabbiest men it's ever been my witness to meet. Almost every question I answered according to him was a lie. After being examined I was vaccinated by an equally crabby woman named Miss Semitar. A week or two after this I was taken to the captain's office to be assigned to work. Mr. William Rob was at that time acting assistant superintendent. While being questioned by him, Mr. Lunn came in to see Mr. Rob about his residence as he was to be the next assistant supervisor. On seeing me Mr. Lunn advised Mr. Rob to place me in the laundry as I was an experienced hand at the business.

A few days later Mr. Lunn took the job as Assistant Superintendent. Coming down to the laundry he told me that if I would do his laundry, and washed it by hand he would see that I would always have plenty of smoking and chewing and he would help me out anytime he could. I did the washing and ironing for about two months, when Mrs. Lunn decided she would rather have the washing done over at the residence so she could have the clothes out in the sun to dry. Well I never received the smoking but I did get quite a few breaks in the court room.

In the laundry someone was always trying to make me. One day I met a fellow who told me to string them along and then get what I could out of them. This was a new one to me and I asked him what he meant. His answer was make them believe you're going to give it to them, but always stall them off, and play only one fellow at a time. This looked fairly easy so waiting until the next one tried I appeared to yield. That night I told him I needed smoking and giving me a bag he told me to come to him anytime I needed anything. The next night it was a pair of socks and I got them with merely telling him I loved him. The state of affairs kept up for almost two months at about which time he began to get suspicious. So I began looking for a new victim. At about this time this hop head was put in the cell next to mine, and as he had been here I began to make up to him, knowing that nothing serious could ever become of it, all I had to do was sit next to him at a table and let him feel me up and call me baby while I called him daddy.

In the shop the other lad wasn't taking it quite so easy. And he kept insisting that I give him the weed back at once or put out. Not wanting to put out to him I figured on making up to someone else and thereby get protection and weed too. I started hanging around a fellow by the name of P.W.; almost the same day he asked me to be his kid. Thinking I could string him along like the other one I complied. I got my protection as the other boy was afraid of P.W. The hop head protection as the other boy was afraid of P.W.; But how pad somehow heard about my going with P.W. Although nothing serious yet happen. The hop head sent word to P.W. to leave me alone or there would be trouble. That Saturday both came on the yard with a knife and ready to fight. But after talking it over they both came to the conclusion that they had been strung along. The hop head quit me cold, but he never mentioned anything he gave me. P.W. was a different proposition, he acted just as if nothing had ever happened until Monday morning. After we were in the shop next morning we went into a little room to pack as we had done almost every day. But this morning it was different; he had a boy placed just outside the door to watch the man and keep jiggers. As usual we started kissing and loving each other up until his passion got the upper hand. He unbutton my trousers before I knew what it was all about. Telling me to lie down on the floor he took a little box of Vaseline from his pocket. Taking some he put it on his penis and taking the rest he put it on my ass; laying down on top of me he gradually began pushing his penis in me. This was the first time I ever had Vaseline used on me and it made a subtle difference. P.W. did not have a big penis and instead of hurting me as I expected I got a curious thrill. It seemed as if I could lay there all day. P.W. had plenty of weed and I always got what I wanted. But he was a jealous fellow, if anyone made a remark about me he was always ready to fight.

I had been with P.W. about 14 months when he was paroled. He was celling with a boy named W.L. W.L. is what is known as a big shot in the shop. He had a drag with the man in charge. Upon P.W.'s going home W.L. asked me if he could take P.W.'s place. He was a pretty good guy so I hooked up with him. We didn't want to do anything in the shop, so we made up this plan. As he was a messenger he could make some excuse to get out of the shop at whatever time he wanted to. Our play period at that time was at three o'clock in the afternoon. When we went out to play I was to wait on the corner of the playground and if the coast was clear he would come strolling by and I would fall in beside him. At this time he had a friend in the warehouse where cotton and springs were stored for use in the chair shop. W.L. had put the fix in with his friend so we could come in there and he would give us jiggers.

I will just recite here one trip there, as most of the others were the same. Climbing to the top of the cotton we rolled a bale of it out of its place which left a little hollow about 4 feet long and 2 feet wide and 2 feet deep. The space was too small to lay out flat so he told me to lie down on my back and he got down on his knees. He then placed my legs upon his shoulders. After getting it in we started sucking tongues. After he was through we rested for about five minutes all the while kissing and patting each other. He then asked me if I wanted to go again and I told him yes.

Instead of going as we had before he bent me over his bale of cotton. It was in this building and from this boy that I received the greatest thrill I ever had. L and I got along fine for a long time but after about eight months neither of us got the thrill of those first few months.

After this I got to where I hated to go with him anymore. There was no pleasure at all only a feeling of helplessness and sometimes pain. At last he went home and I was glad of that because I blamed him because I couldn't get a thrill out of it anymore. But it was just as much my fault as his. I can see that now. The reason I didn't get thrill was because I didn't try to, for I see now I can get a thrill whenever I want it. After L went home I had no excuse for what happened and then and no one to blame but myself. I had planned to turn public prostitute for a month or so until I had enough weed to become independent and would have to cater to no one. I consider this the biggest mistake I ever made.

I had intercourse with two boys the same day L went home, S and C respectively. And in return I got nothing but promises. S and C called me in the washroom where they were working. One would keep watch while the other one and I would be behind the washers. Waking up to the fact that I was being made the goat, I rebelled and told them I had reformed and wasn't going to do that kind of thing anymore. Both of them being big shots they had me put on the pan or a thing similar to the boycott outside. They refused to wash my clothes. And when they didn't wash them they were worse than before or else they stole them.

I started putting out to first one big shot then the next, trying to get off the pan without putting out to S and C. But it was no use. Sometimes I would put out twenty-four or five at a time. At this time I was so miserable and humiliated I felt like putting an end to my life, but when the time came I could never bring myself to commit the deed.

At other times I would lay awake nights trying to think up some way to get revenge but it never panned out. You may wonder why I never told the man. I have my code and the lowest thing a person can do is to tell on a fellow inmate. And this time I didn't have a friend in the institution on account of my being what I was. Well, to make it short I gave in to S and C again and virtually became their slave. One day S asked me if I would French it. Not getting what he meant I said I would. But I soon found out what he meant. That afternoon we went into an old unused dry house. Telling me to get down on my knees I complied thinking he was going to try a new way. He then pulled out his penis telling me to suck it and I fearing to comply obeyed. This is the dirtiest practice there is and I hope to see the day when S will get his just desserts.

Things came to the pass after a while and almost everyone thought I had to put out to them. So again I quit but I was panned worse than ever. One day a colored fellow I will call Matt said to me if you will quit messing around with those other fellows and go with me steady I will see that no one bothers you again. In the fix I was in this was a godsend. I took him up on it at once. He got my clothes washed and gave me what I needed. And though some of them still pester me none of them ever tries panning me anymore. With Matt my feelings are no different from what I want them to be. I can get a kick out of it if I want to and if I don't want to I don't. At times I hate him with a hate that almost drives me to murder. But no matter how much I hate him I will stick with him till he doesn't want me anymore or until I go home or he does. The code may be a little strange to some but to me it is nevertheless real and I follow it to the best of my ability. And he has done for me a good turn and I feel as if I owe him something in return. And so as long as he wants me I am there to do as he says to a certain degree. And he has never overstepped that degree.

I have been asked could you quit this fame if you wanted to, and if I want to quit. Yes, I could quit it if I wanted to; it is not like drinking or the drug habit and as far as I can tell has no physical harm as an aftermath. Yes, I would like to quit but as I have just stated as long as Matt is in the institution I won't as I feel I owe it to him.

I wish to give one or two more illustrations with me playing the jocker this time. This will also give you a glimpse of a character I can't understand. First I will take the case of True. This is one of the most peculiar cases I ever knew, and I believe he would need constant attention before he could quit. One day shortly after he was put in our shop he came up and asked me to put out to him and I refuse him. A little while later he came back and asked me if I wanted to put him. I didn't like to refuse him for fear of hurting his feelings. But he was so insistent that at least I told him I would put him but under no circumstances could he put me. So going back to the tumbler one day I put him and it was a very agreeable sensation but one I will never repeat. This experience although it was agreeable for a few minutes turned out to be disgusting. It was this way after I had finished he wanted me to keep on going but I couldn't. He then wanted to suck me off until I had aroused my passion enough to go again. This revolted me so much that I could never go with him again although he begged me something fierce for a few days.

This brings to my mind another incident that happened a year or so before this. There was a boy in our shop who had repeatedly tried to make me. Now I had heard from a fairly a good source that he would go himself although I had never known him to do so. A few months after he gave up hope of ever making me, he came to me with the tale that no one had ever done anything like that to him and he would like to try it to see what it felt like. He hinted around for quite a while before I caught the drift of his talk. Plainly speaking he wanted me to make him, and his reason was to see what kick was in it. At this time I needed no urging to do a thing of this kind so I accepted with alacrity first promising never to tell a living soul. We had no more then got in the room and he had his trousers down then in walked a boy already mentioned in this article ... it was L. I got up and went out telling L to do likewise. But L seeing a good chance to make a boy stayed behind and a few minutes later they were caught by the officer in charge. A pretty lucky escape it seemed to me.

Now I wonder if those of you who read this can see where the greatest crime against mankind is being committed and maybe one of you will offer something to change this for there is no greater curse to man than this. It wrecks your physical courage as well as your moral. It makes him ashamed to hold up his head among men who have no honor at all. I often wonder if I will ever be able to ask any girl to be my wife at times I think I will never be able to do it. Nor am I sure if she would hate me if she ever found out. I then sometimes think that if I should ever meet the girl I would like to marry, I will tell her the truth and trust that she may be able to forgive and forget. It's a foolish idea of course, as angels went out of style in the nineteenth century.

For almost four years I have been suffering from a very bad case of catarrh and adenoids. Several times I have gone to the doctor for something to ease the pain, for the most part I have been told there is nothing wrong with me. Once upon going to the hospital I was giving an examination and was told to quit smoking as my heart was beating faster than normal. If my heart was beating faster than normal it was caused by the gas from the terrible odor from my nose. This odor is caused by slinkers forming around my adenoids coupled with catarrah. And if you have ever been around anyone with this dread malady you can see what I mean. One day I went to the hospital and ask Dr. Marshall if he wouldn't cut my adenoids out. He told me that the next time he operated he would do so which would be in a day or so. He then had me put in to the sick cell telling me I could stay there until he got ready for me. The next morning Dr. Lund came by the sick cell and seeing me there he asked me what was wrong. So I told him Dr. Marshall had put me there until he could operate on me. Dr. Lund remarked that he had a lot of laundry for me to do and that he would see the doctor and ask him whether it was necessary to operate or not. That morning I was called from the sick cell and was told not to come over again without there being something wrong with me.

You will kind of wonder if there was anything wrong with me and if it wasn't just my imagination. Yes there is something the matter with me. But that was just one case in one thousand where the officials worked hand in hand to better their conditions at the expense of the inmates. I do not say all of them are of this stamp. Some of them are really nice men. But those you find in prison are few and far between.

I have been asked will you lead a straight and honest life when you get out of here or will you go back to the old life. I will be frank. I don't know. I sometimes think that if conditions favored me there is a chance for me. Otherwise there is no hope. I will constantly have to be with upright companions for three or four months; all my time must be occupied for it is those hours with nothing to do that will ruin me.

The Boy Scout

The neighborhood in which I was born, raised and lived in was near the downtown section. The people living around there were mostly poor people from the old country. They had just enough to barely live. I liked them; they were friendly and they always talked nice to you. The houses consisted of two-story frame houses with a few trees in front of the houses here and there. The houses were very old outside and poorly furnished inside. Some of them needed a paint job; others needed plastering jobs and all were poorly furnished.

The house where I lived didn't have a toilet in the inside. When we had to go to the bathroom, we had to go outside. Sometimes when we got out to the toilet it would be occupied by someone else and we would have to wait. It was very unhealthy. There was no running water in the outside toilet and the place smelled awful. Once in a while we had to take a kettle full of water and pour it around there.

My father was a stout man. He was a common laborer and he had a hot temper. I remember one rainy day, I was outside playing and I got my shoes all wet and then I saw my father coming back from work. He looked at me and told me to go home. When I got home he asked me how I got my shoes wet. I told him they got wet while I was playing. He took a strap and he beat me up with it. I got an awful beating that day but I did not mind. I was used to his beating by that time. I believe I used to get beaten up about twice a week.

My father used to drink a lot. Sometimes he would come home drunk and he would want to start something. Sometimes his arguing would result in a fight with my mother. So us kids would have to break it up. We would throw my father on the bed and he would fall asleep. Sometimes when he came home drunk he would take a strap and beat me up or take me by the ears and throw me down and step on and kick me. Sometimes I would have scars and blue marks. Sometimes when my father got through beating us up we used to hide from him, or go to bed or under the bed, anything to get away from him.

My mother was a nice woman. I liked her a lot. She always stuck up for us kids regardless if we were right or wrong. Once in a while she used to give us pennies to buy candy with. She would also try to stop my father from beating us up all the time. My mother always had a lot of work to do. She would clean the house, wash the clothes and iron them, keep the kids clean, and cook. She worked very hard.

I had two brothers. One, Jerry, was older than me. The other one, Dick, was younger than me. My brother Jerry was a thin built fellow and tall with black wavy hair. He was much smarter than me and he went to school every day. Him and I would pal around a lot. We used to go to shows together. My father had a lot of faith in him. Anytime he would tell my father something my father used to believe him. But when I would tell him something he would think I was lying right or wrong. I remember one night my brother and a few of the boys from the neighborhood got caught breaking into a place. The coppers came over to our house and told my parents about it. They went down to the station to get him out. When he got out and came home my father beat him up with an iron bar. He was crippled from this beating for a couple of days. After that my brother Jerry didn't fool around for a while.

My brother, Jerry, had an awful temper when he was a kid. I know he did a lot of fighting in his days. Most of his fights he won and some he lost. I had a lot of arguments with him and he used to kick the hell out of me. I never made a pass to hit him back because if I did I would've gotten more. A lot of the times my brother used to tell me what to do and what not to do but I never paid any attention to him. Jerry and my mother got along very fine. My brother liked my mother a lot. When my mother told him to run an errand he would gladly do it for her. For some of the errands my mother used to give him a penny so he could buy some candy. I never ran errands for my mother. She used to ask me to go but I never did go.

When I was a young punk about eight years old my family brought me to school. I liked the first four years of school very much because it was easy. As I started to get older I began to dislike school very much. I remember when I was in fifth grade a few of us boys from the neighborhood would play hooky. We would go home, get an empty potato sack, and go through an alley looking for bottles and rags. After we would get a sack filled up with junk and take it to the nearest junk shop and sell it. With the money which we received we would go out and buy candy and lemonade. Then at noon we would go home to eat so our mothers could see us. They would think we would be coming back from school. After we got through eating we would leave the houses again and all of us boys would probably go out for a walk. The fellows who went with me on these days that we played hooky were Marvin and Eddie. They were neighbors.

We would walk down Halsted Street and as we approach stores with fruit outside we would all pass by and grab an orange or an apple a piece. Sometimes the stores had sweet potatoes outside. We would pick up the whole bushel and walk away with it. We would take the sweet potatoes down to or hang out in front of Bennie's house. There a few of us boys would go down the alley, find some fence, rip it down, and take the wood back to the hangout and build a fire. There we would roast sweet potatoes. As the sweet potatoes were cooking we would all hang around and talk and talk until the potatoes were ready. After they were all cooked we would take them out and eat them. We would hang around for a little while and then my brother and I would go home. He and I would be walking on the street we would talk to each other like this: "I hope to Christ the old man don't wake up because if he is up when we walk in the house he will kick the shit out of us." Sometimes we would get in the house and he would be sound asleep then we were safe that night. But other nights when we would come home we would find him up. He would ask us where we were. We would try to lie to him. We would tell him we just left the house about 15 minutes ago. But just the same he would beat the shit out of us. He would always tell us, "After supper none of you are to leave the house." I don't know why he used to tell us this.

Madison Street is a street were all the hoboes and buns hang. We would walk around there looking for drunks, and we spotted a few one day. They were sleeping under the "L" station. We walked up to them and we frisked them. We emptied the contents of their pockets and we found about forty cents on them. One of the boys kept the forty cents and we decided to continue walking. We approached an abandoned house. We had intentions of stealing the lead pipes. Casper, Bennie and Ted were with me. We boosted Casper up to a window. He said, "Hey, there's a woman lying on the bed." Right away, we all wanted to look. So we all climbed into the room.

We heard men's voices up in the front. Casper right away wanted to give the woman a lay. So Casper just laid on top of the woman and he blew. The woman was so drunk she didn't know what was going on. Then Bennie was just about to get on top of her when we heard the men coming toward the room, and we all had to run. On the way walking home Casper laughed and said he was the only guy who got laid and the rest of us were all mad because this was the first time we had a chance to get laid and it had to be ranked.

One morning me, Casper and Smiley were walking down an alley in the neighborhood. We passed a barn and in this barn was an old stripped Model T Ford. So we went inside to investigate. We looked at the car and finally we pushed it out of the barn and into the alley. Bennie said, "This barn is a nice place to make a club in." The place was pretty dirty, so we got a few shovels and brooms and cleaned it up. Then we decided what we needed to fix the club up with was a lot of lumber. So the next day we got an old wagon and Bennie bar and went up on Clark Street. When we got there we ripped a fence apart, took the lumber, put it on the wagon and brought it back to the club. With this lumber we made chairs and tables. That day a few of the boys went up on H and R and there they stole about six blankets off a truck and brought them back to the club. With these blankets we made cushions on the chairs so we had soft seats.

One day while we were in our club the boys in the gang decided we would go out and raid the J school. That Friday night we got the jimmy bar which we had in the club and we all went over to the J school. We spotted a window, opened it with the jimmy bar, climbed through the window and after we were all in the school we close the window up again. We walked around the inside of the school building. We looked in a few rooms and into the office and couldn't find any money. We decided to go to the lunch room. When we got in the lunch room, we took all the good food, packed it up into boxes and sacks and each one of us carried a sack or box back to the club. Every morning we used to go to the club and scoff up on the eats. The members of the club were: Bennie, Joe, Cliff, Casper, Thomas, me and Smiley. Up on Madison Street there used to be another gang of boys there. They would come around our clubhouse and tried to break in and sometimes they would make a lot of racket on the outside. We didn't like this. When we were in the club we wouldn't make any noise because the people next-door to the club were very nosey and we didn't trust them.

So whenever these boys from the other street would come over to our club house we would come out and chase them away. Sometimes we would get hold of one of the boys and we would beat the hell out of him.

On Sunday morning Casper and Thomas came over to my house and called me. They said, "Let's go see a show." As we were walking down Halsted Street we met a few of the boys from the gang. They asked us where we were going. We told them that we were going to see a show. While we were walking, Casper spotted a store on Halsted Street. So he decided that we should try to burglarize the store. We looked the store over carefully and saw that there was a big padlock on the front door. In order to get this padlock off we would need an iron bar. So we told Casper, "Let's you and I take a walk over to my house and get a bar." I went into my house and down into the basement. There I found a good size bar. I took the bar, wrapped it up in some newspapers and walked out of the house. Then we walked back to the place up on Halsted Street that we were going to burglarize.

When we got there we took the bar out of the newspaper, stuck it into the lock, and used force to break the padlock open. Finally, we succeeded in opening it. And we walked into the store. We looked around for money but couldn't find any so we piled up a lot of chinaware and we're just about to leave when one of the boys spotted coppers outside the store. So we made a dash for the back of the place. There we opened the door, ran out into the yard, and into the alley. We saw a few more coppers in the alley, so we decided to run and try to get past them. So I ran and finally got past the coppers but one bastard started to chase me. I ran about three or four blocks and then I got tired. So I went to a yard and I hid behind a door. A lot of people from that neighborhood saw the commotion going on and it just so happened that a woman in the building saw me hiding behind the door. She told the copper that was chasing me that I was behind the door. The copper grabbed me and took me back to the store which we had burglarized.

There in the store I saw Casper and Thomas. They had got caught before I did, so the coppers asked us how we got in the store. We told them we had broken the lock off. Then they took us down to D Street police station. They brought us in front of the desk sergeant. There they made out juvenile slips for the three of us and they put us into a cell for a while. This was the first time I was in jail and I admit that I was pretty scared. So in about an hour they took us to the Juvenile Detention home. While I was in the juvenile detention home I was interviewed by a probation officer by the name of Max West. He had a talk with me and he said, "I see this is the first time you've been arrested. Why did you go out and do this?" I said I don't know. He asked me how I liked the home and the eats and I said, "Well, the eats aren't so bad but I'd rather be home than be here." He told me the day I was to go to court and told me not to worry because I would get out.

The day finally came when I went to court. They took us to court through a tunnel and there they put us in a small room which they called the bullpen. In the bullpen were a lot of boys and we talked and fooled around. Finally they called all of us and brought us up in front of the referee. There we all formed a line with our parents behind us. Then they read off the charges for each of us which was burglary. Finally the referee had a talk with us. He said, "Well, this is the first time you boys have been in trouble. If I give you boys a chance to be good will you be good? Each of us answered, "Yes!" So then he said, "Case discharged!"

When I got out of the court room I got a bawling out for my father. He yelled, "Why do you want to go and steal?" I said, "I didn't go out and steal, it was the other boys." When I got home he kicked the hell out of me. That following night us boys that were in this jam met and we started to talk. The conversation was about if we were ever going to go out and steal again. They asked me, "Are you going to go out and steal again?" The guy who asked me was Casper. I told him, "No. I think I had enough. Those two weeks in the juvenile really taught me a lesson." So I took it easy and went to school and behaved myself.

After a while I went back to the old hang out by Bennie's house. There I started to indulge in petty thievery again. I used to hang around in the C-Club again with the rest of the boys. The first thing you know summer was with us again and our game was going to Sheridan Park to swim in the pool they had there. We didn't really go for the swimming. We were going there to steal out of the lockers. The way we used to work it was this way. We used to steal by being way behind in our dressing, like putting our swimming trunks on. After all the other boys were out of their lockers we used to walk into them and search the clothes for money. When we found money in the lockers we used to take it back to our locker and hide the money in our shoes. On some occasions some of the lockers were closed but Bennie used to boost me through an opening at the top of the door and I would climb in and open the locker from inside. When we open the locker we would ransack the clothes for money. We did this all summer long and made a few dollars. With some of this money we used to buy hotdogs. Sometimes we used to go and take in a show. In this park we also stole towels for the club. The reason why we stole these towels was because we had a shower in the club and needed the towels. We also stole some swimming trunks. We use these trunks to go out to the beach. When we were out on the beach we would pick the pockets of the clothes that were out there. After we would get through swimming the boys would walk back home.

The first thing you know summer was over and we had to go back to school. Well, the first month of school I went every day but then I started to bum school again and go and hang in the C-Club. There we played cards practically all day. We seldom left the club to go out walking, for fear if we did go out we would get picked up by the police and taken back to school.... I went bumming a lot and the first thing you know the school sent over to my house a truant petition for me to appear in court. When I got this petition I got scared. I said to myself, "Well, it won't be long before I'll go to the bad house (Parental School)."

Finally, the day came when I had to go to court. I went in front of the judge and he asked me, "Why don't you go to school?" I don't know exactly just what I told him but anyway I was freed and I went home. So I made it my business to go to school every day, which I did. One day I decided to go bumming again and I went to the C-club. There in the club was my brother and a few other boys. We were in the club all morning. In the afternoon about 2:30, I heard some commotion outside the club. I told Thomas, "Do you hear that noise outside?" He said, "Yes, it's probably some stalled car up there." I said, "No, it can't be. There's a lot of people out there I can hear them talking." Then all of a sudden I heard somebody coming through our secret door. So the boys who are in the clubhouse ran upstairs to see who it was. We had a secret compartment upstairs; we lifted up a board to see who it was and we saw a few coppers out there. So all of us boys got frightened.

The club was in an uproar for a minute or so. Inside the club we had a window and this window led to the yard. So we broke open the window and we all jumped out into the yard. We started to run through an old building that was in front of the club but here were coppers in this building. The coppers grabbed me and Ted and they took us back into the club. There they searched around and found a lot of stuff which belonged to some public schools. They asked us where we got the stuff and at first we told them, "We don't know nothing about it." They said, "Where did it come from?" Then they asked, "Who stole it?" About ten minutes went by and I saw a copper bring my brother into the club. So that made three of us fellows that got caught. But Thomas got away. So the coppers took all the stuff we had in the club and piled it up, took it, and put it into the patty wagon. The stuff consisted of silverware from the school, a lot of manual training tools, school pencils and papers, and a little food. As they were leading the stuff into the patty wagon they put Jerry, Ted and me into the wagon too. But before we got into the wagon we saw Thomas, the fellow that got away, in the crowd outside the club. Just when we were about to go into the wagon and pull away Thomas told them to stop. So they stopped and he told the coppers to open the door and let him in. When we all saw this we thought Thomas was crazy. So the coppers said, "What do you want to get in for?" Thomas said, "Well, I belong with this crowd. I'm one of the fellows." So the copper grabbed him and threw him in the wagon. As we were going down to the station we talked to Thomas. We asked him, "What's the big idea? You got away and you should have stayed away." He said, "Hell, you guys are all pinched. I might as well get pinched too."

Finally we reach the Detention Home. They took us out of the wagon and brought us into the home. In the office they ask us our names and a lot of other questions and then they wrote it down in the big book. Time in the home went by fast. We were there about four days when one morning, about 7 o'clock we went outside for a little fresh air and to play ball before school. While playing we were surprised to see Bennie, Cliff and Mike come in. So me, Jerry, Thomas and Ted went and talked to Bennie and Cliff I asked Bennie, "What are you doing here; how did you get caught?" Bennie said, "I think the principal mentioned something to the coppers about my name so the coppers came to my house and talked to my father and then he brought me to the station."

We were talking and Bennie said, "I called up Mr. H and threaten Mr. H with death if he would testify against us." We thought it was very nice and we all got a kick out of hearing it. I told Bennie, Cliff and Mike that when they go to the school and fill out their cards, they should say that they are in the six grade and in that way they would be in the same room with us.

Finally the day came when we went to court. There in the home we put on our own clothes and went to court through a tunnel. Finally the time came when we went in front of the referee. There we all formed a straight line with our parents behind us. They read off the charge, which was burglary. The referee said, "I will have to sentence all of you boys to some institution because all you boys have records. You have been here before and you were given a chance to make good but you wouldn't take it." So he sentenced Thomas to Saint Charles, me and my brother to Cook County School, and he let Ted go free. Bennie didn't go to court that day. After the referee was through with us we went to the bullpen. After the court proceedings were over we were taken back to the home. Later in the afternoon, my brother Jerry was taken to Cook county but Thomas had to wait to be taken to Saint Charles. So me and Thomas were in the Juvenile for about four days.

Finally they loaded me into the Cook County school bus and took us to the Chicago Parental School. The place looks very nice. They had about ten great big beautiful buildings in there and also a big swimming pool in the middle of the institution. Ben the house officer had a talk with me. He asked me if I ever was a Boy Scout on the outside. I told him, "I never was." So he told me, you'll have to become a Boy Scout because all the boys are members of the Boy Scouts in this cottage. I didn't like this idea of becoming a Boy Scout because I thought that the Boy Scout gang was a lot of hooey. But I figured by being a Boy Scout I would receive a little extra privilege.

The following night the house officer had a few boys in the cottage help me out with the Boy Scout knots. At first, learning these knots was very difficult as I kept practicing them I soon learned to do them by heart. The next night the house officer had the captain of the cottage take me to the Scoutmaster. There I had to perform the knots. I did these knots in perfect order so the Scoutmaster gave me a slip and on the slip was written "Knots O.K." I went back to the cottage with the captain and the house officer asked me, "How did you make out son?" I showed him the slip on which was written, "O.K." And he was well pleased. He talked very gentle but I didn't like him because I felt down deep in my heart that he was a lot of bullshit. That night he told me I would have to start learning my Scout oath. So I asked him, "What is that?" He told me, "You will have to learn at least two every night. Memorize them very well." So I studied these oaths very carefully. At first they were very hard to learn and I got very disgusted because sometimes I would get confused but finally I learn them by heart. The next night I went to see the scoutmaster again and there I recited the scout oaths and I did them well. So the Scoutmaster asked for my slip. I pulled a slip out of my pocket and handed it to him and he put on it, "Oaths O.K. too."

Finally I was a full-fledged member of the Boy Scouts. Boy, was I glad to get over this nonsense. Now that I was a Boy Scout I was allowed go on trips with the scoutmaster on Saturday afternoons. Sometimes we would go to the Forest Preserves and on some of the occasions we would take along a few boxes of weenies and we would roast them in the forest. I liked going hiking because there was a lot of fun in it. We would go out to the woods and there we would play all sorts of different games. We would also have enough to eat.

My job in the cottage was washing dishes. When I was at the Parental School we were allowed to go to school in the morning and then in the afternoon we would go out to the farm to work. In our farm work we would pick string beans and sometimes we would hoe the field. After we were through with our day's work, we would go to school again. In the morning when the boys used to get up from our sleep we were allowed to make our beds. After making my bed I had another job ahead of me. I was working in the House Officer's room. My duty was to dust the room out, clean the floor and arrange the room neatly. I was doing this work for about a month when they found someone stole some money out of that room, and the house officer blamed me for taking it. It just so happened that I was to go home the next week. On account of the money stealing I was kept over for another month.

One day the house officer called me and he told me that they had found the fellow that stole the money. He was sorry that he blamed me for taking the money. So I said to myself, "This is a hell of a time to feel sorry." Just because he blamed me I was held over for an extra month and I didn't like that. He also told me that he would send my name to the office and recommend me to go home.

The day came when I finally went home. My sister came up there to call for me. We both left the institution and went home on the streetcar. When I got in the neighborhood things were pretty dead. The rest of the fellas and the gang were still inside serving their terms. I was home about a week and finally I made friends with a newcomer. This new friend of mine was Constantine. So me and Constantine were hanging around the park. There we would stay all day and play ball and pass the time away. One morning as we were playing in the park a girl happened to come along and Constantine talked to her. He knew this girl very well as she was his next-door neighbor. After they got through talking Constantine came over to me and asked me if I wanted a lay. So I said, "I don't care." This girl happen to be his study chalk (which means an intercourse partner). So me and Constantine went to his house and there we stayed in the house for about twenty minutes. Finally the girl came around the back way, knocked on the door, and Constantine let her in. After she was in the house, he took her into a room, and he gave her a lay. After he got through I went in there and gave her a lay myself. After that him and I laid this broad steady.

One day Constantine suggested that we go out and steal and make some money. So I agreed with him and I took him off on R and H. There we waited for food trucks to go by. When we would saw a truck loaded pretty well we would both jump on the truck and each of us would grab a box of fruit and jump off the truck. Of course these trucks weren't going fast. After we had the fruit we would walk down an alley and we would take them to some fence I had known before.

So me and Constantine were stealing together for a while. One day when I was in school I was called down to the principal's office. There in the office I saw a probation officer from the Parental School. So I knew there was something up. This probation officer told me, "I come to take you back to Parental School." The reason for that was that I was playing hooky a great deal. So he and I left the building and we went down to his car which was parked near the school. He opened the car door and he let me in the car and when I got in the car I noticed that he had his door handles off. So we rode to the Parental School and there we got out and we walked into the office. When we got in the office there was nobody there so we had to wait until the Superintendent got there. The Superintendent finally came in and he talked to me. He asked me, "What's the matter? Can't you go to school every day and behave?"

After I got out of Parental School I went back to the old neighborhood and there was the old gang. So I was hanging with Thomas, Constantine and Tiger one night as we were sitting in the park, suggested we go and burglarize some places, so I asked him if he had a good place on the line. He said he did. I asked him, "Where is this place at?" He said, "Up on Halsted Street." So me, Constantine, Tiger and Thomas walked over to the place.

We walked into the alley behind it. We looked the place over to see which way we would go in. We spotted a window and found a brick and waited for streetcar to go by. When the street car went by we took the brick and broke the window with it. After the window was broken, we took all the pieces of glass out with our hands. After the window was clear we took and pushed Constantine through the window. After that I followed and Thomas went next but he couldn't get in because he was too fat. So he told me to open the door for him. I did this. After the door was open both Thomas and Tiger walked in. After they were in we bolted the door again. The four of us looked around for money. We turned the draws inside out, but we couldn't find any money. So Thomas said "We might as well take off the telephone box because we will get a few dollars out of it." So he started to rip it down but the telephone box wouldn't come off of the wall.

We were just about to leave the place when we heard a noise in front of the door. So we all got excited and were wondering what this noise was. Finally, we heard voices outside and the voices we heard were coppers. One of the coppers said, "Open the door in the name of the law!" So Thomas said, "Fuck this son of a bitches; let them wait out there." So we let them wait out there for about twenty minutes and then Thomas said, "We might as well let them in." So Thomas opened the door and let the coppers in.

The coppers took all four of us and put us in a patty wagon and took us down to the Maxwell Police Station. There they made out juvenile slips for the four of us and took us to the juvenile detention home that same night. There in the home they made us take a bath and they gave us clothes to wear and then we went to bed. The following day we went to school and we all went to the same room. We stayed there for about two weeks and then we went to court. The judge sentenced Thomas and Tiger to Saint Charles. Constantine went to Parental School, and I went to Cook County School. After court we went back to the home to eat. When I got through eating they took me and put me in the Cook County bus and took me to Cook County School. There we were unloaded from the truck and taken into the office. After they got through talking to me in the office they sent me to house number one—this is the receiving cottage. Here I was all alone and it was lonesome! I was here about a week and finally some guy came in that I knew. So him and I got to talking and we decided to run away the first chance we got.

When we got home my father told me that he was going to take me back to Cook County. Before we left I had dinner at home and my father and I took the elevated and went to the Cook County School. When we got there he took me to the office and handed me over to the Superintendent. The Superintendent asked me why I ran away. I told him that I didn't like the place. I remained there for about three months and then I got paroled. When I got home I went to the old hang out in Sheridan Park and in the meantime one of my partners, Constantine, got out from for the School.

We started to hang around together. I must have been out of the School for about two months when one day Ziggy a guy named Georgie, and I were walking down Clark Street and we noticed a parked car. We knew this car was stolen which somebody had parked there before we got there. So I tried the door to the car and it was open, I got in and started trying to start the car but it wouldn't start. I looked under the seat for a screwdriver which I found and told George to go out and find a brick. He found one and brought it back to me. I slipped a screwdriver in the ignition and hit it with the brick to try to start the ignition. I pounded on it for about three minutes and tried starting the car again, but she wouldn't start.

Ziggy decided we should push the car down an alley so we could strip it. So the three of us took the car and pushed it down into some alley and into some yard. When we got there we lifted up the hood of the car and we saw a "muffler." We took this muffler to be a siren. Thinking it was a siren I decided to take it off so I took the screwdriver and went to work on it. While I was taking it off we had Georgie for a lookout man. Before I had the thing off Georgie hollered, "Jiggers the coppers are coming!" So Ziggy and I ran down the yard under some steps to hide. We couldn't run through the yard because it was a blind one with no way out. Finally, the coppers came over and they looked around and found us. They took us to the car that we had pushed into the yard and asked where we had gotten it. We denied knowing anything about it. They took the three of us down to the station. When we got down there I was worried. I was afraid I would go back to Cook County because I had just gotten out of there and I hated to go back in such a short time. I wasn't out long and I was on parole and I knew they would send me back.

When we got to the station they made out juvenile slips for us and took us to Juvenile Detention. I stayed there for about three days when one of the officers from the school came there to take me back to Cook County. When I got there he brought me to the Superintendent's office. The Superintendent said, "You haven't been out very long have you?" I told him I was out for about two months. He asked me, "Can't you behavior when you're at home?" I told him, "I try to behave, but it is pretty hard." After that I went to house number one. In the house an officer saw me, he was surprised to see me again. He had a friendly chat with me and asked me if I was willing to behave myself and try not to run away. I told him, "Well, I'll behave and I won't try to run away."

The first week I was there he kept an eagle eye on me. Finally I heard that he was going to leave on his vacation. I figured that while he would be away would be the ideal time to take another walk around the block. The following week he left and we got a new house officer to take care of the boys. This, of course, was very nice because the house officer was green and I knew I would get a nice chance to run away some day. In the meantime I got acquainted with some fellow from around my neighborhood. He asked me if I was going to serve my time out. I told him, "Hell, no! The first chance I get I'm going to run away from here." So he asked me if it was all right for him to come along with me. I said, "I don't care."

So one night after supper all of us boys went outside to play baseball and we went on the field of the institution. We played ball for a while and then me and this fellow, Phil, went to sit on the grass and talk for a while. Finally we got our chance and he and I ran across the field. The house officer saw us and made a few fellows chase us. These boys chased us for a while until finally we lost them in the cemetery and we walked on our way. I remember we both walked down to Cicero. When we got there we snuck on the "L" and the "L" took us all the way into Chicago.

I went to the park and met all the boys and they were surprised to see me back again. While hanging in the park I made an acquaintance of a fellow named Tontoe. Tontoe wasn't living at home at the time so he and I got to hang around together. During the night he and I used to sleep in an old car in the neighborhood. Some mornings I used to go home when my father wasn't around. I would go there to wash up and eat and clean up.

One night Speedy came around the neighborhood with a hot car and he called me over. He asked me if I wanted to go for a ride and I said, "O.K." We went riding and whipping. One night Tontoe, Tiger and I had a stolen car and we went to Pollock Town. There we went to some girl's house. We know this girl by the name of Sue. We stopped in front of her house and called her over to the car. She came. We asked her if she wanted to go for a little ride and she said, "O.K." After we had her in the car she decided to go over to her girlfriend's house to call her. The girl came out and she got into the car and went riding with us. We rode around for a few hours and found a nice, dark place to park. There we all threw a fuck. After we all got through with the girls we took them back home. Then we went back to the old neighborhood. As we were riding back to the old neighborhood we talked about the girls and I said, "Well, she was a good lay." When we got to the neighborhood we parked the car. All of the guys in the neighborhood had laid these broads before us.

One day me, Bennie and Tontoe picked these two same girls up again and went to riding around with them. Finally we decided to lay them. So it happened that morning that among us three fellows none of us had any rubbers on us. So as we were riding around the neighborhood up on Halsted Street, Bennie decided to see his brother, Joe, to get some rubbers off of him. While Tontoe and the two girls were sitting in the parked car waiting for Bennie to come out, we happened to see a car approaching us. This car looked suspicious, so Tontoe laid it in and tore around the corner. This other car followed behind us. The reason we were scared was because this car which we were riding in was a stolen car. Tontoe takes a turn around another corner and this car was still following us. So Tontoe decided to lose him. Well, we got chased for about ten minutes and Tontoe and I jumped out of the car and ran through this yard. We both got away and went to the neighborhood.

Later on that night we found these two girls were arrested. These girls didn't squawk on us. The coppers arrested them and took them to the station. After that we went to the pool room to see Bennie and told him all about it. The following day we went to where the girls lived and we were surprised to see them both out. We asked the girls how they got out and they said that they had told the coppers that they didn't know the fellows that were driving the car. They had said we had just picked them up, and given them a lift, and that they didn't know the car was stolen. We asked the girls if they were mad at us because we had jumped out of the car and ran that night. They said, "No" and that we couldn't help it and did the right thing by running. Well, next night we took the girls out for a spin and laid them again and took them home. We used to go around to their houses and pick them up anytime we wanted to get laid.

One night Tontoe, Bennie and I had a stolen car, so we decided to go down to Pollock town to see if we could pick up some different girls. As we were passing a house down there we saw two girls in front of it. Bennie said, "Hello!" The girl said, "Hello" right back. So we stopped the car and started to talk to them. Finally Bennie asked the girls, "Do you girls care to go for a ride?" At first the girls hesitated. They said, "We hardly know you boys." Then they made up their minds and got into the car. We drove away. One of the girls in the car asked us to take them to some house where her girlfriend lived. When we got there she went upstairs and called a girlfriend. The girlfriend came down and came over to the car. We were introduced. She got in the car and we drove around for a while.

Finally Tontoe decided we were crowded in the car. So he drove us to a spot where we had another stolen car parked. There he got off and took one of the girls with him and drove away with her. That left me, Bennie, and Tontoe with two girls in the other car. We drove around until it got real late and after it got late we drove to the old neighborhood to the J-School. Coming down the street the boys that hanged in front of my house spotted our car. They saw us pull into the school yard. No sooner were we in the yard then we saw all the guys from the neighborhood coming into the school yard. Some came in through the front and some came through the back. There must've been about fifty guys in the schoolyard that night. All of the boys got in line waiting for their turn to fuck.

One of the girls was willing to lay but the other girl was kind of stubborn so me and Tontoe took this girl that was stubborn over to the park near the boy's toilet. There we asked her if she is going to lay both of us. She said, "No." So Tontoe and I took and kicked the shit out of the girl. We beat her up silly and she still wouldn't give in. Finally she broke away from us and she started to run down the street hollering. Tontoe and I chased her and we caught up to her and then we kicked the shit out of her again. Then we took her back to the spot where we had her and we went to work on her again and still she wouldn't give in so she broke away from us again and this time we let her go. Thomas said, "It's no use fooling around with her because she won't lay."

After that we went back to the school yard to see if the boys were still there but they weren't. They had all gone. Tontoe and I went to the front of my house to wait for the boys. Finally, someone came around and we asked him if he had laid the girls he was with. He said, "No." So we told him what had happened to us. So Tontoe decided that we should all take a ride and get out of the neighborhood because we were afraid the coppers would be coming around later. We rode around for about two hours. Then Tontoe said, "Well, things ought to be cool by now." So we turned around and rode back to the neighborhood. Tontoe dropped us off and then he drove away to park the stolen car. Later he came back to where we were and then we talked for a while and then we all went home to go to sleep.

The following night I saw Speedy and he asked me if I wanted to go out that night and make a little money with him. I said, "All right." I asked him, "What are we going to use for a car?" He told me that he had a hot car parked near the neighborhood. That night we both got in the car and we went out south, riding around looking for a store to break into. Finally we spotted a store. Speedy and I parked the car about a block from the store. Then we both walked over to the place. We looked it over and it looked all right. So Speedy and I went into an alley to look for a house brick. With this house brick we were going to break the window of the store. After we found a brick we walked back to the store and Speedy told me, "You break the window while I go to the corner and look out for coppers." I was standing with the brick in my hands by the window of the store waiting for a streetcar to go by so I could break the window.

The reason why we waited for the streetcar was that when a streetcar goes by you can break a window and nobody will hear the crashing noise. As I was waiting I saw a car creeping slowly so I took a walk away from the store into some yard until the car was out of sight. I saw the car go by and after it was gone I came out to look at it and the car had stopped where Speedy was at. I saw a fellow talking to Speedy and I knew this fellow was a copper. I was waiting for this fellow to go away but he didn't go away. He took Speedy into the car with him and drove off. I waited there for a while figuring this fellow would bring Speedy back to where he picked him up. I waited there for about twenty minutes and I saw no sign of him. Then I walked over to where the car was at and the car was still parked where Speedy and I had parked it. So after that I decided to walk home.

When I got home I went to sleep on my porch. I must have slept for about an hour and a half and then I felt somebody trying to wake me up. I got up and saw it was Speedy. Speedy asked me, "What happened to you?" I asked him, "What happened to you?" He told me that the fellow who stopped him was a copper and that the cop asked him what he was doing on the corner. Speedy had told him that he was looking for his brother that his brother had gone bumming from school today and hadn't come home. Speedy asked me which way I walked and I told him the streets I had walked on. So he said, "That's funny, I rode down there with the car looking for you. I don't see how I could've missed you." After that we both went to sleep.

The next day when we got up we went to the pool room and played a couple of games of pool. That night Tontoe came around the pool room and asked me if I wanted to go for a ride because he had a hot car on the outside. I said, "Alright!" As we're walking out I met Thomas and he asked me where we were going. I told him, "For a ride." He asked us if he could come along and we said, "Alright." We went riding for a while around the neighborhood.

As we were riding around there some fellow, Pepe, called me and asked us where we were going. I told him we were just going for a little ride. We decided we should go out on a stick-up that night. We all agreed and told Pepe that we didn't have any guns. So he said, "That's all right. We'll go out and get some." So he went to some garage in the neighborhood and he borrowed a pistol, but we still needed a couple more. So I went over to Joe and asked him if he could get a couple of pistols. He said, "What are you going to do with them?" So I told him we were going on a stick-up. So he asked, "Who is all going on it?" I told him, "Well, there is me, Pepe, Tontoe and Thomas in the car." He asked me if he could come along. I said, "I don't care." So I took Joe over to the boys and we planned what we were going to do. This guy, Pepe, decided that we should go out and stick up a drugstore. He told us we would have to get another car so we could clean the place out and take all the cigars and cigarettes. He said we would also need another man. So Joe went out and got Tiger. After we got Tiger we went out and stole another car.

Just before leaving we stopped in the neighborhood to talk to some fellows we knew and asked them if they had a couple of pistols which we could borrow for about an hour. This fellow Joe went home and got a rifle and an automatic and then brought them over to the car. This fellow wanted to come with us too, so we went and took him with us. As we were riding down to the drugstore, me, Tontoe, Tiger and Thomas drove in one car while Joe and Pepe drove in the other car. The guy we got the pistols from drove with us. As we approach the place, Joe parked his car across the street from the store we parked our car five feet from the place, on the same side of the street that the store was on. Tontoe, Thomas, Pepe and Tiger got out of their car while the guy we got the pistol from, whose name was Joe, stayed at the wheel to drive for a getaway. I remained in the back of the car to open the door when the fellas would come out in a hurry. Tontoe, Pepe, Thomas and Tiger walked into the place to stick it up. I remained in the car with Joe.

Then we heard shots from the drugstore. This guy, Joe, got scared and he wanted to drive the car away but I told him to wait until the boys came out. We waited for about a minute or two and finally Tontoe and Tiger came out and ran into the car. They were both excited and I asked them, "What was all the shooting about?" They told me that there was a copper in the place. So we waited for a while and then I saw Thomas run out of the store and into some yard. Then Pepe ran across the street to the other car. We drove back to the neighborhood and we waited around there for about 20 minutes for Thomas to come around. While we were waiting my brother came over to me and told me that Thomas had gotten shot and that he was dead. I told my brother, "it can't be true because I seen him run out of the place." After all of us boys heard about this we were all sorry for what happened to Thomas.

That night I went home to sleep and the next day I read in the papers about it. The neighborhood started to get hot so Tontoe, Tiger, and I stayed out of the neighborhood for about two or three days waiting for the neighborhood to cool off. One night Tontoe, Tiger, and I went to see a show. After the show we were coming out and we met Bennie outside. Bennie told me that my brother wanted to see me. I was wondering what he wanted so Bennie took me over to where my brother was living. When I got there my brother told me to hang around his flat for about a week until the neighborhood cooled off. So I went to my brothers flat to stay.

We were in the flat for about a week and everybody was broke. We didn't have any money. We didn't have anything to eat. So one night Tontoe, Tiger, Bennie and me went out to steal a car. With this car we went to the neighborhood which we were living in and there we spotted to store. We parked the car and we all got out and walked around to the back of the store. There we looked around but we couldn't find a spot to break in through the back. We went back to the front of the place and spotted the door with a padlock on it. The door led to the basement. So we took and broke the lock off and went into the basement. There we looked around and finally we found a spot to work on. Bennie held the flashlight while I broke my way through the wall. After we had made a hole through the wall we all climbed in. Once we were all in we scattered around the store looking for money. We didn't find much money, only about five or six dollars and change. We decided to take all of the best food they had in the store and take it back to the flat. We packed up about fifteen or twenty bushels of choice food. After we had it all packed Tontoe went out to get the car and drove it to the back of the store. There we piled all the food into the car. When we got upstairs we looked over the stuff and picked out some good things to eat, and ate it. Then we put the rest away in the pantry. We had enough food there to last us for about a month.

One night all of us boys were playing cards when Bennie decided that we should go out and make some money. So Tontoe called me and said, "Let's go out and get a car." So I got mad and I asked him, "What's the big idea, I always go out with you to steal a car. Why don't you get somebody else?" So Tontoe said, "Well, we'll draw cards and the lowest man goes with me." It so happened that Tiger got the lowest card and he had to go with Tontoe. Both went out and were gone for about an hour and in the meantime me and Bennie and a few more of the boys were playing cards. All at once Feather came into the flat, excited. I asked him, "What's the matter?" He said that Tiger was pinched when they were trying to steal a car downtown; some copper grabbed him. When we heard this, we got scared because we figured if Tiger squawked the coppers would come up to this flat we would all get arrested. Most of the boys in the flat were wanted by the police. That same night my brother went out to look for a new flat. He found a new flat and we packed up what belong to us and put the stuff into the car and drove away to the new flat that same night. When we got to the new flat we found it was a very large place. There was plenty of room for all of us boys.

One night, Bennie, Tontoe, and I went out north. We went to spot an A&P store. Finally, we spotted one. We parked the car about a half block from the place and the three of us walked over to the store. We walked to the back of the store and there we talked over our plans. Bennie told me, "You go in front, break the window, go in and open the door." Then he said, "If everything is all right you'll yell O.K. when you open the door." So I run around the front and waited until the streetcar came by. Finally a streetcar came by and I pulled the jimmy bar out of my pants and broke the window with it. After the window was open I took the pieces out with my hands and made a hole big enough for myself to crawl through. I went into the place and before I open the back door I looked around very carefully to see that there was nobody in the store. Finally, I saw everything was all right and I went to the door and opened it for Bennie and Tontoe. I said, "Everything is O.K." So they both came in. After they were in, I bolted the door again and we started to look around for money. We found a little money. In these A&P stores we went for the cigarettes, and we took and packed up and brought them to the rear of the store. After that we started to pile up sacks of sugar, butter, and eggs. After we had everything we wanted, Tontoe left and got the car and brought it to the rear of the store. There we packed everything into the car and drove off to the flat. After we had everything moved into the flat we went to sleep.

The following morning we got up and went to the old neighborhood. Went to see some fellow we knew. This fellow owned a couple of restaurants and we went there to transact our business. We told him what kind of stolen groceries we had and we made a price. He agreed to the price and we said that we would bring the stuff there at night. He told us we could use his truck to deliver the stuff to the restaurant. When we got to the restaurant we unloaded the stuff into his place. After we were all through the man paid us. With the money we got we went back to the flat. In the flat we still had the cigarettes we had stolen. We took them and piled them into one of the cars we had parked nearby, drove back to the old neighborhood to a certain store. We knew the fellow in the store was a good guy. We asked him if he wanted to buy the cigarettes. Bennie did the talking and asked for $.75 a carton. This fellow try to chisel us down, so Bennie told him, "There's just one price, $.75 a carton. Take them or leave them." So this fellow knew he was getting a bargain and said, "O.K. I'll take them all."

The three of us left the store and got back into the car. Then we drove back to the flat. When we got there we parked the car in the alley nearby and went into the flat to get the cigarettes. We each grabbed a bundle of cigarettes and carried it back to the store. When we got there we took and parked the car in the alley and I unloaded the stuff. In the meantime, Bennie went around to the front to tell the fellow that we were ready to sell the cigarettes. So this fellow came to the back of the store, open the door, and let us in with the stuff. After we got in we laid the stuff on the floor and counted it up and made our price. The fellow paid us off and we left the store through the rear door. We got into the car and drove back to the flat. There we split the money up into three equal parts. After that was done we all dressed up and went to see a show in the neighborhood. After the show, we went back to the flat, played cards and listen to the radio until it got late. Then we went to bed.

On another night, Tontoe, Bennie, and I went to our garage where we had our cars and our guns. We got into the car and drove out north. It was about 1 o'clock in the morning and we were riding around looking for a good A&P to burglarize. We drove around for about an hour-and-a-half looking for a place to take. We passed so many that we didn't know which one to take. Finally, we came to a store and decided to burglarize it. We drove the car about a block from the place and parked it. Then Bennie and Tontoe went to the back while I went to the front and broke the glass with my Bennie bar. I took out the pieces of glass, and then crawled into that place and broke the lock off the back door and let Bennie and Tontoe in.

After we were all in we bolted the door again and we all took our positions. I went to the front to look for money and the cigarettes while Bennie and Tontoe packed up all the good merchandise. We were in the store about ten minutes, piling things, when I heard a noise outside. I looked to see who it was and I seen a copper standing in front. I told Bennie and Tontoe about it. When they saw the copper we all got scared.

The first thing you know the place was surrounded with coppers. We didn't have a chance to run or get away from the cops. So Bennie, Tontoe, and myself got excited. For a moment the three of us didn't know what to do. Now we could hear the coppers at the back door. They were saying, "Open the door in the name of the law!" But we didn't pay attention to them for we had experienced the same thing at other times before. Finally, Bennie decided we should hide the guns. So Bennie found a place in the toilet where he hid them. In the meantime, the coppers we're still trying to get in the place. So finally us boys made up our minds to let the coppers in. Bennie opened the door and when the coppers finally came in they told us to stick them up, which the three of us did.

The coppers lined us all together against the wall and searched us. When they couldn't find anything on us they told the three of us to put our hands down. Then the coppers asked our names, so the three of us gave them phony names. The coppers asked us how we got out there because we were a long way from our homes. We told them that we rode the streetcar out there. Then a copper said, "Are you sure you didn't come out here in a car?" So one of the coppers told the other copper, "We better look around here because maybe these boys have got a car." Then they took the three of us outside and put me and Tontoe in one squad car and Bennie in the other one. Then we all drove down to the police station.

Finally we got to the police station. There they questioned us one at a time. The coppers ask me how we were going to move the stuff. I told them the same thing Bennie had told them that some guy with the truck was going to come around and give us a hand. So one of the coppers told us that they had found a stolen car about a half block from the place and they asked us if we knew anything about it. We told him we didn't. In the meantime the coppers hadn't found the guns which we had hidden in the store. When the copper was done cross-examining me about the car which they had found, he told me he didn't care about the car being stolen because all he was interested in was getting the backseat which was missing. I told him, "I don't know what you're talking about." He said, "Come on now son, we want to help you out. We know you didn't want to go out with them boys. They made you go. Now you just be nice and talk to us and tell us all about it and will let you go."

I knew they were all lying and I still said, "I don't know what you're talking about." So, the coppers really began to cross them and me about the car and the seat, and they were throwing question so fast at me that I was getting all confused. And they asked me where I had thrown the seat and I made a slip and said, "I threw the seat in some alley coming down to the store." They asked me who was driving the car so I gave them a line of crap and told them some fellow by the name of Joe was driving the car. I told him that he had stolen it and then drove us down to the store. They asked me where this fellow was at and I told him that he probably got away when we got arrested. They asked me if I knew where this fella lived and I told him that I didn't know as I had just met him.

After they got through cross-examining us they took us back to the Juvenile Detention Home. Here we remained for about two weeks and then we went to court. We went in front of the referee who gave us a continuance for a whole month. Bennie and Tontoe got out on bonds, but I had to stay in the home. I got acquainted with some fellow by the name of Bobby and this fellow and I hung around together a lot. One day we went down in the gym to play. As we were playing there some guy came over and put me wise to some kid who was a punk, and took it in the ass. After this fellow left me I went over to this kid and tried to get around him, to get on his good side, and see if I could fuck him. I talked to him for about a half hour and we finally went upstairs and ate supper.

After supper the superintendent of the home came into the playroom and called my name. They took me out into the hallway and there he told one of the officers to lock me up in Blackstone. Blackstone was a place where they locked the guys that started trouble in the home. They would feed you bread and water for about three days. I asked him, "What's the big idea of locking me up in there?" He wouldn't tell me but I knew why I was going there, it was because I was trying to get around this kid that was a punk and lay him. In Blackstone I'd stay there all day long doing nothing but sleeping. This was getting monotonous. I must've been in there for about a week before they let me out. After that they sent me to school and I was allowed to work in the kitchen. They kept me away from all the other kids when we were in the home. I believe they didn't trust me with the kids because they were afraid I would moon some boys. After supper they would take and lock me up in Blackstone and I would stay there until the next morning when one of the guards would come and open the door and let me out. Then I would go into the dining room to eat my breakfast and after breakfast I would remain in the kitchen to do my work. I didn't mind this job in the kitchen because I was finally getting plenty to eat.

The day came around when we all went to court again. I went alone but Bennie and Tontoe came with their folks later. I was sitting there and Bennie and Tontoe came over to talk to me. While we were talking I noticed the coppers who arrested us had three packages. I told Bennie, "I think the coppers found the guns." We remained there for a while and finally we were called into the referee room. There we all formed in a straight line with their parents behind us. I forgot to say that my folks showed up too. They started to read all of our charges and our probation officer was telling the referee, "These boys are all first-time offenders." This was not true because we were all under false names and we had been in the juvenile before. But of course they didn't know anything about this. Tontoe hired a lawyer who defended us and this lawyer didn't do a damn thing to help us. The referee sentenced all of us to Saint Charles.

We had to remain about a week in the detention home before they would send us away. While we were in the home, Tontoe got a job working in the kitchen with me. Bennie went to school. One morning me and Tontoe got through with our work in the kitchen and went over to the isolation room where they kept the sick boys. We knew some fellow in this room so I started to kid him. I told him that he was to go home tomorrow. I told him, "Don't tell nobody that I told you." He told me that he would be out of the isolation room tomorrow morning. The next morning this guy got out of the isolation room and Tontoe and I told his fellow that he should give us something because we had told him that he was going to go home. He said, "I haven't anything to give you." I told him, "You can get us a piece of ass before you go." So he said, "No, I don't want to do that." So I started to con the kid. I said, "Well you're going home. Nobody will know nothing about it." Finally this fellow gave in and we went to the bathhouse. There Tontoe remained at the door to give jiggers while I went with the kid into the corner where I pumped him. After I got through Tontoe went while I gave jiggers for him. After Tontoe got through, some fellow passed by the toilet and I knew this fellow, so I told him about it and he went in there and got some too.

After we all got through Tontoe and I went to school and there we saw Bennie as we were all in the same room. We told Bennie about it so Bennie says, "Well, after we go to recess I will go in the back of the Home and see if we can find the kid." So after recess we left the room and we walk toward the home. As we were going a guard stopped us and asked us where we were going. We told him we were going to the Home to get a drink of water. He said, "You can't drink water in there. What's the matter with the water in the yard?" I told him, "I didn't know the water in the yard was running." We left him and walked to the sink to take a drink of water to make it look real. After that the recess bell rang, we went back to the school but we never found the kid because we couldn't get into the Home. Bennie was mad because he couldn't get in there to get the kid. So he said, "That's all right, we'll go there and get him after we eat our dinner." Dinner time came and we went to the Home to eat and the kid wasn't there because he went home already.

We remained at the Home for another three or four days and finally one morning we were called down to the office and there we got our clothes and put them on. I knew we were going to Saint Charles. We were glad to go there because we wanted to get it over with and start serving our time. Maybe when we got there we would run away from the joint too. We were loaded into a bus. There was about six of us fellows and there must have been about four or five girls that they were taking to the Geneva school. On the bus the girls were smoking and we got to talk to them and we kidded around with them. We asked the broads what they were going to use for a cock and they said they would have to use bananas, if they could get them. We were on the bus for about one hour and finally we came to the institution. The institution looked like a giant palace. They had about 12 buildings there. Finally the bus pulled up in front of the administration building and there we all got off and went into the office. After that they sent us to the receiving cottage.

When we got to the receiving cottage we saw Robbie and Bird working outside the cottage. They were expecting us to come out there because they knew what was going on in the city. We were lead into the cottage and there we ate our dinner and it seemed that the food was good. I liked it. After that we were put to work swabbing the floors. They gave us a rag and we got on our hands and knees and we just kept pushing the rag back-and-forth until the floors would shine. We would do this for about an hour and then we would quit. Then we would go into the reading room and there we would read books and play checkers. In this reading room we noticed that the windows wouldn't open all the way. We also noticed that they kept all the doors in the cottage locked. Tontoe, Bennie and I had intentions of running away from this place. We didn't figure on hanging around here. It wasn't easy to run away, and we had to wait for a good chance. We stayed in this cottage about two weeks and then they sent me to McKinley Cottage.

When I entered the cottage a fat woman came and opened the door for me. The woman asked me my name and I gave it to her and then she asked me why was sent out there. I told her that I was sent out there for burglary. She told me that she treated the boys very fine in her cottage and asked me to be good. I told her I would behave and try to keep out of trouble. My first job in this cottage was swabbing the floors for two or three weeks. I didn't like this job because it was very hard on the knees. In the morning we would work half the time and then we would go to the kitchen and there we would peel potatoes. In the afternoon we would go to school. After school we would go back to the cottage and we would stay there until supper. After supper we would go to the reading room and read until bedtime. We would read there and we were all allowed to talk easy, that means not so loud, in whispers. When the time would draw near we would go to bed and sleep.

One morning as we were going to work my house officer sent me to the laundry to work. I was supposed to iron shirts and all sorts of things. When I went to work in the laundry I didn't like the work. I worked there for about two or three days and then one morning after I got to the laundry I refused to work. The woman who was in charge of laundry told me, "Are you going to work or shall I send you to the guardhouse?" I told her, "Well, I'm not going to work, so that means you'll have to send me there."

Finally I was taken to the guardhouse and in there I was severely punished and put on a strict diet. We were fed three times a day. In the morning they would give you a slice of bread dipped in cocoa for your breakfast. In the afternoon they would give you a slice of bread with a tablespoon of food for your dinner. At suppertime we would get the same thing we did in the afternoon. During the day we were ordered to stand on line and we were also made to work on the coal pile. There with an empty stomach we remained for about three or four hours to work. After we got through working we went back to the cottage. There we would eat our dinner and after we got through eating we would have to scrub the floor on our hands and knees. This we would do for about an hour and after we got through doing this we would stand online until bedtime. When bedtime would come we would go up to the dormitory and there we would put on our nightgowns and we would have to stand online until 12 o'clock midnight. Then we would go to bed and this was sure a relief after standing online for three or four hours.

I remained in the guard house for about two weeks and finally I got out and went back to my same cottage which I had come from. When I got back to my cottage the women seemed mad at me for going to the guardhouse. She asked me what happened and I told her that I didn't like to work in the laundry she told me, "It isn't what you like, it's what you've got to do." I noticed that this woman started to have it in for me. She would give me all the hard jobs in the cottage to do and she would punish me for the least little thing I did.

After that I went to work again peeling potatoes. Here I remain for about another month and finally I got a job working in the barbershop. This job I asked for because all the boys I knew in Saint Charles were working there. The barber here in the barbershop would instruct us on how to cut hair. The first week I was working there I sure ruined a lot of boys' hair because I wasn't accustomed to the work here, but as time went on I got to know it real good. The barber instructor was a very nice fellow. He used to let the boys in the barbershop smoke cigarettes. After we would get through cutting hair a few of us boys would talk and walk around the institution. Sometime we would go into the kitchen to look for some food to steal. Every morning us boys in the barbershop would get a bag of cookies from the bakery which we would have to pay for with cigarettes. Some mornings we would buy some weenies from the butcher shop and pay for them with cigarettes. We used to take these weenies and roast them on the steam pipes and eat them.

One afternoon me and a couple more fellows that I know were outside playing ball. After we got through playing ball we sat down on the grass and started to talk. One of the boys said, "Gee, it's getting warmer out. I wish I was home." I said, "Yeah, I wish I was home too!" Well, when the boy heard me talk like this he called me over to the side and then he put the idea out to me about running way. Of course I didn't have any idea of running away but since it was warm outside I figured, I'll lam this place. All together there were about four of us guys planning this run away. It so happened that our house officer was going to go on his vacation and we figured we would wait until he left. Then we would get a new house officer who would be green. Finally our house officer left. After he had left one of the boys that was in the plot with us went to work on the window in the basement. We started to take the bolts and some screws off the window. This he did during the day when he was off.

One night after we got through playing ball we came in from the field just as it started to get dark. We all went down to the basement of our cottage and the boys who were in the plot got together. We waited until it got really dark and then us boys snuck down to the basement one at a time, because we had to come upstairs again after we'd seen that everything was ready. One of the boys pushed the screen out and we all jumped out the window. Since we had first planned this thing, the word had went around so we had three new guys who joined us and now we were seven altogether. As we were standing outside and started to walk across the field the boys in the hospital who were sitting outside saw us and started to chase us. All of us boys started to run across the cornfield and during this chase I got tired and took a rest in the cornfield. While I was resting here I decided to wait until morning before I left. The institution would be looking for us all night. I slept in the cornfield all night. When dawn came I started to walk down the highway and finally I came to a town near there and I walked through town. As I was walking I spotted a bicycle in front of the house. I was just going to grab it and go away with it when some guy in the building saw me and hollered at me. He said, "What are you trying to do there?" I didn't pay much attention to him, I just ran.

Finally I was out of town and on the highway again I must have walked for about two hours when a car drew up alongside of me and the driver asked me if I wanted a lift. I told him I did and got into the car. As we were driving he asked me where I was from, and I told him, "I'm from Chicago." He also asked me, "What are you doing here?" I told him that I had come out to look for a job on the farm. As we were driving I notice he kind of stared at me and seemed kind of suspicious and I figured he knew I was from St. Charles because of the clothes I wore.

We drove around for a while and finally we stopped near some house and talked to some fellow and after that we drove off again and made another stop in front of the firehouse and a man came over to the car and started to talk to this fellow whose car I was in. This fellow asked who I was and the guy I was driving with said, "He's just a fellow I picked up on the road." I saw the star under this fellow's coat and I knew he was a sheriff. The sheriff asked me if I was from St. Charles and I played dumb and told him I wasn't. So the sheriff tells the guy I'm driving with "Well, I'll hold the kid here and I'll call the school and find out if he's a runaway from there." He called up to school and came back and told us, "I think you are a run away from Saint Charles because they said there was some fellows still missing from there."

I was locked in the cell and later the sheriff came and took me out to dinner. The sheriff treated me very nice and I think he was a swell fellow. Then some guy came down from school and took a looked at me and said, "Yeah this is one of the boys from the school that ran away last night." When I got down to the guardhouse I saw a few more of the boys there and the first thing you know we had the whole barbershop down there, all the fellows who had cut hair off were down there. We were put on severe punishment for a week, and then we all went back to our cottages again.

One day the house officer called me upstairs and he had a little talk with me. He said, "I see you're behaving and haven't been getting in any trouble, so I'm going to give you a good job. Do you think you will be able to take care of it?" The job he gave me was to take care of the dining room to see that the boys who did the cleaning did their work. "I'll take it!" I said, "and I will see to it that the boys do their work." I took the job and made the boys work for a while but later on I let them take it easy. Finally one morning as the boys were working in the dining room the house officer pass by and he saw the boys were taking it easy and loafing on the job. He came over to me and said, "Well, what's the big idea of letting the boys take it easy?" I told him, "I'm letting the boys take it easy because they're tired." He said, "Well don't let them take it easy when they're working on a job." I could see that the house officer was mad and I didn't give a care because I didn't want the job anyway. The following night the officer's wife heard about it and she took me off the job. She put me in the kitchen scrubbing floors again, and there I remained for a few months, and later got back into the barbershop.

One morning when I was down in the barbershop the telephone rang and the barber instructor answered the phone, and when he got through he told me to go down to the main office. So I was wondering what they wanted me for down in the office so I went down there. And so I entered the Superintendent's office and he asked me what my name was and I told him. He handed me a blue slip with my name on it. This blue slip meant that I was going home the following day. So I left the office and went down to the barbershop to tell the boys about it. They were all glad to see me leave the following afternoon. With this blue slip I went around to the shops to get my clothes and after I got all my clothes I walked around the institution visiting my friends.

When I got home my family was glad to see me and they also told me to behave. After that I took off all the institution clothes and put some of my own clothes on. I ate supper at home that night and then I went to see a show with my kid brother. While I was in the show, Tontoe and Tiger came in and they called me and asked me if I saw the whole show. I said, "No" and they said, "Well let's go out anyway." So I left the show with them, but my brother remained. When we got outside I saw that Tontoe had his car out there so we went into the car and drove off. We went to Pollock Town to see if we could pick up some girls. We were riding around Pollock Town for a while and we couldn't pick up nothing, so Tontoe told me, "Don't worry, I'll get you a fuck someplace." I asked him, "Well if we can't pick up no girls, what are you going to do." He said, "That's all right. You just leave it to me." So we drove up and down the street to some Can House. Then we parked the car and walked into this house.

We got in the house and they had six or seven girls. You picked out the girl you wanted. I picked out a girl and Tontoe paid my way. This girl and I went into her room and there I gave her a fuck. It was a good one because I didn't have one for a long time. After Tontoe and Tiger got laid too, we all left and went to the car and drove off. We rode around for a little while and then we went to a restaurant to eat. After that we all went home to sleep. Well, it sure felt good to be out again, to go where you wanted to go and to do what you wanted to do.

When I left Saint Charles I stayed home and I believe I didn't fool around for about two months. One day I met some kid which I knew from the neighborhood. He just got out of Pontiac a month before I got out of Saint Charles. Him and I got to talking and he asked me what I was doing. I told him, "Ain't doing nothing." I asked him what he was doing and he said he went out and stole a car once in a while just to make a few dollars. I asked him, "Who are you going with" and he said, "Well I go out alone." He asked me if I wanted to join up with him, And I said, "Well, I don't care." So I joined up with him.

The following day he and I went out to steal a car. We would walk around the factory districts looking for a car to steal. When we would spot a car he would walk over to it and open the door and I would follow him. We would both get into the car, start her up, and drive away. We would drive down to Riverside where this partner of mine had his garage. Here we would strip the cars of all its accessories. Then we would wait until it got dark and then we would drive the car out of the garage to some lot. There we would strip the car of its tires and would carry them back to the garage and leave the car in the lot. Later on in the day some fellow would come down there with the truck and look this stuff over, and buy it off of us. I hanged around with this fellow for a while and finally he broke away from me and joined a different gang.

Then I decided to hang around with some fellow named Georgie. One day Georgie and I spotted a store around the neighborhood so he suggested that we burglarize the store on Sunday when it would be closed. In the meantime, we cased the store and got the layout of the place. One Sunday afternoon him and I went down there. We walked to the back of the place and broke a window. After we had broken the window we both crawled into the place. This place we had broken into was an empty store and there was a door which led to the place we wanted to get into. We drilled a hole in the door and got it open. When we got in we started searching for money but we couldn't find any money so we started to pack up all the cigarettes and cigars into boxes and sacks. After we got everything packed we started out with our first load. We both walked out of the store and into the alley.

As we got into the alley we spotted a couple of coppers in the alley. As we saw these coppers we threw the stuff away and started to run. I ran for a while with one copper chasing me while the other one chased Georgie. Finally the copper pulled out a gun and said, "Stop, or I'll shoot!" So I figured it would be best for me to stop or this copper would shoot me. After this copper had me he took me to a place where they had a paddy wagon and there I found they had caught Georgie and they threw him into the paddy wagon with me. When I got down to the station they asked me my name and I gave them my brother's name and his age. The reason why I gave my brother's name was that I would go to the Juvenile Home and probably get a chance to get out. So we both went to the Juvenile Home and there I remain for about two or three days and then the home found out who I was and my right name and age. So they transferred me back to County Jail. I remained in County Jail two days and then was taken down town and photographed and fingerprinted. Then I was returned to the Des Plaines station where I remained four days and then was brought up in Boys' Court.

In the court room I saw my father and he looked kind of mad. Here I was in front of the judge while a man standing alongside the judge read off my charge. The judge said, "Frank you have a very bad juvenile record with many charges a burglary and here you are before me charged with another burglary. I am not going to give you a chance for probation but I am going to send you to eight months in Bridewell." So I was tickled pink to get only eight months. I was figuring that the judge would have me bound over to the grand jury and if I face them I would get a sentence of one year to life in the penitentiary.

When we got to Bridewell we all went into the receiving room. There we had to take all our clothes off and we all took a bath and they gave us some Bridewell clothes. The clothes they gave me didn't fit so good and were all baggie and looked terrible. Then they took us to the mess hall. There on the table were beans. I took one look at the beans and I lost my appetite because they smell terrible and the mess hall was filthy. Even the table had a very terrible odor. Then they took us to the cell house where they locked us up for the day.

The next morning we left our cell but before we left we had to carry the toilet buckets out. The buckets had a terrible odor. We carried these toilet buckets out into the yard and then dumped them in the sewer. When I was transferred from the receiving cell to the north cell house I was surprised to see Tontoe and Dazzo his partner. They were doing a year each. They were surprised to see me. Most of the time that I was in Bridewell I was locked up in my cell. Of course it was hard to get used to at first but later on I got used to it and I didn't mind it very much. Down in the A Block they had a lot of fairies. Well us boys down there used to get a kick out of them. They used to sing during the night and we also got a kick out of the way they used to walk.

One morning after we got through working, Tontoe came over to my cell. He asked me if I wanted to get fixed up with some fruit and I asked him, "Where is the fruit at?" He said, "He's up on B Gallery and I will go over and open the break for you." He did and I got out of the cell and I walked with him upstairs to where the fruit was and Tontoe told him I was his brother. And the fruit took care of me through the bars. The inmates at Bridewell were allowed one visitor every month and once a month my brother, Jerry would come down to see me and would ask me how I was getting along. Then he would leave me some money to buy stuff with. Tontoe's time was almost up and one morning he went home. I was glad to see him go even though it would be lonesome without him.

Time was passing by. The days seem to go by fast and one afternoon I got a visit and who should it be but Tontoe and Joey. So I asked Tontoe, "What's the matter? Why didn't my brother come down to see me this time?" I noticed that Tontoe was sad and he hesitated about talking. I asked him again, "Hey, Tontoe tell me—is my brother pinched or something?" So Tontoe told me my brother was killed with another guy when they went out to heist a jug. When I heard this I started to cry. I asked Tontoe if my folks were trying to get me out for the funeral and he said they were trying but it doesn't look like they are going to be able to do any good. I had a warrant on me to go to court again when I got out a Bridewell, so that's why I couldn't go out to go to the funeral.

In the Bridewell I had another two months to go before I would be released to go home. Time was now dragging. During the next few months I was always thinking of what happened on the outside and it always seemed impossible. I just couldn't believe that my brother and this fellow had died. When time came for my release they shifted me from the Bridewell to the County Jail to wait for another trial. There I went to court and I was charged with malicious mischief, and since I had already done time and Bridewell the judge gave me three months probation. I went home and it sure was a relief to be out on the street again.

THE BEAVER

I WAS BORN ON THE WEST SIDE OF CHICAGO. I don't remember much of my early days but I do remember that I started school when I was five years old. I went to kindergarten, there I met Whitey and we played with the horses. After school was over, we'd go out and play in the playground till nine o'clock. Then we'd go home and sleep.

I was in kindergarten for about a year and then I went to the first grade. I used to get along good in school, I was the teacher's pet. She was a good teacher. One day I was sick and could not come to school so the truant officer came there. My mother said, "What do you want?" The truant officer said, "I want Theodore to come to school." My mother said, "He can't come to school. He is sick." So the truant officer said, "I want him to come with me." My mother got mad, she took the broom and hit him with it. From that day on he did not come to my house anymore.

Whitey and I used to go around the alleys picking up bottles and selling them so we could go to shows. He said to me, "Let's go and get milk bottles and make money and go to the show." I said, "Alright." So we started to go around the alleys picking up bottles and selling them to the junkman.

One day, we wanted to go to the show on Halsted Street. We didn't have enough money so when we passed by a fruit stand and swiped some apples and oranges. We sold some of the stuff and got enough money to go to the show. Whitey and I started bumming school when I was about eight years old and in the third grade. This teacher didn't like me so well. So I says, "Let's go bumming." We met the kids on the corner who never went to school. We went around the alleys jack-rolling drunks; we'd search them and take their money away and then go to the show.

For a while we went out of this neighborhood when we moved to the North Side. We lived there for about two years. My mother took sick when we were out here and had to go to the hospital. She stayed there for about six months before she came home. During this time I was living with my grandfather because it was the doctor's orders. My grandfather lived in the old neighborhood and I used to go junking with him.

Whitey and I used to smoke, I think I was eight years old when I started to smoke. Before I was ten years old Whitey and I went into a candy store and took cigarettes and candy. We brought them down in the basement and sold them to my stepmother and got two and a half dollars apiece. She used to buy stuff from the other guys in the neighborhood too.

While I was running around with Whitey we used to go out on Halsted and Van Buren for "winos." We would see a wino and would ask him to come and follow us and we would show him where he could get some whiskey. Then we used to take the money off of them, run around the corner, making as if we didn't know anything about it. After that we would go to a show and then go home. One guy chased us. He was pretty drunk. But he knew what he was doing. We took a watch off of him. He chased us all over. Whitey would catch the watch and throw it to me and I'd throw it back to him. Finally, I picked up a rock and I hit him over the head. So we sold the watch to a guy on the street. A couple of other things that we used to do was go around old buildings looking for old stoves and iron. We'd take the stuff and sell it to the junkman. We used to go around on porches in the night about one o'clock and take milk bottles, if there was a full bottle we would take them too.

When I was ten years old my mother died. She had been in the hospital for six months. When she came home she seemed to be alright, but two months later she died. While my mother was sick I started to stay at my grandfather's house. At this time I was in the fifth grade and Whitey was in the same grade with me. I had gotten along pretty well in school but then I had a little trouble with the teacher and after that I started going bumming around two times a week. The principal threatened to send me to the Parental School and sent somebody to see my father. I thought it was no good that they should come to the house. That made me go on.

Then Whitey was picked up and was sent to the Parental School. I went with some boy named Gilbert to Polk Street . Gilbert and me would do the same thing. When we were in an alley and saw a bum Gilbert would always give him the arm and I would take the money. We made pretty good at this. I went to restaurants to eat and went to a bunch of shows. I hung out on the corner of Polk and May and shot craps. We would go to the show nine in the night and come home at twelve. One day I went with the boys and I didn't go home. In the morning when I came I told my father I was at a party. He said, "Why didn't you tell me?" I said, "I told the boy to tell you."

The second time I ran away from home I stayed out for three days. I was picked-up and taken to the Detention Home. My father came and got me. Next I was picked up for robbing a store with some guys named Butch and Bulldog. They let me go home this time though. Then I met some more boys around the neighborhood. First I met Eddie, at the playground, then later, I met Captain Jack. The third time I was picked up it was for stealing with Lumpy. The probation officer told me and Lumpy that he would give us a break next time, but this time he would send us to St. Charles, but, Lumpy got out on Thursday of the same week and I got out one day later. I did not steal for two weeks. In the meantime Whitey had gotten out of Parental School and so we started going together.

One day Chip, Whitey, Gilbert, and I tried to make a candy store. We were reaching through the bars, when the coppers came and put the gun on us. They took us to the station and kept us there till four o'clock. Then they took us over to the Juvenile Home. We were there for a day and a half. Then our fathers came for us. Some guy in the building said they'd give me probation. I said, "Alright." We went downstairs and went home.

They told me to join the Community Center. I did. I stayed there for a while playing with the boys at night, basketball, handball, and other games. They gave us free tickets to go to the show at the Opera House. I got sick of the place. I wasn't making money. I started going with Wally, Eddie, Sestino, King-of-the-Birds, and Jakie. We rented a flat and I didn't go home. Captain Jack was in St. Charles.

We started making schools. Eddie had made schools a couple of times. We made the Jackson School about four or five times. We would take all the stuff out and take it to the flat. We also made the Marquette School. We found butter and eggs on the third floor in a storeroom. One guy throwed an egg. So we had a food war. Then we threw cakes. We then went downstairs, took the stuff, took a street car and went to the flat.

We made the Goodrich School after that and went around hardware stores making them. We were sneaking into shows at the same time. We were also junking in the day time. Another thing us guys did was to rob trucks. I was going to the Jackson School at that time. At twelve o'clock we would go out to lunch. Instead of going home we would put on roller skates and go on Morgan street. We would see a truck and take bananas and oranges and go back to school. We sold the stuff to everybody.

One day we got chased by a squad while we were taking stuff off a fruit truck. They said, "If you don't keep off the corner we will get you." We stayed off the corner for a while. It was too hot. We hung out on Blue Island. Then the squad hung there. So we had to go on Polk Street instead of Harrison. One night Eddie, Cadoodles and I crashed a window. We were on Halsted and Roosevelt Road at a Florshiem shoe store. We crashed the window and grabbed shoes, took them to the flat. We sold them in the morning for about three dollars apiece. We did that four times. Once the squad came and put the spotlight on us. We went through the alley. On that job none of the shoes fit.

We never hung on the streets at that time because our fathers were looking for us. One night my father caught me near Halsted and Adams. He said, "Come home." I didn't want to go home. He said, "Alright, I'll call the cops." I went home. I stayed three nights.

I was going with Gilbert, Bulldog, and those guys. We decided to make the Dante School. We tried to drill holes through the wall and get the suits and shoes that were in there. All at once we heard about four shots. So we jumped out of the window and ran away. Then I started stealing stuff out of cars. I was with Eddie and Chicken Man. We'd go down Canal Street and look in the cars. We would see the stuff, hit the door handles, take the stuff out and bring it to the flat. We did that quite often.

We made crashes too. We used to make a little dough looking in cars so we started making joints again, crashing windows. We crashed one on Halsted Street, took suits and coats. We brought them over to the flat. We also made a couple more shoe stores. Whenever I brought shoes home I used to tell them I bought them. They told me to bring them back. I made as though I brought them back only I put them in the flat.

When I was fifteen years old I started making cars. l rode in a stolen car with Chip's brother, "Chacha." We used to go riding around for the fun of it. We were chased by the squad. We would drain gas and all that. One day there was a Chevrolet parked on Sangamon. We went to get it. The squad came and we stated running through yards until we got to the elevated and got away. Another time there was a Chevrolet by a hospital. They couldn't start it so I said, "Let me get in and try to start it." I pushed the switch and started it up. I tried to drive it, put it in first and second and went around the block. I went back down the street again. I asked a guy if he wanted to buy a car. He said, "Yes," so I sold it to him. The next car we took was a nineteen twenty-seven Hudson. I opened the window stuck my hand inside, and opened the door. I started it-up, but I didn't know how to drive so good. That was my second car. I went around Taylor and May Street. I called Gilbert and took him with me. We got tickets for the Civic Opera House so we dressed up, put on a clean shirt and tie and we went. When we got on Ogden and Lake Streets the light said, "Caution." The brakes were no good. I pulled up the emergency but we hit a guy. He took my license number and he said, "My father is a politician. You'll have to fix it up." Some cops came and I gave them a false name. Then we went to the Opera House.

We stayed there for two hours. We saw a bunch of guys from Polk Street at the opera. We heard some songs. We left there. Went for the car, but there was two coppers on horses right by the car. They had a ticket ready for us because we were by a no parking sign. The cops didn't go away, so we took a street car home, The guys asked what I did with the car. I said, "The cops got it."

We went after a different car. I went with Eddie. We made a Dodge roadster. After we made the roadster we made the McKinley School using the roadster. Kingy, Jakie, Augie, and Eddie broke in and took about thirty parade rifles and a bunch of other stuff and took it to the flat. We got three dollars a piece from a guy across the street in a restaurant. The next day we wanted to use the car but some guy took the key and we couldn't start it. We tried to jump the wires. The lady across the street called the squad. We saw the squad car coming so we walked away. I went with Eddie down Canal Street, got a Ford and picked up Chicken Man. We went on the West Side and parked it and started taking the spare tire off. The squad came and asked us what we were doing. I said, "Nothing." We turned the corner and ran away. The cops got the car. We decided to raid a candy company. Me, Wally, Sestino, Eddie, Captain Jack, and Lumpy. We went there and started breaking in through the back. There was candy, gum, money, and everything. We packed the stuff up. Sestino and Eddie was working on the cash register. It wouldn't open. When we packed the stuff we heard the change fall. Sestino found thirty dollars in change. We put it in our pockets. We started taking the stuff to the flat. We made three or four trips.

The next morning we so sold one carton for twenty-six dollars to a guy on Polk Street. All together we made about two hundred dollars. We went to a show. A few weeks later we the same place again. This time we made it through the front. We found about twenty dollars and gave it to Wally to hold. We started packing up cartons and filled the store-room with candy and chewing gum. We made a lot of money on it. We decided the place was too hot.

We went around to make cars. On Canal we made a four-door Ford. Whitey, Eddie and Chicken Man were with me. The next day we took another car and stripped it. We sold the tires. Kingy came over with Jakie and lived in the flat with us. Kingy's mother came after him and took him home. I went home the next day. We thought nobody was in the flat anymore.

The next day Augie got caught in the flat. We thought that Augie might squawk to the coppers so we didn't go back to the flat anymore. We started hanging around a candy store. Then I started going around with Jam, Cat-Eye's brother. Wally was going with him at the time so I went with him and Wally too. The next day we looked for a car and made a stick-up. We parks the car by Jam's brother-in-law's house. I started driving the car around the block. I stepped on some button. It was a three-chime horn. Wally and Jam had gone out and made forty two dollars. They gave me about ten dollars because I wasn't with them. I gave the car to Kingy. He stripped the tires and sold them.

Me, Eddie, and Freddie went on Wacker Drive looking for cars. We couldn't get none so Eddie went home. We still went around and me and Freddie spots a car, I looks in it and said, "The ignition is open." So I drive to Wacker Drive to a gas station. Freddie got out, took the gas line off and started running it. Then we went on Sholto Street and sold the tires for forty dollars.

Me, Jam, Wally, Cadoodles, and Jimmie went out to Cicero to make A&P stores. We'd go over there and crash a window. Jam was right in front. We'd go in and take cigarettes, candy, and cigars and put it in the car. Jam had told me to go for a car when we started on the job. Jimmie and Chip came around; they had a four-door Ford. They said, "We'll go with you." So we said, "Alright." We piled in and got in front. We went to Cicero. It was dark. We spots an A&P, break a window, take all the stuff. I go in for a second time, the Lincoln Squad passed by. Then the Flivver Squad came, so we jumps in Jam's car. They started taking shots at us so we jumps out of the car and started jumping fences. We started going through alleys. We scattered all over. I lost Tony and Freddie. I got on Harrison and Cicero and I says, "Them guys got the money. I might as well walk." Then I seen them guys on a street car. I whistled. They knew my whistle. They got off and paid my fare.

I got on and we went around the neighborhood. We seen Jam was not

Six. Institute for Juvenile Research Oral Histories

there. His brother said he went to look for us. It would be two hours before they came back. They had a Ford coupe. I took it and went driving. At three in the morning we got lammed from the Hudson Squad. I was going like anything. We lost them when I got on Morgan and Jackson. We went and had coffee at Monroe and Halsted. When we left there it was five in the morning. We went to Racine Avenue and robbed bread boxes and paper stands. In the morning we stripped the car that we had. Later that day Step and me had a Ford roadster. We were driving on May and Aberdeen when the Lincoln Squad from the Maxwell Station came by. We lost them. That Ford was good. It would make forty five in second and sixty five in third with the wheels out of line. We parked it and somebody took it from us.

Three days later we went to the Loop with Jimmie. We stole a two door Ford on Wells and Lake Street. We were driving around when a Chrysler 77 came after us. Jimmie stepped on the gas and was going fifty five through stoplights. It was raining. When we got on Wood and Huron Street we stopped the Chrysler and we took it home with us. We went on a dress shop job with it. I took two tires off the running board before we went on the dress shop job. Some other guys went on that dress job, I didn't go. When they come back they had fifteen dresses. They parked but in five short minutes the Lincoln Squad had the car. Ben gave some of the dresses to his sister and Jam gave some to his sister-in-law. I made five dollars on the tires.

One day me, Step, and Chicken Man went on Canal street to get a Ford. We got a roadster which belonged to the government. We went around with it until we met a man named Jimmie. He said he wanted to buy a Ford for twenty dollars. We went on Sangamon and Van Buren and Chicken Man and Hank stepped in a Ford. Chicken Man started it and Hank jumped in. I followed them with the roadster. We got back on Sholto street and we saw Willie coming. He took the car over to a garage on Roosevelt Road. We were riding down Congress and Loomis when a squad starts coming. I puts it in second and we went around a corner. The squad was right after me. I whipped a couple of corners and lost them. We asked Kingy to put the car in a garage. He comes back and says he can't put it in a garage. So we went riding with it. We were looking for a car when a big shot copper in a Lincoln Squad started chasing us. I was on Harrison and Green and was going to take a corner when a truck comes and turned the corner. We smacked into the truck. The Ford was knocked on the sidewalk. We jumped out and ran.

They started chasing us. We went in an alley and hid there. In twenty minutes I came out of the alley and started walking innocently. I went by the Ford and saw the squad was there. I went home and ate dinner and came out.

Later in the night I went out with Willie to burglarize a store. We went at about one o'clock. We broke the window but someone was looking. We went to the restaurant. Then we came back but that guy was still there. So we went home and called a boy named Al and went back. When we got there we saw three squads there.

In the morning I was in a pool room and a man says to me, "You stole my car." I said, "No." So he hit me. Chicken Man ran away. Then he said, "I'll let you go if you get my car for me. So I said, "Yes, tomorrow morning." He said, "O.K."

One day we went on Canal street and got a Graham Paige. We picked up three girls. We took them on Sixty-Third Street to their house. When we came back the tank was empty. I asked the boy by the name of Whitey if he had any gas. He said he did so we so we bought some gas from him. We were driving down Sholto Street when we ran into the school. We jumped out and ran. A few minutes later a squad came and took the car away.

I went over to Ben's house and stayed there till ten o'clock. Then I went home. The next day I went on Sholto street and waited on the corner for someone to come. Hank and Eddie came. We went on Van Buren and Jefferson streets and made a Whippet with a radio in it. I went and parked it. The car only went about forty in third. The radio was no good so we gave it to a guy in a Ford roadster. I gave the car to Jake and we went on Aberdeen Street driving around with it.

It was a lemon. We left it and the squad took it. Then me, Eddie, Captain Jack and Lumpy went to rob a candy factory. We went at night. We broke open the door and went in. We took about eighty-five packages of gum. Then me and Lumpy went away to Kedzie and Madison. We went away so not to get caught. As soon as we left, two Lincoln squads came. We went and ate chili con carne. Then we went to the show and after that we slept in a hotel.

For the next few weeks I went on a vacation to the North Side. We played dice and poker for money. Then I came back to the neighborhood. There was a garage on Grand and Wood where they kept laundry trucks, Fords and Chevrolets. I went to the laundry and spotted a truck. When I went out I closed the door in such a way that I could open it when I came back that night. I figured we could get the truck tires and sell them for ten dollars apiece. That night we went back, but the door was closed with a lock and a dog started barking so we went away.

We went to a show on Chicago Avenue and Wood Street. We came out at about eleven o'clock. Then I went to sleep at my friend's house on the North Side. The next morning I went with Ambrose to look for a car. We could not get one, so we went home. That night we went to make a store on Jackson and Sangamon. We got a jimmy and broke the wood from the door. We went in. We got all the cigarettes, candy, cigars, and gum. I found a suit there and took it. Eddie also found one. After that we went to the flat and played cards all night. In the morning l went to my cousin's house and we sold the cigarettes and cigars. We got twenty dollars for them. With the money we got from this job we went downtown to a show.

When we came from the show we went to a restaurant and bought porter-house steaks, coffee, and cake. Then we went to the Hub Theatre on Chicago Avenue and Wood street. When we came out it was twelve o'clock. I slept in my cousin's house again that night. In the morning we went to a bakery, bought some cakes, ate them, and then went home. My father asked me where I was and I told him I was at Mike's house. My father was suspicious, but Mike came over that afternoon and nothing happened.

One day I went to the Cubs Park with Whitey, Butch, and Tony. On the way there we saw two bikes. I went up the guy and asked him for a ride. He said, "It ain't my bike." So I took the bike and went home. Whitey and Butch got a bike and went home too. We were riding around the house when my father came and hit me. He took me by the ear and brought me home. He said, "Where did you get the bike and why didn't you go to school?" I said that I went to school, but he showed me a paper from my teacher. Boy, did he hit me. I went on the corner and saw Butch and Whitey. They sold the bike for six dollars. So we went two dollars apiece.

We went to school that day. After school we went to the Star and Garter and then to the restaurant. We went home that night. Two days later me, Eddie, and Fred went to get some shoes. We went on Halsted and Roosevelt and broke a window and took ten pair of shoes. We sold them at two dollars a pair to a guy on Jackson Boulevard. I had one pair left and Captain Jack said that I should sell them for a dollar. I did what he said. Later we saw a truck with coffee on it. We jumped in it and took some coffee and sold it around the street. I played dice with the money I had made and I lost all my money. Wally had to treat me to a show.

One day I had fifteen dollars. I played dice and lost it. Was I sore! My friend Butch had some money so we went to White City. We had lots of fun. We went on the Bobs for twenty minutes. We tried some games and Butch won an elephant. I brought it home. When we got on Harrison and

Racine we went to the pool room and shot pool for a nickel a game. When we were going out of the place I broke the trunk of the elephant. Was I sore!

I put it in front of my house and went to a friend's house for the night. We stayed out till three in the morning and then went to sleep. The next night me and Freddie were on the corner and we heard a wreck down the block. We ran over there and saw that a Hudson driven by a Mexican had hit a Lexington owned by a friend of ours. We looked in the car and the keys were still in there so I took the keys and put them in my pocket and started going away. The Mexican started looking for the keys. He said to me, "I'll give you a dollar if you will find my keys." We waited until he went away and then I got in the Hudson with Fred and started it up. We passed by the Mexican and he jumped on the running board. I took the key out and "Here is the key." He said, "Please do not start it. I will give you a dollar if you will put it in the garage." I said, "Give me the dollar." He said, "When we get to the garage." I thought to myself, "He can't fool me." So when we get to the garage I started going. He was on the running board until we came to Sangamon and Congress. I stopped the car and said, "If you don't get off of there I'll smack you." Freddie had a pipe in his hand and he thought we would do it. He said, "I'll call a policeman." So I started the car and knocked him off.

Me and Fred went driving on the North Side. We drove around for about two hours. Then we came home. We got out of gas, so we let the car go and walked down Morgan Street. We saw a Ford truck and so we got in it and drove it away. Fred went home and I parked the car on Vernon and May. Butch came around and we went riding in the neighborhood.

About four o'clock in the morning we parked it and went to sleep. The next morning we went riding again. We passed by the squad. Butch started lamming the corners until we lost it. Then I got behind the wheel and went driving. I saw Gilbert and some of the boys who were going to school, so I said, "Jump on." They jumped on. We were going along when Gilbert said, "The Chrysler squad is coming." I put it in second and started going about forty when the squad turned the corner on Vernon and Sholto. I stopped and let the boys out. I put it in second and started going around the corner wlth the squad right in back of me. I turned two corners and into an alley and lost them.

I parked it and got out. I was lucky not to get in it again or I would have been pinched. That night we went to an A&P; broke the window, and took cigarettes, candy, soap, and coffee; and brought them to the flat. At the flat we had a storeroom with about four locks on it because Sparrow and his friend raided the flat and took some shirts from Eddie. Boy, we were sore. When we came to the flat Benny said, "Somebody was in there." So Eddie and me hid in the closet. This fellow was looking all over but he couldn't find us. Later we went out and went to a show.

When we came back me and Eddie stole two chickens. We fried and ate them. That night two police men came in Wally's house. Wally ran out of the house with his pants to the flat. He said, "Open the door. Its me, Wally." When he came in his feet were cold. He went to bed. In the morning his brother came with shoes and shirt for him. He stayed there for two months. We used to clean the flat two times a day. We would scrub the dishes and silverware and the floors. Then we used to go on the corner of Congress Street and rob candy from the truck. We'd get Cracker Jacks from the Cracker Jack wagon.

One day Kingie had a Pontiac sedan. We made the Jackson School, broke into the storeroom, and filled the car with stuff from it. We took the stuff to the flat and left it there. We then went on Oakley and Ohio to another school. When we got there, we saw that it was being watched so we decided to go to the Buckingham Fountain on Michigan. Wally didn't want to go so we went home. In the morning the car was gone so we had to get another one.

I went on Vernon and May and saw a Dodge there so 1 got into it and got away. I parked it by the flat. That night we went to the McKinley High School and we took out a bunch of guns and band instruments. We sold them at four places. We sold the band things to a man in a restaurant on Morgan. He gave us five dollars apiece. We made about forty dollars. We went to the Midnight at the Haymarket on Madison. We were hollering. Eddie was with us two. A copper was sitting in back of us, It was two o'clock when we got out.

We went to the flat and saw it was lit up. We didn't know how come. When we got upstairs the door was open. We went in and saw Augie on the bed. We said, "Why didn't you put out the light?" He said he had just come. We had money so we played cards all night. In the morning we went on Morgan and Harrison to a Greek restaurant and bought a dime hamburger. We had gotten up early, about five thirty, so we could go out and get a truck with eggs and chickens. We got two dollars for the chickens and five dollars for the eggs.

Wally did not steal because he had just come away from Cook County School. We didn't want him to go back so we made him stay in the flat and watch it. He would clean it and cook the spaghetti we had robbed from the trucks. One day Kingie and Page came to the flat to sleep. They did not go home. Their mothers went to Wally's house and asked Wally's father where the boys were. Wally's father said he did not know. So they went away.

We were on Halsted and Adams getting a shine when my father appeared on the other side of the street. He was looking at us, but he didn't see us. Eddie said, "There is your father." I looked around and saw him and he saw me so he came over and said, "Come on home." So I said, "I don't want to come home." So he said he was going to beat me so I went with him. The next day I went by the flat and I saw that Kingie's sister and mother came there and got him too. The next week the flat was raided by the coppers. I think Kingie's mother squealed.

One day we went by Sparrow's house to rob a store. We got Gus and a friend of Sparrow's. Then we saw Eddie on Kenzie. He had opened a window and was getting some shoes from this store when a man came out. We ran away. We went to the "L" and went to the flat. Another time we had a sack and we crashed a fruit store taking out potatoes, pears, tomatoes, and everything. We went to the flat and ate them.

One day Eddie robbed a bike and I asked him for a ride. He wouldn't give it to me because he was afraid I was going to run-away with it. Well, finally, he gave me the bike and so I went for a ride and didn't come back for an hour. Then I took the bike and sold it to a kid I knew for a dollar.

Another day a boy by the name of Mike gives me a Chevrolet roadster. I had it for about two weeks. I went to the YMCA with it. Then I was driving around and l ran out of gas. Two days later I went to look for the car where I had left it and it was gone. I said the cops had taken it. I was right, the cops were in the garage with the car.

One day we were going to the show on Madison and Halsted to see the Wonderland to see a gangster picture. There were ten of us guys in the gang, some got in for nothing, and some paid. Some had seen the picture. There was a colored lady there about twenty years old. One of the guys, named Gilbert said, "Let me fuck you. I will give you dresses and shoes." She said, "Alright." We went out and she followed us. We got on Green Street and she was walking with Gilbert and Chip.

She said, "Tell the other boys to go home." Chip came by us and said, "Make like you are going home." We went around the corner. They went up to an old house. They went on the third floor, but a lady saw us so we said, "Well, let's go to another house." We went on Green and Van Buren Street on the second floor. Gilbert went first. He put it in her cunt and she said, "Come on, Gilbert." He said, "I am coming," and he was, coming. After he got off Chip got on and then I got on. There was another fellow also named Gilbert who got on. She was crying because his prick was big and made blood come out of her cunt. I took her money and ran downstairs. There was a dollar and a half. I took it and brought the purse back up to her. She said, "Give me my money." I said, "I'll give you a kick in the cunt." So she went away.

Another time we made the Jackson School again. We found forty dollars and two electric irons. We sold them for a dollar and a half so we had forty-one fifty. Me and Willie went fifteen dollars apiece, Eddie got seven dollars, and Step got four and a half bucks. Me and Willie went on Halsted street and Van Buren to see a show. When we got there the show was closed. We went in the back and up to the roof. We took off the window and went in. We cracked open the telephone box and got five and a half dollars. There was also a candy machine. This we broke open and took the money and candy. There was also some Baby Ruth candies and Hersheys, which we took. When we told Eddie about it he was sore that he didn't come with us. The next day we were looking for something to take.

We walked for an hour and a half. We saw a man with a Ford truck. He had a box with money in it. When he went into the store we were going to take the money out or the truck. The box had about a hundred dollars in it. We started kicking the door of the truck when the lady from the store came out and said, "If you don't get out of there I will call the man." So we went around the corner to wait for him. He came out and went up to Miller street and stopped. We went there but we couldn't get anything. He was looking for us. Then he went to Morgan street end stopped, he went in a store and left the door open. I opened the door and Eddie took the money. We ran into a house and opened up the box. There was twenty dollars in it. We gave Whitey and Chicken Man a half dollar apiece. They did not want it so me and Eddie kept it. We went in the alley, shot craps for it. I lost five dollars and had five dollars left.

About a week later we went to a show. On our way we saw a Buick in the alley between Vernon Park and Sholto. Me and Eddie had a screwdriver. We were going to get a Ford when a boy said, "Give me the screwdriver for a minute." We gave him the screwdriver and he took the tire off of the Buick. I got in the car and started driving anyway with it. Eddie got on. The car had no tires on it. I pulled it out of the alley. We were going around the corner with it. The people said, "If you don't get that car off the street we'll call the cops because the kids will get hurt by the car." I pulled the car in the alley and took the battery out and sold it to a kid on Polk and May street for a dollar and a half.

That day I went on the North Side to my cousin's house. We went to the show and after the show we went to a Greek ice-cream parlor to eat. There was a slot machine there which would grab either a watch, a cigar lighter, or some candy. My cousin tried it and only got some candy. I took the machine and put it upside down and took the watch, cigar lighter, and pipes out.

The man from the store came and was going to hit me but my cousin was going to hit him because he had it in for the man. We took the stuff to his house and split it. It was Christmas time. My father was there so I said to him, "I'm going to stay here," so he said, "Alright." When I came home I saw Eddie. We went by a haberdashery shop. It was 12 o'clock. We crashed the window and took out two boxes of ties and stockings. There were forty stockings and twenty-five ties. We sold them and bought eats for the flat.

One day Me, Eddie, and Willie went looking for a car. We were on Harrison and Racine Avenue when we saw a kid with a box. He saw us and started running away. We went for him. We caught him on Congress Street. We took him to Laflin and Congress streets to a haunted house and put him on a bed. Well, we fucked him and then I made him suck me off. He had seventy five cents on him so, we took it and said, "Go home now." We went to the show with the money and to the restaurant. On our way home we got a Chrysler. It was a good car.

Another time me, Chip, Koots, and Captain Jack went for a car downtown. We got on Canal and Jackson Boulevard. There was Ford Cabriolet there. We were going to get it but the squad car came and we ran away. It was July and there was swimming at the pool in Sheridan Park. So we went swimming there with the gang. While we were swimming, we also raided the lockers and got the money from them. We did this for a couple of weeks until the Park copper said if he caught the guy, "it will be too bad for him."

When I came out of the Juvenile Court I went on Halsted and Madison to see if l could get into a show for nothing. Fred and Gilbert were with me. We got up the fire escape but the manager of the show was there. We ran downstairs and out into the alley. We walled down Halsted and I took some apples from a store. The man came out and we ran. I ran into the arms of two coppers. I asked the coppers to let me alone because I had just gotten out of the Juvenile Home, so the copper said, "Let the boy go this time, but the next time I will take him to the station." They let me go. I went around the corner and there I met Red and Gilbert. From that day on I did not pass that store again.

That summer me, Eddie, and Willie went out for a car. We walked downtown but we couldn't find one so we started coming home. We were passing by Van Buren and Green Street when I spotted a car. I kicked the door of the car and Willie was going to go in, but I saw some men looking at us. They were going to call the cops. We were going to run when we saw Chicken Man coming in a Ford sedan. I called him and he stopped. We got in and rode away. We stopped on Aberdeen and Vernon Park and let Willie and Step-and-a-Half off, then me, Chicken Man and Eddie went looking for a Ford roadster.

We came to Congress and Racine and saw Lumpy there. He had a five gallon can of gasoline and was putting it into a Dodge in front of the Paris Garter factory. I stopped there and Lumpy said, "Give me a push," so I backed up and Lumpy got in the Dodge and I pushed him to Loomis Street and he got the car started. I threw it into second and swung around in front of the Dodge with Lumpy coming after me. We were going through alleys and streets. Lumpy was in back of me. I turned on Laflin and then turned into the alley and Lumpy could not catch up to us. Then we went on Vernon Park and Sholto and picked up Step-and-a-half. Step said, "Let's get some bananas." We went over to Vernon and Morgan street to see the banana man. Step asked the man for a dozen bananas. The man gave them to Chicken Man. Step threw it into first and we started off. The man jumped on and was getting in the car when Eddie hit him on the hand with his hammer and he got off. Chicken then gave the car to a man for nothing because it was his car.

The next morning we went on Halsted and Van Buren to a White House hamburger joint and got hamburgers. I ate ten hamburgers and two cups of coffee. Then we went to see a show.

One day me, Willie, and Eddie went out for a car. We went down to the Loop to look for one. We were looking for a Chrysler and we saw one on Wacker Drive and Dearborn street. We couldn't get in it because we didn't have a screwdriver. We saw a Ford roadster. We went into the Ford and looked for a screwdriver. We found a screwdriver and went back to the Chrysler. When we got there the car was gone. So we were looking around for another one, but we couldn't find any so we went home. There I saw Hank and he said that he wanted to go for a Ford so I said, "We just got back from looking for a Chrysler and didn't want to go." He said I was yellow. I said, "Let's go." So we walked down Jackson near the Union Depot and we saw a Ford sedan. But there were two men standing there that looked like coppers, so we went up to Lake Street till they went away. When they went away Hank and me got in to the car, started it and went away with it. It didn't have any brakes on it so we put it in a garage on Sholto and Vernon Park Place. We put some candy in it and took out some cans of paint that was in it and gave it to the colored man in the garage because he let us keep the car there for nothing.

In the garage was a Ford coupe, a hot car. I told the man in the garage. He said, "If that is a hot car it belongs to one of the boys." I said, "Let me take it for ten minutes." He said, "Alright," so me and Step-and-a-Half went riding on Harrison and Congress streets. We were whipping corners with it and then we brought it to a garage and I started looking for Eddie. I saw him sleeping at his house. I called him and asked him if he wanted to come and make some dough. He, said, "Yes," so I went to the garage, got the coupe out of the garage, picked up Eddie and Willie, and went to a shoe store. We went to Congress and Kedzie and broke the window. We took out the shoes and put them in the car. Then we brought them to Eddie's house. After that we made out to make a dress joint. We got fifteen dresses which we took with us in the car over to the garage on Vernon Park and Sholto.

We put the lights out and took the dresses. We gave two to the colored man in the garage and three to a girl who was there. We had ten left. We sold them for three dollars apiece and got thirty dollars for them. We had also taken cigarettes which we got twenty dollars for. That made fifty dollars altogether.

Another time, me and Step went out for a car. We saw Chicken Man and took him with us. We went on Wacker Drive and Dearborn looking for a Ford coupe. We saw one and I kicked the door. Chicken Man went in and opened it. He started it and we jumped in. I got at the wheel and Chicken Man and Step came. We got on Lake and Racine Avenue. Here we saw the Lincoln Squad. I put it in second and was going about forty-five. Chicken Man was looking back to see if they were coming. He said, "They are a block away," so I whipped the corner and they whipped right after us. They were still in back of me. They told me to pull to the side. I said, "Alright," and I was going to the side. Then I put it in second and turned into the alley and started going. They shot at us but they only hit the fenders and we lost them. We got on Monroe and Loomis streets and parked it there.

We went into Jefferson Park and saw two girls there. They were whores. We were asking them about a fuck. One said we were too small, but the other said we was alright. So we started feeling the girls up and they were showing us their cunts and they said they had the clap. Chicken Man gets up and got a piece of paper and went and wiped off his prick because he had come in his pants. The girls were laughing their heads off. When they heard that he had come in his pants they said, "Come with us to the flat," but Step said, "We can't fuck." But they said, "Let's go." So we took them to their flat in the Ford coupe. Chicken Man and Step got in the back and the girls in the front. We took them to their flat and said we'd see them at four o'clock. Then we went on Congress Street and Halsted to the restaurant to get something to eat. Then I told Step to take the car and park it because I was going to go to the hotel and sleep. I hadn't slept for a day.

I was with Eddie and Chicken Man. We were pulling an A&P job and I told him to come and call me at about nine o'clock that night. He said, "Alright." He came that night, called me said, "The car is parked on the corner of Congress and Halsted Street." I asked him if he took the keys out and closed the doors and he said, "Yes." I told him to go downstairs and get some hamburgers while I put my clothes on. I had ten dollars on me. We ate and then we got in the car and went. I stopped in front of Eddie's house and called Eddie and Chicken Man.

Eddie's old man came out and said to go away and leave Eddie alone. So we took Chicken Man and went away. We picked up Eddie on Miller Street. We went on Harrison and Morgan and asked a guy if he wanted some hot tires. He said he would give us twenty dollars for them so we made the sale. We said we would come back at two o' clock as it was one o'clock then. We went on Madison Street and got a Ford sedan. We took it to Congress and Aberdeen Street where we stripped the tires off, put them in our car, and then went to Harrison and Morgan Street with the tires. The fellow there asked us to go with him. We got in his car and went over to Division Street and delivered the two tires. When we got back he gave us twenty-one dollars. The extra dollar was to put gasoline in his car. He gave us the key and we went and put gas in the car. For once we were not afraid of the squad because we were riding in a car that wasn't hot.

Once Paul, Step, and Chicken Man went out for a car. We were walking around the Loop looking for a Ford. When we got on Lake Street we saw a Ford coupe. We kicked the door on it and was going to get in but two kids came in a Chrysler. They were going for another one so we went away with them on Avers street. We saw a Ford roadster so we got a brick and a screw driver. Chicken Man got in and hit it but the ignition wouldn't open so I got in there and hit it and I stepped on the starter and it started.

Paul, Chicken Man, and Step-and-a-Half came and we went on Lake Street. Here we stripped the car. We sold the top for fifteen dollars to a guy. I still got to collect five bucks from him. Me, Chicken Man, and Hank went out for a car. We went near a fire station for one but, we couldn't find any so we went to Jefferson and Van Buren streets. We saw a Ford coupe.

I kicked the door open and Chicken Man went in and started it. I jumped in and went away with it. The next day we went on Congress and Sangamon Street to make a candy factory. When we got there we saw a Ford coupe with the keys in it so Chicken Man came and called me. I jumped in and Chicken Man came right after me. We went on Vernon Park and Sholto Street and opened up the rumble seat. We found some blankets in there so we took them out and gave them to Eddie. He put them in his house and then we went and parked the car. I saw a Pontiac sedan on Vernon Park and Sholto which was a hot car.

I went on the corner and asked if the guy had the keys for it. He gave me the keys and I went to drive it when the squad came. They took the car away. I got in the car that I had and went and got Step and Chicken Man, and then I went to the North Side with it. We went to my cousin's house. I called him and asked him if he could get me a gun. He sent me over to Grand and Western to a kid who lived there. I went there and tapped on the door and his sister-in-law came out. She asked what I wanted and I said that I wanted to see him. She said he was not home and that he was working with his brother. Then I went on Wood and Ohio Street where I saw a friend of mine whom I had known from when I lived on the North Side. He asked me for a ride so I let him go with Step and Chicken Man while I waited on the corner.

He went on Chicago Avenue and Wood Street to an ice-cream parlor to get some candy, then he came back. He almost tipped over with it on his way back. We went back around the neighborhood and I gave the car to Stiff. I didn't go home because my father was looking for me. Step came back and said he had had a flat tire. We fixed the flat and I was riding around with him when we met Tony coming home from work. We picked him up and he drove. We got lammed by the squad and Tony turned a corner and hit a truck. We jumped out and ran away.

Then I went for a car with Eddie. We went on Adams and Green Street and saw a Buick coupe. I put my hand on the door and it opened. I tried to shift and it opened. So I got in and started it and Eddie hopped on. Vie went away with it. We went to Vernon Park and Sholto and took the tires off. Then we drove to Aberdeen and Congress. When we got there the Flivver Squad came and we had to run. It was too late. They had the guns on me. They put me in the squad and asked me my name, address and how old I was. I told them I was seventeen, so they took me to the Deplanes Street station, where I was kept for four days.

Chip, Jim, Jam, and Wally came to see me. They brought me smokes and eats. On Sunday morning, the copper called my name and handcuffed me. I asked him where I was going and he said, "To jail." I got in the patrol wagon and we went to the B. of I. for a show-up. In the morning I went to court and got a continuance. The continuance was for two weeks so I had to go to the County Jail until then.

I had a friend and I asked his father to get me out on bond. Instead, I got out on probation, Two weeks later, I got a Ford Coupe on Green and Congress, I drove it over to Vernon Park Place. Step and Chicken Man were going to sell it to a gang for $20.00. We were taking the car over to them and we were on Roosevelt and Ashland. The Ford Squad pulled up just then and we couldn't get out of traffic, so we jumped out and ran. Chicken Man, Step, and I start going but we got caught seven blocks away. They took us in the squad and brought us to the B. of I. to have our fingerprints taken. Then we went to court. Step and I got out on bonds, while Chicken Man got probation. We went to the Cook County Jail, that is, Step and I, stayed there for a month. When we went to court we were a discharged. The next day l was caught in a car with Chip and Fred, and I was sentenced to one year at St. Charles' School for boys. I will be out in six months.

Conclusion
Delinquency and the End of Boyhood

What does one take away from these particular stories? I doubt the answer would be the same for everyone. What I have attempted to do in this book is to provide a sociological context for these stories in terms of gender, capitalism and power. By doing this I hoped to give historical evidence of the social construction of early twentieth century concept of masculinity and its relationship to the then emerging notion of juvenile delinquency.

The women's movement of the Progressive Era, the simultaneous movement of women into the job market and the influx of immigrants into industrial cities as a supply of cheap labor challenged male hegemony in America. While Clifford Shaw and his colleagues provided us with some important studies of boyhood and delinquency, it is doubtful that he saw the broader implications of his collected oral histories at the time.

The three stories presented here describe boys caught up from an early age in the then narrowly defined system of gender identity and criminality. The definition of what it meant to be an American boy was articulated in literature, science and the popular press. Part of what it meant to be an American boy was a youthful dismissiveness of authority and a disrespect if not disdain for women. Mark Twain was to note that boys are adventurers, rebels and rule breakers. While boys in the city were not able to take a raft down the Mississippi, they were able to steal cars and could see what it was like to be on the other side of the law and chased by the police. They saw West Madison Street as an exotic land that yielded hidden and forbidden pleasures. It was like venturing into some savage, foreign land. While not all of these boys were from immigrant families, most were what Howard Becker has referred to as *outsiders*, or rule breakers. They were poor and from highly dysfunctional families. But what they shared in common was a contempt for the power that confined them to third rate existences.

Conclusion: Delinquency and the End of Boyhood

Many of the stories given to us by Shaw were oral histories of boys who parents had taken bold moves to travel, most often steerage class, from remote places in Europe to a congested metropolis that was alien to them. This was a place where few could even understand the language and culture that surrounded them. While not all were European immigrants, all had come from some other place that was relatively more tame than the harsh urban environments in which they found themselves.

In reviewing these oral histories we can discover elements of *coincidence,* conditions that helped to bring many of these young men together—themes that run through their stories.

Poverty

Shaw and his colleagues interviewed boys from homes that had little or no economic stability. The boys families here exemplify this characteristic. Some had little idea as to where their next meal would come from. Large families were often a carry over of ethnic and class social norms from their countries and regions of origin. The Catholic Church in the United States furthermore advocated strongly against birth control. And large families that might have been useful in peasant societies that valued sons became dysfunctional in twentieth century American cities.

Early on we have evidence of some of these children eating from garbage cans. For most, theft became a means of early survival, but it was not their sole or even primary motivation to misbehave. These boys viewed criminal behavior as a challenge to authority, they did not see their resorting to crime as unmanly—just the opposite. Crimes of theft would be better seen as mini-adventures. Getting caught was part of the excitement.

The type of work fathers were able to secure was both unstable and low level. Often men had to work in noxious, unsafe conditions of slaughter houses and factories. They were maltreated by their employers and could not always rely on bringing home a pay check. The informal familial support systems upon which one might be able to rely in Europe was not available here. Both women and men worked to support their families. For these particular families and children, there was no strong communal support or identity.

Child labor was part of the experience of being poor. Opposition to it came from a number of quarters; while most were concerned with the exploitation of children, others were concerned with marginal workers such as children negatively impacting the living wage of unionized adult workers. The possibility of children working to supplement their family income was a violation of new laws being developed to protect children, but also to protect unionized workers.

Alcohol Abuse

The vast majority of homes from which these boys came were beset with parental alcohol abuse. This was primarily associated with their fathers who were usually marginally employed. Labor abuse frequently was correlated with alcohol abuse which in turn was associated with an enormous degree of domestic insecurity, beyond financial insecurity, and could result in depression, domestic violence, physical abuse and neglect of children and a general sense of fatalism.

Temperance movement promoted an agenda of abstinence. It consisted of powerful groups that saw urban ills as related to a lack of sobriety. This was seen as an important issue for the Christian Church, the Women's Movement, and industrialists who wanted more from their workers. These groups feared that alcohol, not dangerous and unsanitary working conditions, not the stress of poverty, not the lack of clean water, not the lack of health care and quality education for children, was the chief cause of most social problems. Today we realize that alcoholism was much more of a response to these conditions than a cause of them. And while alcohol was correlated with family disorganization, familial violence and crime, it was the exploitive, dehumanizing, industrial system that created many of the conditions that would lead to high rates of alcoholism among immigrants and non-immigrants alike.

Absent Mothers and Fathers

Frequently mothers were absent from the scene. Many poor young women died of tuberculosis or in child birth in the early 1900s. Few had medical doctors available to them to help in the birthing process and often relied on untrained and inexperienced midwives. Abortions were outlawed and many poor women died in attempts to end their pregnancies without the help of trained medical doctors. The infant mortality level was exceedingly high and birthing often resulted in postpartum depression which was not even recognized at that time as a health issue.

Many children grew up in one parent families. And frequently a single parent with few supportive relatives would see it necessary to put their children up for adoption, or to simply house them in an orphanage "for their own good." Fathers were often absent and not involved in the lives of their children. For most of the boys in these stories, fathers would beat them. We have no story of ever attending a Cubs game with dad.

From the evidence presented on immigrant labor and the hours parents were forced to be outside of the home working well into the night, many of their children remained unsupervised. These were indeed the first "latchkey" children, and Persons in Need of Supervision. (PINS).

Poor Health

The transitioning from one's home country to another was frequently associated with the lowering of resistance to new germs and diseases not found in their home environments. New foods, new climatic conditions for which many were not prepared and new cultures which meant new languages and new values added to the immigrant's already stressed system. Anthropologists and epidemiologists such as John Cassel (1976) provided substantial research to show the negative health consequences of immigrants adapting to an alien environments and cultures. Given the physical quality of the neighborhoods in which they were forced to reside, those living in poverty were exposed to hazardous toxicity and overcrowding. Living in cities under such conditions increased not only stress but the likelihood of stress related health disorders, including alcoholism.

Physical Abuse and Trauma in the Household

While trauma theory was not fully developed until after World War I, little was known about the impact of domestic violence and physical abuse of children and women in the home (Terr 1992).

The advent of the first wave feminist movement challenged one of the two characteristics that gave men a particular advantage—gender and race. Often men, especially those otherwise economically disenfranchised, responded to this movement with greater violence against women. Children witnessed physical abuse of their mothers. Not only did this violence against women help define masculinity for the boy, but it signaled that women could be an appropriate target of abuse and violence.

Excessive Absence or Truancy from School

Many of the boys who were exposed to violence could not find safety in their homes. At local schools immigrant children were often targets of bullying and violence by other school children, particularly boys, and seen by some teachers as disruptive and incapable of learning (Grant 2014). There classrooms were overcrowded and underfunded. The quality of teaching was poor. A need for boys to find companionship and meaning outside of the home frequently brought poor boys from different ethnic groups together.

Few Communal Supports

Aside from churches that were experiencing rapid transition in the ethnicity of their parishioners, as one ethnic group was displaced by a later arriving one, it was difficult for church leaders to connect to people who were not at all like them. Likewise, it was difficult for many of these immigrants to connect to these clergy (Cox, 2013).

Racism and Discrimination, Tensions Between Immigrants and African Americans

The twentieth century brought a large exodus of African Americans from the south to northern cities. In Chicago they experienced a different type of discrimination including residential segregation and blocked access to labor unions and good paying jobs. There was also a lack of recreational facilities for these newly arriving groups.

Chicago's Race Riot of 1916 was one of the bloodiest in American history. These groups of black American migrants and white foreign immigrants clashed around the scant resources available to poor and working class peoples. Mexicans, Asians, Filipinos and other groups were turned against each other as the tabloid press stirred racial unrest by frequently promoting negative racial and ethnic stereotypes. Many of the services provided by social welfare organizations were aimed at assisting whites only.

Excessive Incarceration Rates for Nonviolent Activities

Putting children into reform facilities was better than putting them in jail. However, reformatories degenerated into training centers for criminal life. Children who failed to go to school were treated no differently than those accused of more serious offenses. They were brought into a system that was supposedly designed to help them, but produced the opposite outcomes. The production of a system of juvenile justice was in some ways a political jobs program for unlicensed social workers, counselors, teachers, house parents and staff. It became a mere extension of the prison industrial complex where patronage trumped professional credentialing and training. These facilities exposed children to greater violence than most experienced on the street. There was more than a very good chance that they would return to places like this again and again.

Young black male children were disproportionately consigned to detention facilities and prisons that served an adult population. Even though these boys were often less troublesome as whites, and less violent, they were arrested for lesser infractions and their incarceration rate was disproportionally higher. Though African American boys, Mexican boys and Asian boys were nearly invisible to Shaw, they would soon come to constitute an important component of the community of juvenile delinquents. And the importance of gendered crime was reflected here as well.

While there is considerable evidence that masculinity in many of its variant forms historically has been given unequaled access to power and wealth in most societies, like whiteness it also stands closely allied with social privilege and crime. This is not to say the females have not achieved a few advantages, but that the unequal distribution of opportunities and possibilities is still quite staggering.

Raine Dozer (2005), in a brilliant research essay on gender transitioning female-to-male, speaks of social interactions before and after FTM physical transitioning. Presenting oneself physically as male elicits reactions and behaviors that are quite different from the individual who presents as a female. He quotes a reflection of a transman in this regard:

> I remember one time walking up the hill; it was like nine o'clock, and this woman was walking in front of me, and she kept looking back, and I thought, "What the hell is wrong with that girl?" And then I stopped in my tracks. When I looked at her face clearly under the light, she was afraid. So I crossed the street [Dozier 2005, p. 305].

Dozer also relates incidents wherein a transman is treated more respectfully and with greater deference by both men and women. Once the transition is physically obvious, social interactions change. Anyone who has taken a gender course in school or studied sociology even briefly knows that one only gains a sense of oneself through the reactions of others. But if gender is indeed performance or a social construction, so too is criminal behavior. The point here is that juvenile delinquency occurs at a time one is attempting to understand the meaning of oneself and this meaning is only gained through human interactions. Early experiences are therefore critical to identity formation.

The relationship between gender and crime is not a new area of study. But given rapid changes taking place in both of these registers, gender and crime, there is value to reflecting historically on how lower working-class boyhood of the 1920s was closely linked to preditory behavior. And as the gender binary further weakens, and as "hard" masculinity further softens, we might find new gendered pathways leading us away from this fusion of boyhood and crime.

Bibliography

Abrams, Lynn. 2010. *Oral history theory.* New York: Routledge.

Adler, Freda. 1975. *Sisters in crime: the rise of the new female criminal.* New York: McGraw-Hill Publishers.

Adler, Jeffrey S. 2006. *First in violence, deepest in dirt: homicide in Chicago 1875–1920.* Cambridge: Harvard University Press.

Alinsky, Saul. 1972. Interview, *Playboy*, 19 March.

Barnett, Cynthia. 2000. The Measurement of white-collar crime using uniform crime reporting. Crime Information Services Division, U.S. Department of Justice, Federal Bureau of Investigation. Report No. NCJ 202866.

Bartlett, Frederic C. 1932. *Remembering: a study in experimental social psychology.* New York: Cambridge University Press.

Baur, E.J. 1933. *Delinquency among Mexican boys in South Chicago.* Master's Thesis, University of Chicago.

Beck, Allen. 2013. Sexual Victimization in Juvenile Facilities Reported By Youth 2012. Washington, D.C.: Bureau of Justice Statistics, U.S. Department of Justice.

Bederman, Gail. 1996. *Manliness and civilization.* Chicago: University of Chicago Press.

Benjamin, Jessica. 1988. *The bonds of love.* New York: Pantheon.

Bennett, James.1981. *Oral history and delinquency: the rhetoric of criminology.* Chicago: University of Chicago Press.

Bereswill, Mechthild. 2007. Fighting like a wildcat: A deep hermeneutic interpretation of The Jack-Roller. *Theoretical Criminology*, 1: 469–484.

Bertaux, Elliot. 1981. *Biography and society: the life history approach in the social sciences.* London: Sage Publishers.

Black, Jack. 1926. *You can't win.* New York: Macmillan.

Bloom, Harold, ed. 2002. *Upton Sinclair's The jungle: the modern critical interpretations.* Philadelphia: Chelsea House.

Bowlby, John. 1944. Forty-four juvenile thieves: their character and home life. *International Journal of Psychoanalysis*, 25: 19–52.

Bradley, April, and James M. Wood. 1996. How do children tell: the process of disclosure of child sexual abuse. *Child Welfare*, 70: 3–15.

Breckinridge, Sophonisba, and Edith Abbott. 1912. *The delinquent child and the home.* New York: New York Charities Publication.

Britton, Dana. 2003. *At work in the iron cage, the prison as gendered organization.* New York: New York University Press.

Brown, Allison P. 2007. Interpretation and the case study: the challenge of a relational approach. *Theoretical Criminology*, 11: 485–500.

Bulmer, Martin. 1984. *The Chicago school of sociology.* Chicago: University of Chicago Press.

Burr, Hanford M. 1910. Studies in adolescent boys. Springfield, MA: Seminar Publishing.

Butler, Judith. 1999. *Gender trouble.* New York: Rutledge.

Cappetti, Carla. 1993. *Writing Chicago: modernism, ethnography and the novel.* New York: Columbia University Press.

Cassel, John. 1976. Contribution of the host environment to host resistance. *American Journal of Epidemiology,* 104: 107–123.

CDC (Center for Disease Control). 2014. *Suicide prevention: Youth suicide.* National Center for Injury Prevention and Control. http://www.cdc.gov/violence prevention/pub/youth_suicide.html.

Chesney-Lind, Meda. 1989. Girl's crime and woman's place: toward a feminist model of female delinquency. *Crime and Delinquency,* 35: 5–29.

Chodorow, Nancy. 1978. *The reproduction of mothering.* New Haven: Yale University Press.

Clapp, Elizabeth. 1995. "The Chicago juvenile court movement in the 1890s." Paper given at the Centre for Urban History, University of Leicester, on 17 March 1995 wherein she quotes from a leaflet, "To the Women and Women's Clubs of Illinois," dated Feb. 15, 1896, pp. 7–10, Scrapbook 3, Lucy Flower and Coues family scrapbooks, Manuscript Division, Chicago Historical Society.

Collier, Richard. 1998/1999. Masculinities and crime. *Criminal Justice Matters,* 34: 21–24.

Corbett, Ken. 2009. *Boyhoods: rethinking masculinities.* New Haven: Yale University Press.

Covington, Jeanette. 2007. *Drugs in black and white.* New York: Routledge.

Cox, Harvey. 2013. *The secular city.* Princeton: Princeton University Press.

Cox, Oliver C. 1965. Introduction. In Nathan Hare. *The Black Anglo-Saxons.* Chicago: Third World Press.

Cressey, Donald. 1932. *The Taxi dance hall.* Chicago: University of Chicago Press.

Dearey, Melissa, B. Petty, B. Thompson, C. Lear S. Gadsby and D. Gibbs. 2011. Prison(er) auto/biography, "true crime," and teaching, learning and research in criminology. *Critical Survey,* 23: 86–102.

Deegan, Mary Jo. 1978. Women in sociology, 1890–1930. *Journal of the History of Sociology,* 1: 11–34.

Deegan, Mary Jo. 1985. Institutionalization, diversity and the rise of sociological research. Review of The Chicago school of sociology by Martin Bulmer. *Contemporary Sociology,* 14: 365–366.

Deegan, Mary Jo. 1990. *Jane Addams and the men of the Chicago school, 1892–1918.* New Brunswick: Transaction Books.

dela Croix, S. Sukie. 2012. *Chicago whispers: a history of LGBT Chicago before Stonewall.* Madison: University of Wisconsin Press.

Denzin, Norman K. 1992. *Symbolic interactionism and cultural studies: the politics of interpretation.* Oxford: Blackwell.

Denzin, Norman K. 1995. Stanley and Clifford: undoing an interactionist text. *Current Sociology,* 43: 115–123.

Dilthey, W. 1985. *Poetry and experience.* Ed. and trans. Rudolf A. Makkreel and Frithjof Rodi. Princeton: Princeton University Press.

Dollard, John. 1935. *Criteria for the life history.* New Haven: Yale University Press.

Dowd, Nancy. E. 2008. Boys, masculinities and juvenile justice. *Journal of Korean Law,* 8: 115–134.

Dozier, Rane. Beards, breasts and bodies: doing sex in a gendered world. *Gender & Society,* 19: 297–316.

Drake, St. Clair, and H. Cayton. 1945. *Black metropolis.* New York: Harcourt, Brace and Company.

Du Bois, W.E.B. 1899. *The Philadelphia negro.* Philadelphia: Publications of the University of Pennsylvania.

Eadie, Robert, and Andrew Eadie. 1911. *Physiology and hygiene for young people.* New York: Charles Scribner's Sons.

Elliot, Jane. 2005. *Using narrative in social research: qualitative and quantitative approaches.* London: Sage.

Fallows, Samuel. 1900. The Illinois State Reformatory, in *The Reformatory system in the United States, Vol. 2.* International Prison Commission, House of Representatives, Document 495. Washington, D.C.

Ferri, Enrico. 1900. *Criminal sociology.* New York: D. Appleton and Company.

Ferrie, Joseph and W. Troesken. 2008. Water and Chicago's Mortality Transition, 1850–1925. *Explorations In Economic History,* 45: 1–16.

Fivush, R. 2008. Remembering and reminiscing: How individual lives are constructed in family narratives. *Memory Studies*, 1: 45–54.

Forbush, William B. 2013. *The Boy problem*. Worcestershire: Read Books Ltd. Orig. published 1902.

Freud, S. 1925. Some psychical consequences of the anatomical distinction between the sexes. In J. Strachey, ed., *The Standard Edition of the Complete Psychological Works of Sigmond Freud, Vol. 19*. London: The Hogarth Press, pp. 241–260.

Gadd, David, and T. Jefferson 2007. On the defensive: A psychoanalytically informed psychosocial reading of The Jack-Roller. *Theoretical Criminology*, 11: 443–467.

Gelsthorpe, Loraine. 2007. The Jack-Roller: telling a story? *Theoretical Criminology*, 11: 515–542.

George, Henry. 1879. *Progress and poverty*. New York: D. Appleton and Company.

George-Graves, Nadine. 2009. Just like being in the zoo—primativity and ragtime dance. In J. Maling, ed., *Ballroom boogie, shimmy sham, shake: a social and popular dance reader*. Urbana: University of Illinois Press.

Gibson, W.H. 1922. *Boyology or boy analysis*. New York: Association Press.

Giordano, Peggy, S. Cernkovich, and J. Randal. 2002. Gender, crime and desistance: toward a theory of cognitive transformation. *American Journal of Sociology*, 107: 990–1064.

Gittens, Joan. 1994. *Poor Relations: The Children of the State in Illinois, 1818–1890*. Springfield: University of Illinois Press.

Gordon, Linda. 1986. Feminism and Social Control. In J. Mitchell and A. Oakley, eds. What Is Feminism. New York: Pantheon Books.

Goring, Charles. 1913. *The English convict: a statistical study*. London: HMSO.

Grant, Julia. 2014. *The Boy problem: educating boys in urban America, 1870–1970*. Baltimore: Johns Hopkins University Press.

Grant, Madison. 1916. *The passing of the great race*. New York: Charles Scribner's Sons.

Greenwald, Ricky, ed. 2002. *Trauma and juvenile delinquency: theory, research and interventions*. New York: Routledge.

Griswold, Robert L. 1993. *Fatherhood in America: A history*. New York: Basic Books.

Godsoe, Cynthia. 2014. Contempt, status and the criminalization of nonconforming girls. *Cardozo Law Review*, 34: 1091–1116.

Grossman, Ron. 2016. When Chicago welcomed the KKK. *Chicago Tribune*. http://www.chicagotribune.com/news/ct-kkk-chicago-flashback-0125-20150123-story.html.

Guerin, Eddie. 1928. *Crime: the autobiography of a crook*. London: John Murray.

Guerin, Eddie. 1929. *I was a bandit: confessions of a super crook*. New York: Doubleday, Doran and Co.

Hall, G. Stanley. 1904. *Adolescence its psychology and relation to physiology, anthropology, sociology, sex, crime, religion and education*. New York: D. Appleton and Co.

Hansen, J.E. 2011. Settlement houses: an introduction. The Social Welfare History Project. Retrieved August 25, 2015. http://www.socialwelfarehistory.com/programs/settlement-houses/.

Hansen, Randall, and Desmond King. 2013. *Sterilized by the state: eugenics, race and population scare in twentieth century North America*. Cambridge: Cambridge University Press.

Heap, Chad. 2009. *Slumming: sexual and racial encounters in American night life 1885–1940*. Chicago: University of Chicago Press.

Hensley, C., and Tallichet, S.E. 2009. Childhood and adolescent animal cruelty methods and their possible link to adult violent crimes. *Journal of Interpersonal Violence*, 24: 147–158.

Higham, John. 1970. The reorientation of American culture in the 1890s. In *Writing American history: essays on modern scholarship*. Bloomington: Indiana University Press.

Irwin, Katherine, and Meda Chesney-Lind. 2008. Girls' violence: beyond dangerous masculinity. *Sociology Compass*, 2/3: 837–855.

James, Henry. 1886. *The Bostonian*. New York: New American Library 1965.

Kay, Kerwin. 2003. Male prostitution in the twentieth century: pseudo-homosexuals, hoodlum homosexuals, and exploited teens. *Journal of Homosexuality*, 46: 1–75.

Kidd, Kenneth. 2004. *Making American boys: boyology and the feral tale*. Minneapolis: University of Minnesota Press.

Kimmel, Michael. 1996. *Manhood in America: A cultural history*. New York: The Free Press.

Kimura, Doreen. 1999. Sex and cognition. Cambridge: MIT Press.

Kitch, Carolyn. 1999. Destructive women and little men: masculinity, the new woman and power in 1910s popular media. *Journal of magazine and new media research*, 1: 1.

Klein, Jesse. 2012. *The bully society*. New York: New York University Press.

Kupers, Terry A. 2005. Toxic masculinity as a barrier to mental health treatment in prison. *Journal of Clinical Psychology*, 61: 713–724.

LeBon, Gustav. 1879. *La Psychologie des Foules, Vol. 2*. Paris: Felix Alcan.

Leonard, Thomas C. 2016. *Illiberal reformers*. Princeton: Princeton University Press.

Leslie, Heather. 2011. Institute for juvenile research. Life histories collection (1910–1940s).

Liberman, Akiva, and Jocelyn Fontaine. 2015. *Reducing harms to boys and young men of color from criminal justice system involvement. A report published by the Urban Institute*. Washington, D.C.

Lombroso, Cesare. 1911. *Criminal man*. Brief English translation by Gina Lombroso Ferrero. New York: G.P. Putnam's Sons.

Matthews, Fred. 1977. *A Quest for an American sociology: Robert E. Park and the Chicago school*. Montreal: McGill-Queens University Press.

Messerschmidt, James. 1993. *Masculinities and crime*. New York: Rowman & Littlefield.

Meyerowitz, Joanne. 1993. Sexual geography and gender economy. In B. Melosh, ed. *Gender and American History Since 1890*. New York: Routledge.

Meyers, Tamara. 2005. Embodying delinquency: boys' bodies, sexuality, and juvenile justice history in early–twentieth-century Quebec. *Journal of the History of Sexuality*, 14: 383–414.

Mishler, Elliot. 1986. *Research interviewing: context and narrative*. Cambridge: Harvard University Press.

Mjagkij, Nina. 2002. *Light in the darkness: African Americans and the YMCA 1852–1946*. Lexington: University of Kentucky Press.

Morison, Samuel Elliot, Henry Steel Commager, and William Leuchtenburg. 1930. *The growth of the American republic, Vol. 1*. New York: Oxford University Press.

Morris, Aldon D. 2015. *The Scholar denied: W.E.B. Du Bois and the birth of modern sociology*. Oakland: University of California Press.

Moses, Earl. 1936. *The negro delinquent in Chicago*. Washington, D.C.: Social Science Research Council.

Nickerman, Kathryn M. The emergence of "underclass" family patterns 1900–1940. In M.B. Katz, ed., *The underclass debate: views from history*. Princeton: Princeton University Press, pp. 194–216.

Nisbet, Robert. 1976. *Sociology as an art form*. New York: Oxford University Press.

Odem, Mary. 1995. *Delinquent Daughters*. Chapel Hill, University of North Carolina Press.

Olzak, Susan. 1989. Labor unrest, immigration, and ethnic conflict in urban America, 1880–1914. *American Journal of Sociology*, 6: 1303–33.

Parker, R.J. 2012. *Women who kill: bitches from hell*. Alberta, CA: R.J. Parker Publishing.

Pasko, Lisa. 2010. Damaged daughters: the history of girls' sexuality in the juvenile justice system. *Journal of Criminal Law and Criminology*, 100: 1099–1130.

Pollack, W.S. 1998. *Real boys: rescuing our sons from the myths of boyhood*. New York: Random House.

Pula, James. 1995. *Polish Americans' an ethnic community*. New York: Twayne.

Purcell-Guild, June. 1919. Study of one hundred-and-thirty-one delinquent girls held at the juvenile detention home in Chicago, 1917. *Journal of the American Institute of Criminal Law and Criminology*, 10: 441–476.

Robinson, Stephen. 2006. "Boys, of course,

cannot be raped": age, homosexuality, and the redefinition of sexual violence in New York City, 1880–1955. *Gender and History*, 18: 357–379.

Salerno, Roger. 2007. *Sociology noir.* Jefferson, NC: McFarland.

Salerno, Roger. 2013. Was there a black Chicago school? In J. Low and G. Bowden, eds., *The Chicago school diaspora: epistemology and substance.* Montreal: McGill-Queen's University Press.

Schulster, J.R. 1995. Memory styles and related abilities in presentation of self. *American Journal of Psychology*, 1: 67–88.

Schwendinger, Heiman and J. Schwendinger. 1974. The sociologists of the chair. New York: Basic Books.

Sedwick, Eve Kosofsky. 1985. *Between men.* New York: Columbia University Press.

Sered, Danielle. 2014. *Young men of color and the other side of harm.* A report published by the Vera Institute of Criminal Justice.

Shamir, Milette, and Jennifer Travis. 2002. *Boys don't cry: rethinking narratives of masculinity and emotion in the U.S.* New York: Columbia University Press.

Shaw, Clifford. 1966. *The Jack-Roller.* Chicago: University of Chicago Press. Orig. published 1930. Chicago: University of Chicago Press.

Shaw, Clifford, and Henry McKay. 1942. *Juvenile delinquency and urban areas.* Chicago: University of Chicago Press.

Shaw, Clifford. 1931. *The natural history of a delinquent career.* Chicago: University of Chicago Press.

Shaw, Clifford. 1938. *Brothers in crime.* Chicago: University of Chicago Press.

Snodgrass, Jon. 1972. *The American criminological tradition: Portraits of men and their ideology in a discipline.* Doctoral dissertation, University of Pennsylvania. http://repository.upenn.edu/dissertations/AAI7225673.

Snodgrass, Jon. 1976. Clifford R. Shaw and Henry D. McKay: Chicago criminologists. *The British Journal of Criminology*, 16: 1–19.

Snodgrass, Jon. 1982. *The Jack-Roller at seventy.* Lexington, MA: Lexington Books.

Snodgrass, Jon. 1984. William Healy (1869–1963): pioneer child psychiatrist and criminologist. *Journal of the History of Behavioral Science*, 20: 4.

Snodgrass, Jon. 2015. *The occulted history of The Jack Roller: research ethics in lifewriting.* A paper presented at the Fourth IABA Europe Conference in Mederia, Portugal, May 27–29.

Spillane, Joseph. 1998. Making of an underground market: Drug selling in Chicago, 1900–1940. *Journal of Social History*, 32: 27–47.

Spivak, Gayatri Chakravorty. 1988. Can the subaltern speak? In C. Nelson and L Grossberg, eds., *Marxism and the interpretation of culture.* Urbana: University of Illinois Press.

Stockton, Gary. 1983. Institute for juvenile research. Life histories collection (1910–1940s) Descriptive inventory for collection at Chicago history museum, research center.

Stoller, Robert. 1965. Passing and continium of gender identity. In M. Judd. *Sexual Inversion.* New York: Basic Books.

Strecker, Edward. 1926. What constitutes mental health in children. *American Journal of Diseases of Childhood*, 32: 409.

Sutherland, Edwin. 1924. *Criminology.* Philadelphia: J.D. Lippincott.

Sutherland, Edwin. 1932. Review: natural history of a delinquent career. *American Journal of Sociology*, 38: 135–136.

Sutherland, Edwin. 1947. *Principles of criminology.* Chicago: J.B. Lippincott.

Tanenhaus, David S. 2004. *Juvenile justice in the making.* New York: Oxford University Press.

Terr, Lenore. 1992. Childhood trauma: an outline and overview. *American Journal of Psychiatry*, 148: 10–20.

Thomas, William I., and D.S. Thomas. 1928. *The child in America: behavior problems and programs.* New York: Knopf, 1928, pp. 571–572.

Thomas, W.I. 1923. *The unadjusted girl.* New York,: Little, Brown.

Thomas, W.I., Robert E. Park, and Adolphus Miller. 1921. *Old world traits transplanted.* New York: Henry Holt.

Thornton, William, and Jennifer James. 1979. Masculinity and delinquency revisited. *British Journal of Criminology*, 19: 3.

Thrasher, Frederic M. 1927. *The Gang*. Abridged Version, 1963. Chicago: University of Chicago Press.

Tracy, Sarah W., and Caroline Jean Acker. 2004. Introduction. In Tracy and Acker, eds., *Altering American consciousness: a history of alcohol and drug use in the United States*. Amhurst: University of Massachusetts Press.

Thompson, Alistir. 2010. Memory and remembering in oral history. In D. Ritchie, ed., *The Oxford handbook of oral history*. New York: Oxford University Press.

Tulving, E. 1983. *Elements of episodic memory*. New York: Oxford University Press.

UCR. 2013. Arrests by sex. FBI, Criminal Justice Information Division. Washington, D.C.

Vice Commission of Chicago. 1911. The Social evil in Chicago. Report of the City of Chicago to the Mayor and City Council.

Walcott, David. 2005. *Cops and kids: policing juvenile delinquency in urban America*. Columbus: Ohio State University Press.

Walklate, Sandra. 2003. *Understanding criminology—current theoretical debates, 2nd edition*. Maidenhead: Open University Press.

Wall, Tim. 2013. *Studying popular music culture*. London: Sage.

Ward, Geoff. 2012. *The Black child-savers*. Chicago: University of Chicago Press.

Watson, John, and R.A. Watson. 1928. *Psychological Care of Infant and Child*. New York: W.W. Norton.

Widom, Cathy, and Michael Maxfield. 2001. An update on the Cycle of Violence, Research in Brief. Washington, D.C.: U.S. Department of Justice, National Institute of Justice, February 2001, Department of Health of the City of New York. 1921. *Annual report of the department of health of New York City*. Board of Health, NY.

Willrich, Michael. 2003. *City of courts: socializing justice in progressive era Chicago*. New York: Cambridge University Press.

Wilson, William J. 2011. Poor black and American, the impact of economic, political and cultural forces. *The American Educator*, Spring, pp. 10–23.

Yow, Valerie Raleigh. 2015. *Recording oral history, 3rd ed*. New York: Rowman & Littlefield.

Zimmerman, Jonathan. 2002. *Whose America? Culture wars in the public schools*. Cambridge: Harvard University Press.

Zimmerman, Gregory, and Carter Rees. 2014. Peer networks and delinquency. In Richard Wright, ed., *Oxford Bibliographies in Criminology*. New York: Oxford University Press.

Index

abandonment 19–21, 71; in Snodgrass narrative 61; of Stanley 37
Abbot, Edith 72, 73; *see also* Breckenridge, Sophonisba
addiction 21, 69, 71; drug addiction 86–88; drugs and alcohol 68–69; parental alcoholism 69; role of the saloon 69
alcoholism 67–69; immigrant men 81
Alger, Horatio 50–51
Americanization movement 24, 73; and mandatory education 24

Becker, Howard 88–91, 182
Bennett, James 3, 5, 8
Black, Jack 32, 34
Black-Belt Chicago 59, 79, 80, 108–109; drugs 87; segregation 92; *see also* race relations
Blotstein, Sidney 64–70, 74
Bowlby, John 103
Boy Scouts 33, 73, 92; history 43
boyhood 12, 14, 31, 63; aggression connected to business 55; and alienation 2; definition of 2, 182; as delinquency 5; in literature 53–54; *see also* boys
boys: abuse of 36, 51–52; aggression of 43; auctioning of boys 20; bad boy trope 50; of color 58–59; disdain for dependence 7; in fiction 53–54; homosexuality 42, 97; homosocial desire 113; lack of empathy 5; rape of 52; socialization of 8, 15; as victims 4, 52; *see also* boyhood
Breckenridge, Sophonisba 21, 65, 72, 73; on girls 82; *see also* Abbot, Edith
Bridewell Prison Farm 73
Burgess, Ernest W. 1, 24–25, 27, 30, 65, 81

Butler, Judith 15, 100; gender melancholy, 15

Cayton, Horace 96, 109
Chicago Area Project (CAP) 59, 89; lack of black youth workers 93
Chicago Juvenile Psychopathic Institute 27, 30
Chicago Parental School 30, 74, 75; abuse at 76–77; antisemitism 74
Chicago Reform School 21, 22, 73, 77; abuse of children 21; history of 21
Chicago school of sociology 1, 81, 108; alienation theme 65; crime research 24–26, 59
child savers 12, 59; Shaw's role 51; and social control 12
Corbett, Ken 15, 36; boyhood 35
Cox, Oliver 95, 186
cultural conflict 66, 72, 77

dance and music 13
Deegan, Mary Jo 82
Denzin, Norman 39–40
Dollard, John 89, 112; *see also* narrative interviews
Drake, St. Clair 96, 109; *see also* Cayton, Horace
drug addiction 86–89; black males 88; Harrison Narcotics Act 87; prostitutes 87; *see also* addiction
Du Bois, W.E.B.: *The Philadelphia Negro* 94
Durkheim, Emile 25, 77; anomie 78

environment and urban crime 2–4; housing conditions 72; noxious environment 21; Stanley's impoverished environment 44–45; zones in transition 65

feminist movement 7
Frazier, E. Franklin 96
Freud, Sigmund 12, 55, 85

gender identity: construction of 6; and deviance 2, 3, 5; fluidity of 16; identification 11; performance 6; socialization 17
girls: age of consent 14; better memory 11; of color 14, 58–59; control of sexuality 12; and delinquency 82–83; gender socialization 15; moral offenses 13; sex work 84; sexual abuse of 86; and violence 4, 14
Guern, Eddie 32, 34

Healy, William 27, 28, 30, 34, 35, 48, 57; on autobiography 34; concept of "own story" 34; as director of Chicago Juvenile Psychopathic Institute 27–28; influence on Shaw 29; interview with Stanley 30
Heap, Chad 100
homosexuality 97–102; cross dressing in gangs 101; drag balls 100; lesbians 99; problems of gay boys ignores 98; prostitution 99; runaways 98; street children 98; Tower Town 99
Hull House 2, 23–24, 27, 56, 79, 82, 89; African American delinquency 58; Americanization of immigrants 56; Jane Adams 23

Illinois Institute for Juvenile Research (IJR) 27; *see also* Chicago Juvenile Psychopathic Institute
Illinois State Reformatory 22
immigration 4, 49, 105, 107; abuse of immigrant labor 70, 185; discrimination against immigrants 70; immigrant children in Chicago 19; Polish immigrants 49; poor health 185; working conditions of immigrants 72

Jack-Roller 29–30, 34–41, 44–47, 50, 59, 61; homosexuality 46; race 57
juvenile courts 4, 20, 22–23, 72–73, 83, 96; attitude toward African Americans 96; denial of *habeas corpus* 22; designed with boys in mind 82; judges mostly male 82; Shaw employed 26; *see also* juvenile justice

juvenile justice system 23, 41, 56, 72, 79; designed for boys 11; Juvenile Court Act of 1899 22; treatment rather than punishment 23; *see also* juvenile courts

Kidd, Kenneth 12, 14, 50

Landesco, John 2, 25
Lombroso, Cesare 1, 3, 25

masculinity 3, 6, 7–8; Chodorow's thesis 15; fear of feminization 7; male narrative 6; toxic 8
McKay, Henry 2, 9, 25, 27–29, 36, 59, 62, 108; collaboration with Shaw 27
Mead, George H. 25, 29
Mexican delinquency 91, 187

narrative analysis 10–11; Jane Elliot on life narrative interviews 11

Park, Robert E., 1, 2, 24–25, 66, 81, 94; directs Urban League 95; influenced by Booker T. Washington 94; opposition to NAACP 2

race relations in Chicago 12, 79; arrests of black boys 5; black migration to the city 48; Chicago Race Riot 1916 48, 80, 92–93; housing segregation 48, 92–93; treatment of black boys in juvenile detention 187; violence and bombing of black homes 49; YMCA segregation 92; *see also* Black-Belt
racism 79; directed against immigrants 108; Jim Crow laws 79; KKK meeting in Chicago 93; *see also* race relations
Reckless, Walter 2, 25

St. Charles School for Boys 26, 30, 68, 77, 103
Shaw, Clifford 2, 8, 9, 13, 16, 21, 25, 27–36, 40, 44, 47, 63–67, 74, 76, 80–81, 89–93, 102–103, 108, 182; as a child saver 51; humanizing delinquents 62; influence on Stanley 29–30; named director of Institute for Juvenile Research 27; rural perspective 51; and St. Charles School 9, 26; work with juvenile court 30; work with Nathan Leopold 9
Snodgrass, Jonathan 11, 16, 40, 44, 47, 49, 61

Stanley (Michael Majer) 30, 34–40, 44–47, 49; absence of father's protection 45; betrayal narrative 39; on homosexuality 46; influence of step-mother 38; misogyny 46; possible trauma 49; on race 57; Snodgrass interviews 49; as a textual production 40
Sutherland, Edwin 2, 3, 25, 34, 108; critique of *The Jack-Roller* 34

Thomas, W.I. 1, 25, 30, 57; definition of the situation 29; *The Polish Peasant* 29; symbolic interactionism 29; Thomas theorem 57; *The Unadjusted Girl* 107
truancy laws 73
true crime genre 31; criminal autobiography 32; influence on Shaw 31–32; *see also* Black, Jack

Washington, Booker T. 1

www.ingramcontent.com/pod-product-compliance
Ingram Content Group UK Ltd.
Pitfield, Milton Keynes, MK11 3LW, UK
UKHW042008140426
5217IPUK00015B/1041